SIXTEEN SEASONS

A little over a decade ago, a shy, unassuming, and tenderhearted young man left a profound impression on me when I first met him among a classroom full of students on the first day of class at Wheaton College. It was simply unmistakable how David embodied Christ's love. For the next few years, I had the privilege to witness him blossoming in the Lord with integrity, simplicity, purity, and singularity to delight in the Lord and His people.

Then, I learned that he was going to embark on a "low-profile" cross-cultural ministry in an "undisclosed" part of the world with Ann, his newlywed wife. I wished them Godspeed, not knowing whether I would ever hear from them again. To my delight, David and Ann have "emerged" to grace us with ten short poignant episodes narrating how God has graciously met them and faithfully made His presence known through them.

In this book, David invites his readers to walk alongside of him as he masterfully describes the complexity of his encounters with a people and culture so foreign to him, yet very much the object of God's love. With self-reflective and audacious honesty, David offers God's transforming work in and through him in that "remote" part of the world as a reminder for us Christians in the West that His light still shines bright in darkness. In this book, David in his unassuming manner causes me to reflect deeply on whether that same light shines bright in my life and through the church in a post-Christian, Western world. Thank you, David, for teaching me through your life.

S. Steve Kang, PhD,
professor of Educational Ministries and Interdisciplinary Studies,
Gordon-Conwell Theological Seminary

Having devoted my life to missionary service, I love a good read that captures the heart of another culture. Now I have a new favorite—*Sixteen Seasons* by David James. The author combines the storytelling of Hosseini (*The Kite Runner*) with the observation of Dalrymple (*From the Holy Mountain*) and adds his own spiritual reflection to the cultural interplay. The result is an insightful, entertaining account of the infusion of good news into a dark environment.

Don Eenigenburg,
church planting director,
Christar

This book captures what happens when youthful enthusiasm encounters the day-to-day grind of very ordinary mission work. The author has a remarkable eye for observing and noting the events of everyday life with humor and insight. He has chosen to follow the adage of "show don't tell" as he communicates his message without being the least bit preachy. This eye-opening narrative shows the reality of life in a post-Soviet country.

James C. Wilhoit, PhD,
Scripture Press professor of Christian Formation and Ministry,
Wheaton College

SIXTEEN SEASONS

Stories from a missionary family in Tajikistan

DAVID JAMES

WILLIAM CAREY
LIBRARY

Published by William Carey Library, an imprint of William Carey Publishing
10 W. Dry Creek Circle
Littleton, CO 80120 | www.missionbooks.org

Kelley K. Wolfe, editor
Kate Hegland, copyeditor
Josie Leung, interior design
Alyssa E. Force, cover design
Mikhail Romanyuk, cover photo

William Carey Library is a ministry of Frontier Ventures
Pasadena, CA 91104 | www.frontierventures.org

23 22 21 20 19 Printed for Worldwide Distribution

Library of Congress Cataloging-in-Publication Data

James, David.
 Sixteen seasons : stories from a missionary family in Tajikistan / David James.
 p. cm.
 ISBN 978-0-87808-473-9
 1. Missionary stories. 2. Missions--Tajikistan. 3. Tajikistan--Social life and customs. 4. Tajikistan--Social conditions. I. Title.
 BV2087.J36 2011
 266.0092--dc23
 [B]
 2011023905

To my love Ann and to my beautiful Grace and Silas.
Though Tajikistan was very difficult, I would not change anything.
I consider it a treasure beyond measure to have seen
your perseverance lead to character and character to hope.
Though we settled on the far side of the sea, we never left His hands.

CONTENTS

FOREWORD

Sixteen Seasons contains captivating vignettes taken from the life of
a young missionary, David James. The reader is transported into a
world unknown, strange, wonderful, often confusing, and surprisingly illuminating as the author provides cultural understanding.
This book is not only a good read, a page-turner, really, but filled with
color, warmth, and cultural charm. Tajikistan was home to the James
family for several years and we are invited to share in their story—one
filled with customs, traditions, daily patterns, politics, transportation,
and experiences that both challenge and intrigue. Life in Tajikistan
could hardly have been more opposite than the American life the
author knew and loved. But success in cultural adjustment—never
easy—begins with suspending judgment, embracing the differences,
and learning to "dance to the rhythm" that makes life meaningful
and sensible to the people who will soon be neighbors, friends, col-
leagues, and, by God's grace, followers of Jesus.

James takes the routine and turns it into the wondrous, humorous, and sometimes sad—much in the tradition of James Herriot,
the English veterinarian surgeon (*All Creatures Great and Small*) who
drew us into his world of animals with both laughter and pathos.
Both Herriot and James possess the gift of creating images that ex-
plode in the reader's mind, creating the wonder of "experiencing" the
very event itself. From observing a "goat pull" match to dealing with
electrical outages, from fussing with a temperamental air conditioner

to being spontaneously inducted into a wedding party as a grooms-man, James helps us see the mundane and the oddities of life with an inquisitive, but discerning eye.

While fighting the natural tendency to dismiss, even criticize, many of these cultural peculiarities, he keeps an open mind, seeks to understand, and, in time, makes sense out of seeming chaos. Learning to "dance to the rhythm" demands patience, mental tenacity, and physical and emotional engagement—rare commodities among those settling into such an exotic culture for the first time. Perhaps even more rare is the respect and love evidenced in James' captivating account of living among the Tajiks. Yet, he does not shy away from marking the deficiencies, dangers, and biblically unacceptable practices. People living in a new culture often come to see more clearly the defects in their own (home) culture and those among the Western Christian community as well. With the same grace in describing failings in Tajik society, he helps us see more clearly where we, too, fall short in being Christ-followers.

One chapter recounts the astonishing circumstances surrounding a Tajik wedding. Getting married is the author's friend, Bahriddin. After describing all the customs of parental matchmaking leading to the bride and groom's marriage, James finds himself stuffed in a taxi with Tajik music blasting at an ear-splitting level. It is the night before the wedding.

> *The taxi driver flipped the tape over, which gave me a moment to assess the severity of the ringing in my ears. Maybe the Mullah [in the front seat] was already deaf or surely he would have been complaining. . . . As the music started in again Bahriddin leaned over and yelled something in my ear. "What?! Speak English!" I yelled at Bahriddin hoping that would give me a better shot at understanding him over the music. "Will you be my second man?!" Had I heard that right? "You mean tonight and tomorrow for your wedding?!" I screamed hoping I had heard incorrectly. "Yes!" Bahriddin*

screamed back, smiling. "Uhhhhh, okay!" I said. Drat.
What just happened? Was I a groomsman now? What am I
wearing anyway. . . . I was having serious doubts that I was
a good choice.

Such are the wondrous adventures of the James family.

Some stories are marked by sadness. The author expresses sorrow on a number of fronts: the historic Russian domination of Tajikistan that has limited its ability to grow and experience the freedoms such a country might expect; the grip of Islam on the minds of people who understand so little, but pay homage nonetheless; the corruption that keeps the masses in poverty; the oppressive government that dictates life in severe ways. The sadness goes beyond these daily realities to signal the ultimate sadness—that the Tajiks face a Christless eternity unless someone tells them about the God who sent his Son, Jesus, to die for the forgiveness of their sins.

By way of James' amazing powers of observation and description, it is my hope that the reader will be drawn into the drama of daily life and the romance of learning to love a new culture, a new people. Additionally, that the reader might become deeply connected with the present state of pioneer missions among least-reached peoples and in so doing be spurred on toward greater engagement in our Lord's Great Commission.

Throughout these stories, one is constantly aware that only by God's presence and the work of the Holy Spirit is the otherwise-impossible task of building a church accomplished. At the end of the day, we join the James family in proclaiming, "To God be the glory for the things He has done."

Duane H. Elmer, PhD,
G. W. Aldeen professor of International Studies,
distinguished professor of Educational Studies, PhD program,
Trinity International University, Deerfield, Illinois

PREFACE

When Ann and I married before the beginning of our senior year of college we had never heard of Tajikistan. That year God worked not only to introduce us to the country but to pair that introduction with a changing of our hearts so that we miraculously began to warm to the idea of going and serving our Lord there. That was the fall of 1999.

After much preparation we finally arrived in Tajikistan in the spring of 2001. In the years we have spent in Tajikistan since that spring, our love has grown to embrace more fully not only each other and our two beautiful children, Grace and Silas, but also the Tajik people whom, by the grace of God, we now hold and will hold forever close to our hearts.

We can testify to the fact that it is not easy to take our selfish, sinful hearts and grow them in love for Himself and a new people. We know we still have a long journey toward maturity, but God has been and continues to be gracious in our lives and in the lives of the Tajiks.

This book is not chronological but instead examines our lives in Tajikistan from several topical angles. These true short stories are taken from the experiences we had in the four years (sixteen seasons) we lived among the Tajiks. I have chosen various places and events because of their usefulness in portraying certain elements of the interplay between the Tajik people's lives and our experiences as Western Christians living among them.

This book is not primarily focused on the work of church planting (the starting of churches) although this was our team's main work and the passion of our lives in Tajikistan. I have left writing about this most important of themes to more capable hands. I have felt my special contribution was to attempt to capture the humor and the gravity, the clashes and the common humanity we have found in the living out of our daily lives with our Tajik friends and neighbors. I hope that in so doing to perhaps more clearly show many Christians in America that missionaries are just human beings and thereby more fully awaken the church to the reality that the Great Commission is the calling of every disciple of Jesus Christ.

This book is humbly offered with more than a little trepidation, knowing that later I will no doubt be embarrassed about something I have written. Hopefully it is not too many "somethings." But it is offered nonetheless, knowing that there can be great benefit in following another's journey.

I must mention that due to the nature of the work the book recounts, the names of all people and many places have been changed. Security concerns are also a major factor as to why our teammates and the local Tajik believers do not play a more prominent role in the book.

Finally, in order to prevent confusion, the reader should know that in Tajikistan we had two primary work relationships. First, we were sent by and served under a missionary organization. Additionally, while in Tajikistan we worked for an international nongovernmental organization (NGO). The stories contain glimpses of our relationships and responsibilities with both organizations.

It is our family's confident prayer that God would continue to glorify His holy name in us, in you, among the Tajiks, and throughout all nations. May this book in some way serve these purposes.

ACKNOWLEDGMENTS

I must thank my incredible teammates for their years of companionship and faithful service in Tajikistan. You taught Ann and me so much. You are truly living sacrifices. We miss and love you more than words can express.

To all at headquarters, thank you for your constant love and support. We serve joyfully knowing you are behind us! And a special thanks to all at our NGO for giving us the opportunity to serve alongside you in Tajikistan.

I must thank the Tajik people, especially our new brothers and sisters in Christ, for opening their lives to us, for accepting the strange creatures who had no manners or understanding. The Lord has placed you forever close to our hearts.

And to our families, thank you for letting us go. But you did far more than let us go. Though you were sad, we knew your hearts were in our work. Having your prayerful support means the world to us. Please understand that we know you sacrifice dearly, especially when your grandchildren are so far away.

We are so grateful for the hundreds back home who have given of themselves so that we could go to Tajikistan in the first place. Thank you for sending us and sustaining us with your giving and prayers. We especially thank our special prayer partners who took it upon themselves to pray daily for us and for the Tajik people. Your faithful prayers over the years have been our strength. When we were too tired to pray, we were so grateful to remember that there were many still lifting us up.

I must thank Cindy Nienaber. Thank you so much for pouring over the manuscript time and time again. Thank you for all your countless hours of editing! You have pushed me to make this book much better than it otherwise would have been.

Thank you to Alyssa Force for your friendship and your wonderful designs!

Duane Elmer, Don Eenigenburg, James Wilhoit, and Steve Kang, your words of encouragement during this project have helped me to press on. I can't tell you how blessed I am to have had your support.

And finally to everyone at William Carey Library, thank you for believing in this project. I know we hope together that this book impacts many for the furtherance of Christ's kingdom.

I

A DAY IN PURSUIT OF
AIR CONDITIONING

Morning

*One watch succeeded another through the day, though how
the rabbits judged the passing of time is something that
civilized human beings have lost the power to feel. Creatures
that have neither clocks nor books are alive to all manner of
knowledge about time and weather.*[1]

Nature is master in Tajikistan in a way that, during my youth,
my farm-born and bred Grammy tried to convince me was true in
southern Missouri. But with her central air conditioning strongly
allied behind my way of thinking, with its beautiful silver registers
whispering me to sleep a little later, I suppose I never really got the
point. How could any teenager be expected to get up before ten on
an AC-cooled, summer day? The watermelon we ate on the porch in
the evenings came courtesy of someone's reliable shipment to the
local Walmart. No, she was talking about a necessity of other times.

As I poured sweat until I could no longer see what I was supposed to be digging, Grammy used to tell me that it would be
much easier to pull the thistles if I woke up with the sun instead
of timing my work to coincide with its apex. When my eyes were
burning with sweaty salt I could blurrily see the great wisdom in
that. But somehow between the suffering of work at noon and

the cool breezes of another perfectly climate-controlled morning, something would happen to make me forget. Maybe it was instant showers or ever-present utilities. Maybe it was David Letterman the night before, speaking out from another world and uprooting my Grammy's wisdom.

However, Tajikistan has proven to be a much more persuasive teacher, and I was up at 5:30 a.m. already sweltering. My wife, Ann, and I have decided that we don't like sweltering. The neighbors find it odd that we always have to scramble to put proper clothes on when they knock on our door while we find it odd that they are already wearing presentable clothes, complete with headscarves for the ladies, when we knock. But when you are living with some combination of your grandpa, grandma, father, mother, brothers, sisters, aunts, uncles, and cousins all stuffed together into one apartment, maybe going without appropriate clothing is not a legitimate option.

I went to the fridge and grabbed some extremely refreshing watermelon, and even though, just like the Missouri watermelon, I had not lifted a finger to make it grow, at least I was now aware that this fruit had indeed been grown—grown in real ground with real water and real sunshine during real seasons. I was reminded of this as I sat at the table eating the watermelon while wishing for cherries—cherries we had thoroughly enjoyed the previous week. Unfortunately, as the reality of seasons and weather came storming down around us, we had been informed that the year's cherry season was over. The bazaar was out! How could that be? When was the next shipment from Venezuela? How could a place be just as unlikely to have bananas for sale as monkeys? Maybe Afghanistan wasn't the best buddy to work with for importing. And I suppose that having some of the most uplifted, formidable mountains in the world did not help trade, but still, why did cherry season only last like three weeks? What's up with that? I took a comforting, juicy gulp of watermelon, knowing that these would be with us for a couple more months. Now that's a growing season! Grammy might find it a relief that I have opinions about such things now.

True to the spirit of modern times, far from giving in to nature, I was going to Dushanbe this morning—our new country's capital—for the purpose of finding something that at the time seemed better than a thousand kilos of cherries and more beneficial than a soul mate. I was going to buy a brand-new, imported, LG air conditioner; I took great comfort in the fact that the Soviet Union had played absolutely no role in creating it.

Southern Tajikistan is full of dinosaur appliances from Soviet times—an excellent example of one of these relics fights valiantly in the windowsill of our living room, intermittently pumping out moderately cool air that teasingly drops the room to just around ninety degrees while enjoying its favorite pastime of destroying conversation with an immoderate thump or pop which we always think might be its last. However, we think it enjoys being the bane of conversation too much to ever think of passing on to becoming a part of the *former* Soviet Union. Our air conditioner seems bent on outliving the statues of Lenin that still stand in our city's parks. Personally, I think Lenin would seem greater if our air conditioner gave up the ghost and stopped dishonoring his past empire.

Since I had thrown my stuff in a backpack the night before, I kissed a sleeping Ann goodbye and was still out the door before 6:00 a.m. As I stepped out into our crumbling stairwell with its prevalence of shocking, yet impressively creative wiring and plumbing—which I might add had been unable to provide water to our second-floor apartment building that morning for my shower—I found myself wondering how we could tap this cool outside air and pump it directly into the sauna that was our apartment without becoming a wasteland of giardia-bearing flies. Screens! Screens! My kingdom for some screens!

I also wondered how it was possible that the water pressure could be so low as to not reach a second-floor apartment. What does the

Sears Tower do differently? Oddly, when house hunting in Tajikistan, one has to consider if the area of town is sufficiently downhill from city water sources. I can imagine a local newspaper advertisement stating: "Excellent downhill location! Water often reaches second floor!"

Our neighbor women, who understand what my Grammy was talking about, were already out filling plastic water containers at the courtyard pump to carry up to their apartments. I always feel sorry for the ladies who live on the higher floors. I think maybe there should be an exception made in the Tajik culture for anyone who lives on the third floor or above, allowing for men to haul water without having it bring an intolerable social shame upon them. But there I go again thinking Western, forgetting that men must be saved for higher pursuits such as religion, driving cars, conversation, and backgammon, not necessarily in that order.

The not-so-subtle bit of frustrated sarcasm in that last sentence is a big step for me as I was taught the principle—and I exaggerate it—that when coming into a new culture one should withhold judgment at all costs until criminals are questioning your sense of morality. At that point perhaps, one might start thinking about the possibility of judgment. That's the basic idea. This is in order to avoid hasty decisions on things one doesn't understand, like why this particular government official is taking that orphanage's money or why that drugstore is selling the internationally donated medicine to the highest bidder instead of giving it for free to the intended tuberculosis patients.

Ann never really bought into the "withhold judgment" theory for cultural interaction. She is firmly in the "I hate this" school of thought, which makes for some interesting conversations between us. Here are a couple examples, which are invented but representative of our normal conversations.

A Day in Pursuit of Air Conditioning

On the Muslim call to prayer:

Ann: "This drives me crazy!"
Me: "If you forget the context and everything it stands for, it's actually kind of pretty in a highly stylized, Arabic sort of way."

On the irregularly timed, four-hour summer afternoon nap during work days:

Ann: "How do they expect business to work if they are closed anywhere from like 1 p.m. until dinner time? And they don't even post a schedule! What? Is it just how they're feeling whether they open at 3 or 5 p.m. or never? This drives me crazy!"
Me: "It's nice that things are so easygoing here."

I made my way up to the taxi stand where I selected an army green, Russian-made Lada that inevitably was older than I am, which is maybe why I felt like I might have had more horsepower. Being the world's worst haggler, I negotiated, no, nothing I do deserves the respect of that word; rather, I agreed to the equivalent of a one-dollar fare. Soon we were puttering off toward the central transport station/bazaar. We ran a couple red lights on the way as we dodged the noteworthy potholes—capable of swallowing us— and coasted downhill whenever possible to prevent the use of gas. This is why sometimes one's taxi is passed by the odd bicycler or unusually determined pedestrian.

As we arrived at the "station"—picture a bazaar filled with unnervingly zealous taxi drivers and ancient vehicles haphazardly parked within the commotion of haggling revolving around a large Russian woman apparently of some importance—our taxi was immediately set upon by eager drivers as I handed over three somoni to pay my present driver. So many other drivers were helping me open my door that it was difficult to get out.

I am beginning to think that as a foreigner I exude some sort of odor and like sharks getting a whiff of blood on the waves, they instinctively know to head my way. As introverts, Ann and I could do without this sort of natural phenomenon. It makes us want to migrate. It has occurred to me more than once as I have been walking down the road with groups of people staring at me, that being here is similar to being stuck in an eternal seventh grade where you become excruciatingly conscious of how high you're lifting your feet and how silly it seems that your arms swing back and forth when you walk.

Ignoring my rhythmically swinging arms and procuring a taxi in need of only one more passenger for departure, I hopped into the backseat between a young, slightly overweight Tajik lady, her heaviness being a highly unusual occurrence in this country, and a guy about my age who liked to smoke. I suppose it would have been okay that he liked to smoke if Tajiks had normal, if I may use the word, beliefs about wind. A young adventure writer, describing the very similar neighboring Uzbekistan, describes a public bus trip between Uzbek cities like so:

> The rocking bus smelled like kerosene, and in the aisles it was hot and getting hotter. Most of the windows, covered with thin blue curtains, were closed. Only 10 a.m., and comets of sweat were already streaking along my jawline. Yet not a few passengers on this bus were wearing heavy cardigan sweaters or thick padded coats called chapons. One of the many curious Uzbek health beliefs holds that certain death follows if a breeze happens to blow on one's bare skin. This widely shared conviction made for miserable public-transport experiences.[2]

Fortunately, I was riding with some freethinking Tajiks. We only closed half the windows. And if I may expand upon the "curious health beliefs" theme, I would like to inform all of you who are reading this that drinking ice in any beverage is a potentially hazardous mistake. Hot tea is the obvious solution to quench that summer thirst and air conditioning is fine, unless you have even the slightest amount of sweat anywhere on your body, in which case you must shut it off immediately or risk the worst. And fans, well, fans are just asking for it.

Trying to convince a neighbor that filtered ice with filtered water is safer than putting your mouth directly on the courtyard's absolutely untreated, rusty faucet is futile because you have forgotten the most important aspect of all; your water is cold while that water is warm. All typhoid outbreaks aside, case closed.

Our teammate, who is passionate about incarnational ministry, got really sick and was in a lot of pain a while ago. Being an adventurous sort he decided to go see a local Tajik doctor rather than racing up to the Western-trained foreigners in the capital. The Tajik doctors diagnosed a very serious pinched nerve in the abdominal area that could really cause problems and thus their suggestion of immediate semi-exploratory surgery was justified. In a fit of sanity he raced up to Dushanbe for a second opinion. Two days later he came back with antibiotics to treat his fairly common bladder infection.

An Australian friend, after breaking his tooth on a small rock—unfortunately, yet not uncommonly, inside his bread—flew all the way to Thailand for his dentistry, disregarding the helpful advice of the local Tajik dentist who said that if he knocked out the tooth on either side of the troubled one, things could be fixed up nicely.

Our neighbor's ideas seem even stranger to us than these examples. To take an odd moment from just yesterday, Ann had the following conversation with her language teacher. I think this sort of sums up our mutual misunderstandings:

Nazokat: "Why is your baby sad this morning?"
Ann: "She has a new tooth coming in."

Nazokat: "Oh, we have a treatment to help that. What we do is make up this special food and then we divide up the food among the neighbors. They eat it and the baby feels better."

Ann: "You mean the baby eats the food or you put it on the baby's tooth?"

Nazokat: "No, the neighbors eat the food."

Ann: "How does the neighbors' eating the food help the baby's tooth feel better?"

Nazokat: "I don't know."

Respecting one of my own curious health beliefs, the young smoking gentlemen to my right turned out to be a very nice guy as he offered to stop smoking and even asked if I wanted a piece of gum to get rid of that secondary smoke aftertaste. I accepted. Then feeling some uncontrollable, Tajik cultural pangs of extreme, aggressive hospitality, I turned and asked the young woman to my left if she would also like a piece of gum that was not mine to offer.

This began and concluded my interaction with her on this trip. Tajik women, although to a much lesser extent than most Muslim societies, are quite reticent in such social situations, and the four of us men basically completely ignored her for the rest of the trip. During our three-hour journey I don't even believe I noticed what her face looked like, and on all those swerving mountain switchbacks I took a white-knuckled hold on the sides of the front seats to keep, as much as possible, from falling all over this modest, young Muslim woman.

The necessities of life sometimes play practical jokes on religious conviction. Good Pakistani families at times avoid this by banning their women from public transport all together. But, at any rate, she did want a piece of gum so we all chewed together as we began our journey towards the mountains that divided the Kadimobod area of southern Tajikistan from the plains bearing Tajikistan's capital.

A Day in Pursuit of Air Conditioning

I quickly made friends with the young smoker sitting next to me. His name was Suhrob. Unlike his namesake from Firdausi's famous epic, he seemed like a shy, peaceable guy. He knew a smattering of English and insisted that we converse with it. Every time I would revert back to Tajik because of a communicative impasse he would diligently plead with me, "Please, English!" and we would continue our unofficial lesson.

There are two main types of conversation that I have with strangers in this country. First is the stranger who wants to practice English, exhausting all possibilities for conversation during this incredible opportunity—namely, me. The other prominent type is the stranger whose curiosity is aroused to conversation only to the point that it becomes painfully clear I have no personal relationship with Jackie Chan. At this point it is often up to me to continue conversation on local topics.

I am amazed at how many Tajik imaginations, upon probably their very first good conversation with a Westerner, only go so far as to ask the following three fairly standard questions:

1. Where are you from?
2. What state do you live in, New York or Los Angeles?
3. Do you know Arnold Schwarzenegger?

I have learned that if I wish to continue the conversation I should answer, "Los Angeles" and "Yes, he's a good friend of mine" to questions two and three. Many will add the "What is your job here?" question, but that's usually about it before we're back to discussing whether I would prefer listening to Russian or Tajik pop music or if I would mind taking their picture in front of their stereo.

Actually, once I get over the hurt feelings that they are really not interested in where I hail from, I realize that this fairly consistent low ebb of curiosity probably serves my learning needs well, as most of the time we're discussing Tajikistan. Besides, when I am occasionally asked questions like, "Are Japan and Germany states within the United States?" I don't know what sort of stimulating international conversation I am expecting.

One of my favorite conversations ever was when I found myself arguing forcibly with a middle-aged bread seller at the bazaar that I was indeed an American and was not lying. I was not able to convince her as I found her conviction that all Americans are black to be unshakable.

An equally frustrating conversation I have repeatedly had with more educated Tajiks goes something like this:

Tajik: "What are you?"
Me: "I'm an American."
Tajik: "No, no, what are you?"
Me: "No, I'm really an American."
Tajik: "*Nameshavad!*" (That's not okay!) "What are you really?"
Me: "Well, many generations ago my relatives started coming over from Europe and they have intermarried, so I guess you could say I'm English, Irish, French, German, and probably some other things."
Tajik: "*Ana!*" (There you go!)

As we began our ascent toward the main mountain chain between our present location and final destination, my buddy Suhrob leaned over to ask if I knew how to tie a tie. He works for the agricultural department and had some special government meeting that morning in Dushanbe. We spent the next few minutes bonding as I tried to transfer the tie from my neck to his without ruining the knot. I felt so skillful and necessary helping the Tajik government in this way.

It was the same feeling I get at the local internet center when people stare open mouthed as I type at an admittedly less than stellar seventy or so words per minute rate. To my shame, I really enjoy this phenomenon. Tajikistan is great for providing new ways to show off. I feel like Maverick when I shuffle cards in front of the students. And I had never gotten to play center in basketball before coming here. Suddenly I'm the 1.8-meter, 67-kilo monster in the middle. For those of you who are having trouble with the metric conversions, on the American scale that's probably closer to elf than monster.

Ironically, regardless of my dress-tie skills, earlier that week I had been publicly humiliated for being a slob. I was in the middle of teaching volleyball when a sleek new car, signaling to everyone present but me, "Important person! Don't mess with me!" raced across our court and parked under the net. Perturbed and as an outsider not caring who he was, I chased after the uniformed gentlemen into the neighboring refrigerator repair shop to ask if he would please back his car up twenty feet so we could continue playing. He proceeded to yell at me and comment that my tattered jeans and dusty grey T-shirt earmarked me as a poor bum. My first two thoughts were, "I'm teaching sports here" and "Don't you know faded jeans are cool? Some stores sell them brand-new like this!" But due to my insufficient grasp of the Tajik language I wasn't even sure I knew exactly how he had insulted me, so I kept those thoughts to myself, took the criticism, and repeated my request. Incidentally, if you have acquired and can't break the bad habit of sarcastic comebacks, a great cure is to switch your primary language of communication. You'll never feel clever in a verbally abusive sort of way again.

Wishing I could say something sharp as I looked down at my grubby clothes, I reflected on Tajik dress habits. Though very poor, Tajiks take appearance to the level of neurosis. In this highly sensitive, shame-based culture, even our poorest students scrape together the cash to get the latest fashions. They may only own two outfits, but you can be assured that they will be spotlessly presented. At our youth center for poor children, our older girls routinely show up for volleyball in wedding-worthy *kortas* (dresses) and high heels. I keep telling them it's rather difficult to bump a volleyball in high heels, but I think that for them death would be preferable to being seen in tennis shoes. So they play barefoot. I'll go for that compromise. Though I must admit that having the girls constantly sprinting off trying to run down the little thief who has just stolen their high heels is a bit of a distraction.

Upon visiting some of our students' homes, I am often shocked to find that their material possessions do not go far beyond a couple of carpets, dishes, bedding mats, a few clothes, and an old television. Entering the average person's home from a dusty yard, which may or may not have running water, most rooms will be rather empty except for the carpets upon the floors. But when they go out for the day they look razor sharp. No one would ever suspect that they have nothing. Even villagers living beyond the reach of electricity know that appearance is king.

I forget its royalty every other day and thus I get hounded that my jeans look more than six months old, I am not wearing a matching jogging suit and, horror of horrors, my sports backpack has dust on it! As a product of Generation X America among whom casual appearance has become an art form, I struggle with "dressing the part." I have this value on being "real," and upon reflection, my definition of being "real" seems to include looking grubby as a primary postulate. I guess it seems to me that if I'm a bit unshaven I'm more trustworthy.

Recently, I have thought about this difference and come up with the tentative hypothesis that perhaps we, as Americans, can look grubby without fearing disrespectability because we are filthy rich. But if you take one of our students for example, perhaps she feels compelled to present a well-off image because she is, in fact, so absolutely impoverished. My students are fighting in a million ways every day to show they are valuable. They are slaves to shame and pride. But, lest I be unfair, is there anything new about that? It just takes vastly more expensive forms stateside.

Still, seeing the arrogant displays and the local style of conspicuous consumption in a new culture with exceedingly foreign eyes constantly reminds me how shallow and desperately sad humans grasping at worth can be. And we are so cruel to one another as we tread upon our neighbors to grasp after it. How can we get so far from, "So God created man in his own image, in the image of God he created them" (Gen 1:27).

Sometimes when I see a bunch of Tajik rich men dancing out in the prominent places at a wedding, throwing around their one somoni bills so people will call them generous, I just feel like going out there and outgunning them by slamming down twenty American bucks into the groom's hand to mercifully stop the whole ridiculous display. God has really used the tool of economic relativity to bring into sharp focus how ridiculous our pride must be before Him who can create eternal beings with a word.

Afternoon

> Men in the Western governments, who were themselves often modern men, did not understand that freedom without chaos is not a magic formula which can be implanted anywhere. Rather, being modern men, it was their view that, because the human race had evolved to a certain level by some such year as 1950, democracy could be planted anywhere from outside. They had carefully closed their eyes to the fact that freedom without chaos had come forth from a Christian base. They did not understand that freedom without chaos could not be separated from its roots. And when these outward forms are imposed on a world view that would have never produced freedom without chaos in the first place, people will not stand when the pressures increase.[3]

The foothills passed by quietly as the cloud cover increased. For a Tajikistan summer morning it was a perfect day to travel. The ever-present, depressingly intense sun was taking an absolutely lovely respite behind some apparitional clouds. I asked Suhrob if it might rain. *"Tobiston ast"* ("It's summer") was the reply. I guess that answered that. I wondered what he thought when a few drops hit the windshield later on.

As we ascended toward the summits of the main mountain chain separating Tajikistan's south from its center, we hit the switch-back portion of the highway. This is the part of the journey where sane drivers slow down and stop passing on blind curves. I would take as a working definition of a sane driver "a non-Tajik" because it seems like in the switchback mountain passes some sort of derange-ment overtakes them. They begin to behave in such a way as would make Mario Andretti nervous.

Granted, I'm an American motorist and in America if it is three in the morning at some rural four-way stoplight, I, at least, will stop and sit there staring out at the wind playing upon the open fields for thirty seconds or more until the light turns green. If I grow impatient or the rebellion froths over from within, I might buck the system by making a pair of right hand turns with a U-turn thrown in between.

I believe most people in the world would see my behavior of obeying glowing poles in the middle of nowhere's night and chalk it up to insanity. I'm reminded of cultures who think standing in lines takes away your humanity. I guess I would have to agree that jostling does seem more human. Still, couldn't Tajiks find another place to freely express themselves, preferably a place without sheer rock faces?

After a few ridiculous decisions that I will try my best to for-get, our driver summited unscathed. Far below, Lake Norak snaked between the peaks of countless half-submerged hills like one of Tolkein's dragons. Even when queasy and shaken by a driver's lack of common sense, the site has never ceased to amaze me. Norak exudes a mysterious beauty as it meanders gracefully between seem-ingly endless hills that extend beyond view. The romance invoked by the inability to comprehend clearly its directions, depths, and ends, never ceases to captivate.

A Day in Pursuit of Air Conditioning

When the Soviets envisioned and built Norak as a grand hydro-electric source, I am sure they had little thought of beauty on their minds. I love the irony in nature's beauty enhanced accidentally by the Soviets' damming up of a few mountain rivers, creating such a site as Lake Norak.

It is as if God played a great trick on the Soviets for as they were trying to construct functionality, uniformity, and scientific precision they accidentally created art. And to the viewer above on the mountain this art deals a heavy blow to one of the mighty Soviet foundational pillars—atheism. How wonderful to see creation breaking through hydroelectric necessity, emanating stubborn resplendence, abundance, and uniqueness in a profoundly anti-Communist manner.

True, the Communists could never blot out the stars or enforce a policy that would allow each person to see a limited and equal number, but I think they must have taken it as an especial affront when nature's physical creativity so effortlessly invaded what they thought would be solely their own austere engineering. For here Norak lays tempting proletariat to become poetic about something other than the radiance of Stalin in springtime.

However, Norak seems to be an exception where nature won out. The Aral Sea, far downstream from this sleeping dragon, at the hands of the Soviet master planners became a cracked, diseased nothingness, which seems more in the vein of Soviet architecture than the apparition of Norak far below. Of course, even today a person cannot approach Lake Norak without a special governmental permit. So be it. Unapproachable bureaucracy enriches the mystery.

Today the clouds provided the perfect lighting, magnifying the fantastic nature of the surreal lake. And I was sorry to pass it and begin the decent to more common and dusty regions.

We passed a lonesome graveyard upon a high mountain face. Familiarly, our driver wiped his hands, palms to fingertips, from his eyes to chin. Halfway up so many scrubby Tajik hills a few headstones consistently evoke this response. I used to think the custom was observed solely in hopes of receiving blessing or power from the spirits living among the marking stones, but having heard Tajiks speak of *kafan xurdan* ("the eating of the graveclothes"), I have checked that belief. Similar to so many aspects of their lives, I have concluded that this practice has to do with the presence of fear.

Fear seems the ubiquitous spice of Tajik life, and to me, it so overwhelmingly flavors all its aspects as to make living unappetizing and ultimately without nourishment. Fear compelling, Tajiks must properly honor their grandmother at her passing and their father at his death or their deceased too may "eat their graveclothes," becoming so angry at the insult of improper respects and memorials as to be wrathfully aroused and return to murder one or more from among their own living children. If a family experiences a cluster of deaths in a short period of time, their own deceased are often seriously suspected as the cause.

Where is the peace of the omnipresent God who loved us so much that He sent His Son to die for our sins and save us for joy and eternal fellowship? Without nearness of such a God of love, protection, and relationship, even the bonds of family in a family-focused culture end in darkness. And we are left with manipulation, false honoring based in fear, thirst for power, and desperate avoidance of the very spiritual world we were created for.

My heart sank with these thoughts as we descended toward the capital. I was thankfully jolted back to more immediate matters when our taxi suddenly transitioned from driving on a smooth blacktop to a short gravel stretch. Ahh, the fruits of corruption. Occasionally in Tajik governmental undertakings, after the project finances have been skimmed, not enough funding is left for the completion of the project. With a road, the results are quite humorous as you go from brand-new highway to gravel pit and then return again to nice road. I prefer another approach to road completion within a decimated budget: when the cash begins to run dry, the road becomes narrower, shoulders are scrapped altogether as superfluous fluff, resulting in a compressed yet continuous completed product. As we bounced up and down in the gravel pit my preference further entrenched itself.

The Italians, contracted to build this main highway between the capital and the south, left last summer. Evidently the budget ran dry. And now another summer had nearly passed with more than one remaining gravel stretch.

Corruption seems to ensure slow progress and effectively discourage personal enterprise, as most people are too discouraged by the sight of the slippery system to try anything ambitious. The few who do maneuver their way through the seemingly uncontrolled processes appear to continuously get pinched into low quality. Foremen pour 80 percent of the necessary cement while distributing, selling, or pocketing the remainder. Another builder wonders if anyone is really going to miss a few bricks. Besides, the wealthy official's BMW has excellent shocks and his shoes are durable. Might as well put them to good use.

And, might I add, that Tajik people do not riot, strike, write nasty editorials, launch investigations, demand rights, or anything of the sort. The constitution seems to be a compilation of suggestions, and the people seem to be fine with that. Honestly, I don't know if it is the Soviet or Islamic training, fear of retribution, a combination of the three, or perhaps some other factors I have yet to understand. But apart from the Tajik civil war, which admittedly deals a heavy blow to my analysis, the only demonstration I have ever heard of was a group of women who did a short protest locally. The logic, so I heard, was that the government surely wouldn't do anything bad to women so it made sense to send them to protest. So the president here has an approval rating higher than an American president could ever dream of and, aided by some constitutional sleight of hand, is presently serving his third of two possible terms.

In case the last statement sounded confusing, that means he has risen above and beyond the call of duty and out of the originally, constitutionally possible pair of four- or five-year terms, is presently ruling for his thirteenth year. I use the word "ruling" on purpose.

But perhaps something can be said in favor of politically catatonic people. Every once in a while Philadelphia, Los Angeles, or New Orleans experiences a blackout followed by an exuberant pillage fest. Fortunately, Tajik people don't usually behave like that because electricity is out nearly every day. And besides, if your town just celebrated its 2,700-year anniversary wouldn't you be feeling a bit catatonic too?

Democracy is certainly the popular word of our day. But at the end of that day where titles and facades start to fade into the twilight, rulers, human rulers unfortunately, still make the rules. Reading the history of Central Asia, the Soviet Union, or any place on the face of the earth for that matter, could anyone honestly be an optimistic humanist or become excited reading utopian novels whether right, left, just left of left, beyond good and evil or otherwise? As Alexander Solzhenitsyn proclaimed in his dire Harvard commencement address on June 8, 1978, "No one on earth has any other way left but upward."[4]

We managed across the gravel pits and eventually found ourselves fully out of the mountains and passing into Dushanbe. A billboard or two actually began to appear. We passed one of an old woman, pictured palms uplifted to the sky, ready for prayer with the words, *"Duoi Modar"* (A Mother's Prayer). Tajiks widely hold that there is nothing as good, pure, and beneficial as the prayer of one's mother. All in all, a much more thought-provoking billboard than anything QuikTrip has come up with, although low gas prices put to lights are pretty exciting.

If you have ever been to Soviet cities, then upon arrival in Dushanbe you would probably feel a strong sense of déjà vu as you beheld its row upon row of decaying, gray, cement apartment buildings. Florence and Venice are decaying too, but I find their decay so absolutely charming. I would think I'd rather have been penniless

in Bonn than a Communist equal in Berlin, and I must not be the
only one to think so because the Soviets didn't build the wall to
keep the Bonn have-nots from flooding in.

It may seem odd to even mention these things as if I feel the
need to defend the Western side of the wall, but now, living on the
other side, perhaps I have heard old Tajik men call the Soviet Union
heaven one too many times. I have actually heard them use the
word "heaven" to describe it! How can people actually love Stalin?
Surely they are not afraid he will come back from the dead and
exact vengeance if they dare to speak against him. No, these Tajik
elders speak sincerely.

From what I have observed, evidently, as long as there is memory of satisfied stomachs coupled with present times sufficiently
full of suffering, a people abused by invaders who have taken their
possessions, forced them to die in distant wars, torn down all but
their most historic places of worship, scared them into observing
their local traditions only in hiding, and taught their children that
their God does not exist, that people, after the invaders have dis-
solved away into history, might speak of them reverently and long
for their return.

I know in frustration I have simplified the benefits that the
Soviets ushered in, like an unbelievable surge in literacy and an
elevation of women in many facets of life to name just two examples, but as a man who believes in God and absolutes regarding
the dignity and value of human beings, it always shocks me how
much people are generally willing to give away for so little materialistic gain. It appears to me that the lion's share of a generation
of Tajiks to this day believe that the Soviet Union was heaven,
and the continuation of a difficult present has only intensified the
rose-colored vision.

At the moment, Dushanbe was feeling a lot like heaven to me.
Personally, my favorite part of Dushanbe's appearance is its larger
streets lined on both sides with towering, mature sycamore trees.

The Soviets seemed to love lining Tajik boulevards with sycamores. Unfortunately, Tajiks hate sycamores. When talking about the tree, often their faces darken as they speak of those oxygen-stealing, allergy-inducing, filthy things.

Apart from one difficult, rake-filled weekend every fall that strained our relationship, I loved the pair of huge sycamores, their leaves as big as my face, which grew in my backyard in Kansas City. I can't recall ever having to gasp for breath while playing in my sandbox underneath one, even when I was young with small lungs. So I really don't see what the Tajiks are complaining about.

Down south in our Tajik city we had a similarly sycamore-dominated road, which was like an oasis of shade. It used to be my favorite street. I was horrified when the insanity of the local municipality decided that, in the name of the beautification of Kadimobod, the sycamores would all be chopped down. As we drove by the decimation, I asked my Tajik friend why each great trunk was chopped off oddly ten feet above the ground, one trunk every few feet extending to the foothills at the edge of town, suggesting the lost glory. Why?

He gave the normal line about oxygen theft, but he explained further that Tajiks believe sycamores are demon trees. I pointed out that most of the holiest Islamic sites I have seen in Tajikistan have a fair number of sycamores on the premises. Evidently sycamores can be redeemed from their natural bent toward evil and even gain righteous power enough to defy Soviet, street-widening bulldozers set on their removal, as the popular local legend goes. I find it strange how Satan can claim something natural and beautiful like a sycamore and steal it away from the enjoyment of an entire people. As for me, I am glad God made them. They are still His. Surely if the rocks can cry out, so can the sycamores.

We sped through the dappled sycamore shade of Rudaki Street, the main Dushanbe thoroughfare named after the great Persian poet of tenth century renown. I asked the driver to drop me near the LG shop so I could fulfill my quest of finding an air conditioner. I paid him, grabbed my backpack and hopped out into Dushanbe pedestrian traffic.

It was the big city for sure. No more greetings of *asalom*. People were moving with purpose and intensity. I was at home again within the freneticism of modern times. I felt immediate relief that once again I was an ambiguous nobody. Sometimes one gets so tired of being the strange, white creature from beyond the great sea. As I melted into the foot traffic, I couldn't help but smile.

Right away, I noticed a strange pair of female friends walking toward me. One of them was dressed modestly in traditional Tajik fashion. Her friend's ensemble, on the other hand, sent her veering toward the sleazy side of modernity. They strolled side by side chatting away, seemingly unconscious of the war of worlds their clothes were waging.

In Dushanbe, modern values appear to be winning their war against traditional ways. And here before me was a visible representation of the ongoing struggle. Were these two young women friends or perhaps the country cousin had come in for a visit? I wondered what they must think about the other, especially since Tajiks seem to greatly value social uniformity.

I also wondered at the anomaly of such a free-dressing woman living within a Muslim culture. Dushanbe is a world away from the burka. What does a Muslim woman think, who is this far removed from the Saudi Arabian model of her faith? Since she has no doubt seen satellite television, I wonder what she must think of the stark contrast.

Honestly, I have never understood nominal Islam. Nominal Christianity makes much more sense. The Apostle Paul wrote a great deal to show halfhearted humanity how such an anemic understanding of Christianity is absurd. But in Islam there is no grace to misunderstand or abuse. If, as in Islam, salvation itself basically lies in your own hands, what could possibly persuade one to be halfhearted? I have heard that from time to time a few present-day orthodox Jews will take it upon themselves to throw stones at passing motorists who dare to so blatantly disregard the Sabbath. Throwing rocks at disobedience makes sense to me if salvation is found in the law. But most of humanity is bizarrely, yet firmly, in the halfhearted, good works camp.

I finally reached my destination, opened the door and found myself face-to-face with a fantastic display of brand-new air conditioners! I am glad no one present asked me if I would sell my birthright for one because the memory of our town's heat had been brutally burned into my consciousness, leaving me quite at the mercy of the LG air conditioner salesmen.

However, I soon found that none of the many salesmen seemed to be at my mercy or even my annoyance as they flitted all around me talking with well-dressed clients, some of whom, I acutely knew, had arrived well after me. We say, "Customer service with a smile." They say, "Suited customer? Then smile."

I had to impose my grubby self in order to buy an air conditioner. I felt like going down the street to the next air conditioner vendor so, with new air conditioner in hand and in my best rendition of *Pretty Woman*, I could parade by the unfortunate salesmen. But I well knew there was no other vendor, so I swallowed my pride and added a generous portion to my salesman's commissions. It was just as well because the conditioner was so bulky I wouldn't have looked much like *Pretty Woman* as I grunted and staggered past the shop in the summer heat.

I found a European take on a van parked just outside, and oh so gently put my precious cargo, the hope of cool days to come, inside the cramped quarters. Then we were off racing across Dushanbe. I was probably still getting ripped off at a three-dollar equivalent fare. But the conversation was pleasant and that has to be worth something.

A Day in Pursuit of Air Conditioning

The principal errand of the day done, I went to work on a couple of other items I had to tie up before heading back south. Our van sped past the Tajik opera house on the way to the main office of my NGO (nongovernmental organization), the European-headquartered AID International.

It crossed my mind that the Tajik language wasn't a good medium for opera. I quickly thought of three popped or guttural letters that strengthened my impression. But I believe some people told Mozart the same about German. Not that I know a single thing about Tajik opera or any opera for that matter, but I would bet Tajik opera is all in Russian, unless there is a Tajik Mozart that I just don't know about. I can't even keep up with Tajik wedding tunes.

We arrived outside the AID International office and I popped in to do all the bizarre things that one does at international NGO offices the developing world over, like "safe banking" for example. "Safe banking" consists of withdrawing from your large wad of ever-dwindling personal cash that you brought in on the plane with you several years ago in a secret fanny pouch. Our assets now sit in a tattered envelope marked "David" with a slew of crossed out balances penciled in on the front of the envelope. Among a jumbled mess of other envelopes, it's always a relief to find yours is still in the safe.

I stood with the finance department head in a small closet bending over the army green safe hoping we would again find that old "David" marked envelope. Granted, there's no drive-through service, interest, or online updates, and they may have bank holidays for American, British, Dutch, German, Tajik, and Russian holidays, but at least there is no minimum balance to be maintained. I do wish they had one of those change-counting machines though. Love those things.

Now, with the advent of Tajik ATMs, I hope the period of having thousands and thousands of dollars strapped to my stomach is over. I'll never forget the time the customs officer made Ann and I unstrap our wads and count them on the table for him in front of a full room of less-than-well-off strangers, at least one of whom was carrying a semiautomatic weapon. He finally allowed us to sneakily re-hide our Tajik equivalent of three or four years' salary back on our persons and head out alone into the inviting darkness towards luggage check. Should we stay close to the guy with the semiautomatic or avoid him?

We were able to find the old faithful envelope so I could make my withdrawal. Before leaving the office, I had to do my once per two-month mail/care package search, attend to a bit of passport picture and visa work, and try to figure out what's going on in the world, the country, and the office. I often find discovering what's going on in the office to be the most difficult of those tasks.

I think the fundamental problem is that I never know what language to speak. English is supposed to be the de facto language of NGO business the developing world over, but I heard a steady stream of German coming from the child sponsorship cubicles, two European friends chatting away in something else, and a pair of Tajik office personnel, desks adjoining, fielding phone calls in Tajik and Russian respectively. They like to speak an interesting half and half language between phone calls. It so flusters me that sometimes I have trouble talking to the Scottish guy.

With everybody running around like the scene after the Tower of Babel incident, I usually forget where I put my shoes, my socks flopping around like rabbit ears, as I wander down the hallway trying not to forget to do anything that can't wait until the fall. A lot of times I stand just outside the office door for a few minutes after leaving, catching my breath, and letting my mind have fair opportunity to remember things undone. I've found it's easier to go back in from the stairway than from Kadimobod.

My tiny van dropped me at the NGO guest apartment, where I had been told the AID International driver had put a massive amount of international aid that was to be taken down to

Kadimobod with me. I took one look at the spiraling piles of boxes and made arrangements to be picked up by a much larger van.

Upon its arrival, the van, locally called a *mashrutka*, which is not to be confused with anything Dodge makes, looked as if it would serve its purpose. I liked the driver right away as we loaded box after box until the mashrutka seemed like it was about to pop. And might I add that there is nothing quite as nice as sweating profusely to start a long mashrutka adventure. I longingly wondered if it was possible to plug a window-unit air conditioner into a cigarette lighter. Dodge vans probably offer that option in Starlight Blue, Desert Sky, or Sage Green. Mashrutkas, on the other hand, do not offer anything. You have to fight for every bit. Incidentally, a little-known fact is that mashrutka rides are among the world's most effective abdominal workouts. At least the glass in their windows is usually translucent enough to make out the starlight blue sky.

I treated my driver to dinner at Café Merve, a wonder of Turkish delicacies, before heading out of town. I still remember the first time Ann and I went to Café Merve. It was on our first Tajikistan stint before we had children. We were shocked to see that sausage pizza meant chopped up hot dogs on a small circular object. Now, years later, I praised the merits of Café Merve to the heavens with utmost sincerity to this Turkish food rookie as they served up the most magnificent hot dog pizza imaginable. This illustrates why recently when I was asked by a new arrival from foreign soil whether the local Mexican restaurant was good, I felt the need to disclaimer my high praise of the establishment by saying, "But I have bad taste now."

After dinner and before finally setting out toward home, I stopped in at the Dutch supermarket. So many imported items, so little time! Between gawking at Gouda cheese and bananas, I hit the jackpot by finding baby wipes. I would be the most popular husband in all of Kadimobod!

I grabbed a Tajik newspaper at the checkout. Both the newspaper and the checkout were fabulous. The beep, beep of the barcode scanner set my soul to flying. And the newspaper was a great find. We went from information overload in the States, to being intensely interested in painstakingly translating two-paragraph articles from Tajik just to see what David Beckham's picture is doing in the local *Tajik Times*. It took me a half hour to figure out I really shouldn't have cared. Let me suggest as a general rule that it is never worth translating news stories about David Beckham.

But with full Turkish bellies, boxes and boxes of relief, a fantastic air conditioner, hard-gained news of Beckham, bananas, and enough European cheese to last at least a month, we finally set off for home.

Night

> *Do not go gentle into that good night,*
> *Old age should burn and rave at close of day;*
> *Rage, rage against the dying of the light.*[5]

The sycamores, in evening light, passed by all too slowly as we went haltingly on our way out of Dushanbe. In Tajikistan, one gets pulled over by the police many times. But I don't think I have ever been pulled over as often as this night. I believe we were pulled over around fifteen times between the Dutch supermarket and Kadimobod.

The bad luck was a series of factors converging to form a nearly impenetrable barrier against our progress. Between the cooling summer evening, the potential riches of a brim-filled mashrutka with a foreigner in the passenger seat, a day not near enough to the weekend to justify heading home early nor sufficiently hot to haze the law enforcers' minds with drowsy pixie dust, the cops descended upon us like locusts. They have their mandatory roadside posts but that night it appeared that an inordinate amount of turns in the road served the purposes of lone law enforcers, traffic sticks in hand out for the good of the commonwealth or of wealth at any rate.

I think the worst moment came when we were pulled over again before our previous officer friend had disappeared from the rearview mirror. Perhaps he pulled us over for going too slow because we hadn't even gotten into third gear yet from our last pull-over. It was also this particular officer who, after taking the standard thirty-three-cent bribe from the driver and a quick, official look at the license and registration while eyeing the mounds of international aid boxes, asked which box he could take. When I refused, he accused me of getting rich off international food aid. He seemed to actually believe I was making a killing running German soups and expired crackers into southern Tajikistan.

The situation, albeit bizarre, was getting worse, so I was proud of my driver when he did some quick mental maneuvering and came up with, "Okay, take a box, but we'll have to write your name and police registration number down so we can report to the United Nations exactly which box of international aid you took." The words "United Nations" did the trick, and we were on our way again with all the boxes intact.

My driver's tactic reminded me of my friend's strategy for sending packages to less-than-prosperous places. My friend collects lots of vaguely official-looking stamps from hobby stores and the like and goes stamp crazy all over the box. The logic being, if it looks more official than the official looking at it, then it ain't worth messing with. My friend might be onto something with this strategy, because I have noticed that the Tajik checkpoint officers abruptly stop all the junker cars putting by while waving supportively at the strangers speeding past in their shimmering SUVs. Sometimes I wonder if you bought an expensive enough car, if you could drive from New Delhi to Moscow without being stopped at all.

But alas, our mashrutka was shimmer deficient so yet another low point came when another officer forced us to pull over and proceeded to jam a pair of fifty-pound sacks of flour into a non-existent hole between my boxes, asking my driver ever so politely, on pain of something undisclosed I am sure, if he wouldn't mind taking it to such and such a house when we reached Kadimobod. I wonder if my driver still had to pay his thirty-three cents. I'm just glad the officer didn't have three fifty-pound sacks or I would have had one on my lap. I added up all those bribes and realized my driver was losing a great amount of his profit, measly to begin with, to the police piranhas. I felt bad and told him I'd pay him the amount he had lost.

We finally settled into a rhythm outside of Dushanbe. The stops were less frequent, and in the failing light, we were soon ascending into the mountains surrounding Lake Norak. The quiet night was conducive for reflection, and as we passed high above the lake and began our decent towards the southern plains, I stared out the window as my thoughts wandered.

Southern Tajikistan, with its harsh continental climate, is quite barren when left to itself out in the Central Asian sun. There is a short time each spring, now a distant memory as I stared out at the barren hills rolling by, when the never-ending slopes are awash in a healthy verdancy. But the brutal summer sun had summoned endless dust to swallow Tajikistan, leaving scrub and stumpy trees in thirsty anticipation of the distant fall rains.

Even in dying light, Tajikistan's settled places remind me of oasis towns with their sudden burst of mulberry-lined streets, hillsides full of resilient orchards, and hearty pistachio groves. Terraced steep places with remnants of recent wheat harvests turn a dustier shade of brown daily as the unrelenting sun bakes them into oblivion. And beyond the tended browns, an endless sea of forlorn scrub warns every living thing not to stray far from the village's grapevine-shaded relief.Before us, shepherds herded their livestock down the highway, the ever-present mountains unwilling to offer easier routes.

A Day in Pursuit of Air Conditioning

We slowed. Life itself slowed. As we inched past them, weaving among the herd in the twilight, I stared at the enduring mix of cows, sheep, and goats. The animals hardly lifted their heads toward the car, parting unconsciously before us like water gives way to a rowboat in a dead calm. The shepherds stopped briefly, returning my gaze. Their eyes reflected, a shade short of desperation, an overwhelming lethargy that reminded me of the land itself. The whole scene was palpably stoic there in the dusk, our empty stares dueling. No one seemed to possess the necessary vigor for emotional expression. Even the sullen hoofbeats of the cattle reflected the dry and difficult monotony of too many moments like this.

I was reminded of the choice given to Helmholtz by the "Controller" at the end of *Brave New World*, the choice of his place of banishment. When asked if he would prefer a nice tropical island of paradise or something of that sort, Helmholtz replies, "I should like a thoroughly bad climate." He continues, "I believe one would write better if the climate were bad. If there were a lot of wind and storms, for example."[6]

Solzhenitsyn, in the aforementioned address at Harvard, speaks of how suffering has prepared the Russian soul. But the Bible says it best in the book of James, "Consider it pure joy, my brothers, whenever you face trials of many kinds, because you know that the testing of your faith develops perseverance. Perseverance must finish its work so that you may be mature and complete, not lacking anything" (Jas 1:2–4). Judging from the eyes of these shepherds, I believe the experience of Tajikistan has been an exercise in perseverance and I wonder if it may have prepared this people for good news as it has prepared the way for that good news to flow down deeper into my own soul.

As the deep darkness settled in around us, the mountains were immersed in mystery. Tajikistan is an incredibly uplifted land. Mountains generally quicken the soul to a sense of romance born of the unknown, but often Tajikistan's mountains do not summon this excitement of natural drama. Rather, the traveler is pressed toward determination in the face of stubborn continuance as the Tajik ranges roll on daunting and drab, like dunes that will deal the traveler a fatal blow of tedium before he passes them all.

But among the mountains in the new darkness I was reminded that when the sun sets, even to the man for whom childhood has died long ago, the whole world is filled with mystery again. Suddenly barrenness is transformed by an imagination elixir into caves, a stream's deepest pools, dark forests, and high mountain passes. This regular rhythm of life, this nightly transformation of our world to darkness has always called me back from a sleepwalk through existence to a remembrance of the profoundness of God's creation. It forces my senses to narrow, to awaken. It is a beautiful immersion.

The night's pervasion reminds me of how thoroughly China swallowed Hudson Taylor. The China of Hudson's experience was capable of engulfing a man in a way that very few places on earth retain the power to do. Granted, Hudson wanted, even fought to be so engulfed, so perhaps that is still a possibility for the determined today. But even as the Western media presents Central Asia as if it were the end of the earth, the ends of today's earth are so accessible.

When, as a young man, my great-uncle set out for Syria, he took a boat from New York, crossing the Atlantic, and on through the Mediterranean to the Middle East. I imagine every day sailing on the ocean fortified the reality that a new world, a world apart, was looming ahead.

Now, with the early flight on Turkish Airlines, I can depart remote Central Asia and have Chicago deep-dish pizza for dinner that very night in the heart of America, reveling in the frequent flyer miles accrued and probably already posted on my account. And not only to have dinner in Chicago, but, as if I had never left, to be able to sit and share that pizza with a Chicagoan and knowledgeably discuss the state of the Cubs or the range of the latest *American Idol* star who sang the national anthem to open that afternoon's game.

A Day in Pursuit of Air Conditioning

No, we have never been in Tajikistan the same way that
Hudson Taylor was in China. What would it have been like to not
know who the Chiefs have on injured reserve for Sunday or to not
be able to enjoy the tape my dad sent of the Red Sox winning the
World Series?

I wonder what it would be like to have been that unrelentingly
in China. What would it be like to be that completely in Tajikistan?
I hardly think it possible for the modern missionary to experience
Hudsonesque immersion. Perhaps with great discipline and determination it could be self-imposed? Perhaps a little.

But even then with the advent of instant communication
brought about by computers, a missionary's headquarters is always a
second away with its Western values and goals. We are always driving, directing, and daily dividing our presence between two worlds.
I wonder how this modern world affects us, our longevity in our
place of service, our work, our focus on that work, our ability to be
incarnational, especially when all the workers begin with a strong
bent toward instant everything. I do not deny the positives of our
modern world. The gospel reaches millions through technology. I
only wonder what the negatives might be.

Maybe we should pause to examine the positives as well. The example of America should teach us that an almost infinite number of
technologies broadcasting the gospel cannot stop the ever-increasing
cultural slide away from Christ if the Holy Spirit is not moving.
Even as radio, television, and internet make the gospel more immediate than ever, it seems that every casual glance at our customs and
ways reflect a steady drift further away.

As I continued staring out at the black hills passing, I wondered
what many Tajiks were watching tonight on satellite television. I
remember the first time I saw a satellite dish jutting out the back
of a nomad's tent in the desert south of Jerusalem. The Middle East
has certainly changed and perhaps the Far East has ceased to exist
altogether or at least ceased to be far.

But the biggest chasm humanity faces is of course not continental or cultural, but spiritual. Tajiks remind me of this fact every time the sun goes down. During the day people do a much better job of masking their true spiritual state. But the picture often gets clearer as the light dims. I'm reminded of Chesterton's words of the one who was "happier and happier as he approached the earth, but sadder and sadder as he approached the heavens."[7] But I have found that this growing sadness can be observed not only in a people's approach to the heavens, but nightly as the Tajiks' side of the earth grows dark.

Fear sets in as Tajiks are reminded of the spiritual world, of the death that will inevitably come. As the sun sets, as eternity reminds us of its presence, rhetoric slips away, and we're left with the emotions that are the natural fruit of our faith. During the day my Tajik friends might speak disdainfully of what they perceive to be my arrogance at saying that I am convinced that I am a child of God, that God holds me securely in salvation, and by His gracious power will never let me go. But at night when, unsure of the love of Allah, the Tajiks retreat to safe communal places to hide together from evil spirits and their own ancestors, I am thankful that I serve a God who empowers me by His presence to walk alone among sycamores or beside the demon-frequented ashes of a dying fire.

On such a solitary night passage I am alive to God's love. I desire that the Tajiks too could find the peace and joy found of boasting in the solid hope born of the resurrection of the Lord Jesus Christ. It is the content of our faith that determines how we experience the night.

More hills slipped by. After a while I could make out our region's most famous mountain in the distance. It marked the final approach to Kadimobod. Later, as we passed Kadimobod's deserted main bazaar seeing almost no one on the streets, I felt a sense of relief. I knew that I would not be a spectacle, that we could unload the aid at the office and I could carry my groceries and new air conditioner up to our apartment without all the stares, without me and my air conditioner becoming the talk of the town for the next few weeks. Granted, it would leak out eventually, but not arriving at prime *tamasho* (watching) time would rob the neighbor ladies of the visuals necessary for a long-lived legend of the foreigners' new air conditioner.

My driver was gracious enough to help me unload the massive pile of aid boxes into one of our fourth-floor offices. Not an easy task. Finally finishing, we sat our sweaty selves back in the marshutka and drove to our Soviet-built apartment building, thumping along through the courtyard and coming to a stop in front of our stairwell. There was still light coming from a few apartments, but the solitary courtyard water faucet gushed alone in the night creating a pool amid the dominant splashing sound.

I noted that the pressure was pretty good, which led me to hope we'd have water on the second floor sufficient enough for a late-night shower. I ran the groceries up. My driver unloaded the air conditioner and stood waiting for me on my return. I paid him, adding in my estimate of the bribes he had sustained. Picking up my prize, I stood and watched him drive away. My eyes drifted to the *mazor*, the resting place of a revered Muslim saint who lay just across the street from our apartment. I could see the massive sycamore trees gently swaying in the mazor's light. It was beautiful. It was awful. Every day from our balcony window I can see the Tajiks streaming to the mazor to kiss its sides, to pray, to rage against their personal dying of the light.

I have heard it said we must find out where God is working and join Him there. I have also heard it said that we must seek out a place that seems as far away from God's work as possible and begin there. For us, it appears God has chosen the latter. I am thankful for omnipresence.

Night is dark when you pray to a distant power. I understand the raging. We have come here to rage against it, but not in futile death throws but with Spirit-filled good news of peace and joy and hope. As I turned to go inside I felt an inner rage, felt like pumping my fist against this Tajik night and had my arms not been full of air conditioner I just might have done so.

11

TO GET AN UZI

Although we're not learning Russian, we can't help but pick up a few choice Russian words that have infiltrated the Tajik language. For instance, with Ann being pregnant with our second child, we recently had the unfortunate opportunity to learn the Russian word for "ultrasound." *Uzi* is an exceedingly helpful word we just added to our random Russian repertoire. But the process of getting an uzi was far more interesting, that is to say harrowing, than the learning of the word itself.

Ann and I, with our two-year-old daughter Grace in tow, were at first eager to go and, by way of uzi, get our first look at our second baby. But holding on to enthusiasm in Tajikistan is about as difficult as retaining water in your bare hands. We were told, just before we went off on our "Hospitals of Dushanbe walking tour" in search of our uzi, that Tajikistan spends about four dollars per person per year on its medical system. According to our same source, a justifiably horrified Western doctor, the less-than-heavenly Mozambique spends three times as much on its medical system.

Putting this information to good use, upon entering a Tajik hospital one should watch one's step, be extremely hesitant to touch anything, resist the urge to look around or be even slightly curious, and be vigilant of falling objects. For example, on the resisting curiosity front, one should not even pose the question as to why the blood-testing lady uses her mouth to suck the patient blood samples out. Just keep moving.

After some futile wanderings and less-than-stellar directions at scary hospital number one, we were directed to scary hospital number two, conveniently located just down the road from scary hospital number one. Fortunately, the doors were open, allowing touch-free entry. Evidently, the hospital staff at this hospital had resisted the common urge to lock all convenient doors. Perhaps, and I speculate, to protect against falling objects?

Unfortunately, they had also resisted the urge of having a reception area so we were soon met by the solitude of some depressing stairs, a pair of doors we might have to touch, and an open exit that led out back. Dodging curiosity and the need to touch doors, we went out back. Several semi-official looking people were chatting in the courtyard. I decided they must work here and asked one of the men where we could get our uzi. He pointed to a less-than-promising stairway across the courtyard. Fortunately, it didn't have doors. We found a few ladies standing in the stairway in sort of a haphazard blob. Just in front of them a closed door said, "UZI." We made it! Well, almost. Over the next hour and a half we would have the opportunity to hone our standing-in-line abilities.

Standing in line in post-Soviet Tajikistan is a lot like grabbing a rebound in basketball. Positioning is important. Have a wide stance low to the ground, be big, look big, feel big. Know who's crashing in behind and anticipate their approach angle. But more than anything, standing in line is about attitude. You have to want it! You have to want it more than the rich, important guy who is about to shove his aging mother on past you because he is rich and important. You have to want it more than the mean lady who looks vaguely dangerous and Uzbek. You have to want it more than the countless pregnant ladies with their bands of children and neighbors building up behind you who seem to want it pretty bad.

To Get an Uzi

I was never a good rebounder. So it was an hour before we even got inside the uzi room. Fortunately Ann, if she had played basketball, would have been a better rebounder than me. Otherwise we might still be waiting outside in the hall hoping things wouldn't fall on us and wishing Grace understood the wisdom in our prohibitions against curiosity and touching.

Before we entered the uzi room, we were witness to the community-creating powers of children. Our two-year-old daughter Grace breaks down walls. Not literally, though looking at our surroundings that probably would have been a possibility. It doesn't matter how high the cultural walls are, Grace breaks them down. Pretty soon we had formed a happy company in the shabby hallway with the other bad rebounders.

These bad rebounders were usually so because they were either nice, timid, poor, or all three. But I guess I'd rather have Grace play with them and their kids than with the big, rich guy or the vaguely dangerous Uzbek lady. Most Uzbeks seem friendly enough, but this particular lady certainly did not. She would make one great rebounder. I'd definitely let her have the ball.

We finally made it into the room, and then kind of wished we hadn't. The shabby room—shabby more in the sense of extremely alarming than in the slightly melancholy sense of the word—looked as if it hadn't had even so much as a light bulb replaced since Lenin died, with the exception of the new fire escape plan. Behind the door there was a hand-drawn map with the words "Fire Escape Route" scribbled in Tajik onto a scrap of poster board. Beside the plan, there were some dangerous firefighting supplies I definitely would not attempt to use especially in the event of a fire. Why were there supplies anyway? Were they suggesting we fight the fire first and if failing in that then proceed to stop, drop, and roll? I've been here too long, because the main thing that came to mind on seeing the "Fire Escape Route" was "Oh, I wonder where they got the poster board!"

The dingy ten-by-twenty-foot room conveniently served as the scan room, payment room, and waiting room all in one! Tajiks seem to be finding ways to keep those health insurance costs down, one of which is to not have insurance. We stood in the middle of the room trying our best not to notice the twenty-some sardined Tajiks staring at the odd American family. We saw some new faces in the room that we hadn't seen during our hour-long wait in the hallway. We decided they must be bad rebounders too. And we saw the scary Uzbek-looking lady standing close to the curtain. Technically, she should have still been waiting in the hall, but apparently no one thought it a convenient time to bring up technicalities.

As we settled in to watch the proceedings, we noticed the scanner lady was saving time and energy. Between her desk and the examining area she just had to poke her head out and scoot her chair a little bit, thereby eliminating the need to stand up. Every time she flung back the curtain after a scan, I made sure to look up at the wall, as Muslim women aren't exactly happy when their tummy is exposed to a waiting room.

Making it into the room was a small victory, but we still had a long way to go. Several times we forgot to block passing angles and people who seemed upset to have already had to wait two minutes in the hallway slipped past us and the other indecisive unfortunates sitting along the walls. But I thought the real low in customer service came when a hospital staff person, her hospital uniform suggesting at least to me that she should be serving us, slipped behind the curtain and had herself scanned. No one else seemed to mind. Part of her employee benefit package perhaps?

Apart from the cutting in line, it took longer than anticipated because almost every person in the room got scanned. It was clear that most of the people waiting were families; typically mothers with their children and a couple of tag-along women relatives. So we obviously assumed just the pregnant lady would get scanned and not her three children, her sister, and her neighbor. But we assumed wrong.

I guess the thinking was basically, if you had already made it into the scan room, you might as well scan everyone in the family just to make sure all those internal things were in order. So little girls got their livers scanned, and screaming toddlers were scanned against their wills. We heard one family saying that they had come all the way from a distant region to get this scan. Well, if you had traveled several hours and had finally made it into the room, I guess you might as well get the whole family scanned.

Another problem that we faced in getting Ann scanned before the sun set, was that we were unwilling to go and wait behind the curtain with the patient being scanned. Tajiks are extremely communal—which despite the tone of this story is a wonderful thing! And while we do try to adapt culturally as best we can, we just didn't think it appropriate to go and share the moment with strangers getting their first looks at their babies or their livers.

Feeling this way definitely placed us in the minority, and so people kept slipping behind the curtain to, first, to assure they got scanned next, and second, to share the first glimpses of a new life with a total stranger. We moved as close to the curtain as we could without falling through. I clutched Grace, waiting for the first stirrings of the curtain as if it were the Pool of Bethesda. Ann focused on giving dirty looks to the others in the waiting room, her eyes saying it would be our turn next or else. She's my hero.

As soon as the last of the final group in front of us surfaced, we dove in behind the curtain, Ann in the lead and I, grasping Grace, close behind. And afterwards, once again, we kind of wished we hadn't. There was a tiny dinosaur of an ultrasound machine next to a ratty old cot sort of thing that you could evidently lay down on if you were feeling especially immune to diseases at the time. Unfortunately, the person lying down couldn't see the screen, so I had to describe to Ann what the baby looked like. I kind of wonder who thought that one through. Probably the same person who thought it would be a great idea to tape a picture of a scantily clad woman right above the ultrasound machine's screen.

The Russian lady knew enough Tajik to figure out we wanted a pregnancy ultrasound and not liver scans for the entire family, so in a matter of moments Ann was lathered up and laying down, completely unable to see the screen. Grace and I got a great look at the baby though. Although the screen was tiny, the Russian lady was very good at her job and was pretty friendly apart from the "problem" fiasco, which I will elucidate now.

Although no other patients came behind the curtain during Ann's scan, it was less than private. In fact, our scan, thanks to the scan lady and our lack of understanding of the Russian language, became the most public scan of the entire day.

We do know one Russian word for problem. It's "problem" with a sort of funny pronunciation. So we understood that according to the scan lady there was a "prrrrooablem" with the baby. Lovely. Then, with us sufficiently alarmed, the Russian lady spoke on and on about who knows what in mainly Russian with the word "prrrrooablem" popping up every once in a while.

Frustrated that she could neither help us understand sufficiently or write down instructions of what we should do next, she left the room in search of, well, she didn't say. So we waited behind the curtain.

As soon as she left the room, the discussion about our "prrrrooablem" commenced. Everyone had lots to say about it. They seemed especially interested in how we didn't know Russian. Then we heard someone say that we did know Tajik well. It got a lot quieter after that, although there was still intermittent discussion about us. Not feeling the need to discuss it with them, we waited quietly for the scan lady to return.

She came back with a "translator." The translator knew how to say, "How arrre yooou?" which she seemed very proud of. But since we wanted to say far more than, "Fine, except for our prrrrooablem. How are you?" the whole translator situation really went nowhere.

So the scan lady wrote down her diagnosis in Russian and then had the other lady translate it into Tajik on the back of the paper. Our diagnosis riddle in hand, we went directly and talked with our Western doctor friend. He said that the diagnosis was a common one that hospitals like to give here, but the diagnosis doesn't even exist in the West—something vague about pressure. It seems to be in the same ballpark as scanning the liver or being deathly afraid of breezes, unfounded but nearly universally accepted.

The one great thing about the scan was the price. When it came time to settle our bill, the scan lady said two somoni. I handed it over, equivalent to about sixty-six cents. Just imagine if we had been members of their HMO. At that price why not scan the whole family twice?

III
THE GIANT SAINT

Approaching

We saw the Nephilim there (the descendants of Anak come from the Nephilim). We seemed like grasshoppers in our own eyes, and we looked the same to them. (Num 13:33)

In Tajikistan, we have neighbor women who, due to a combination of poverty and the beliefs of their husbands, only leave our street a few times each year. But even the men don't travel often. Apart from those Tajiks who decide to join in the suffering of the semi-legal, manual labor force of the Moscow boom, most don't stray too far from their own turf. So as I met my three buddies outside in the morning light I was not surprised to see them alive with excitement.

My friend and present language coach, Safar, had procured the services of his taxi-driving neighbor for our day trip. Suhrob and Alisher had just finished up their spring semester at Kadimobod University. The four of them were gathered around a dark blue Korean hatchback basking in the freedom of the early summer morning, joyful anticipation visible on their faces. Today, *nasib boshad* (if it is fate) we would see the remains of a Muslim saint.

Ignoring the heat, all four wore pants, respecting the Islamic tradition of a man not shaming himself by wearing shorts.

Unhappily, I had decided to roast rather than be the only one shaming himself. Fortunately, the men didn't need to work on their tans anyway as all four—as typical of Tajiks—were quite a bit darker than me even though I'd been out in the sun nearly every day. The tint of Tajik skin usually hangs around an ideal shade of bronze similar to that of Latin Americans, the hue so prized by everyone from the United States. But every place has its own ideal, so I knew that since Suhrob's skin was a bit lighter than the others, his would be considered the nicest color. In Tajikistan, the rule is the paler the better.

But tall is a more universal ideal, and though even most tall Tajiks would be considered short or at best average by Western standards, in Tajikistan, Alisher was considered tall and had the others beat by several centimeters. Black hair and black eyes, nearly universal among the Tajiks, graced all four. As for features, Suhrob, Safar, and the driver had the more typical Persian or Caucasian features not so dissimilar to many European peoples, while Alisher alone had the slightly almond-shaped eyes and facial structure reminiscent of more Uzbek or Mongol people groups.

In preparation for this day trip, I had raided the kitchen on the way out of the apartment. To satisfy our thirst, I grabbed a pair of liter-and-a-half RC Cola bottles filled with frozen filtered water. And for my food contribution I brought homemade cookies and a sausage I hoped was heavier on beef derivatives than pork, though I doubted they'd care as long as no one mentioned it. As we popped the hatch and loaded up, the guys showed off their own provisions. I eyed a *tarbuz* (watermelon) anticipating rolling it to a crisp fresh-ness in the cold springs surrounding the mazor, the mausoleum that was our destination.

Safar, recently graduated from Kadimobod University, placed a hot *kulcha* (roll) into my hands, proudly showing me the whole batch that his wife and his mother had baked in their outdoor *chag-*

don oven that morning in preparation for our excursion. Beautiful! I grabbed my camera from my backpack and we were off.

The three were abuzz with excitement in the back, eagerly taking turns wearing the lone pair of sunglasses, sharing opportunities to be *fason* (beautiful/stylin'). Of course, being a few years older, the guest, and the payer of gas and taxi fees, I was riding "shotgun" in the place of honor. I was doing my best to resist the contagious urge to be fason while chatting away with our taxi driver. At the moment, our driver was extrapolating on his theories about Bush, Iraq, the world of Islam, and his years of Soviet military service in Eastern Europe.

We shared the car, the camaraderie, but to each of us the trip held a different potential. Suhrob, the true pilgrim, alive with the legends, the potential powers, and blessings of the holy mazor, was spouting the knowledge of the initiated at his two nominally believing friends. His uncles had told him the stories of this place. He unsuccessfully tried to control his excitement at his first visit to the site of the remains of the great Sulton Uvais.

Safar, by far the most natural wearer of the sunglasses, approached Islam as one would imagine an inherently cool guy would, with nothing so passionate as might ruin his charisma. But my attention was gathered on Alisher. All three of the young men had heard the gospel, but Alisher, as the most responsive, most serious explorer of the gospel among the three held my curiosity. I was anxious to see how he would react to the holy site.

As for the taxi driver, he seemed pretty excited to be getting paid and receiving religious pilgrimage points at the same time. Scoring in this world and the next simultaneously is the best double-points scenario. To him it was like giving to the United Way on a rewards credit card. As for me, I hoped for a great day to relax with friends as I observed part of Tajik religious experience.

The sun, already brutal, was ironing out my khakis as we pulled into a gas station on the outskirts of town. Beside the decorative pumps, there was a rusty barrel brimmed with gas, a plastic scoop and funnel hanging at its side. Since there didn't appear to be a second rusty barrel filled with ultra, mega, mocha premium, we went with regular gas. We welcomed the shade as we hung out under the awning while the full-service staff, funnel in place, topped us off in preparation for the unwelcoming road ahead.

Apparently Visa, despite their advertising slogan, is not everywhere my family wants to be, as my wife and I have not been able to use our credit cards in Tajikistan for a couple of years. So I gave the taxi driver the first half of our agreed-upon price for the day. He passed the somoni to the attendant who wished us *rohi safed* (white road, hope for a safe journey). And we were on our way, windows down, circulating a slightly relieving breeze through the car. I was thankful that the manifestation of the universal college student's belief in personal invincibility allowed my friends to disregard local superstition about breezes. Even the knower of all things, superstitious Suhrob, who had recently informed me of the great danger of contracting epilepsy while walking the night hills alone in spring, was all smiles as our personal gale blew directly into his intrepid face.

The city fell away and we were soon completely out of the valley and among the foothills of the Pamir Mountains. The mountains go on rolling until reaching formidable size to the east and into northern Afghanistan. The Pamirs give the Himalayas a run for their money. If they were just a tad more strategically located, it would bring Tajiks an assuring sense of isolation from their perpetually warring southern neighbors. They knew the Afghans lived just over a few of these hills and across the Daryoi Panj (Five River). I remembered back to my fascination with the land when I was first attempting to understand our family's new home. A few years earlier I had written:

The Giant Saint

The parched and barren hills loomed on the horizon in every
direction. Beyond them and far to the north, Kazakhstan
sprawled boundless, with its endless history of steppe
nomads, clan upon clan. To the south, Afghanistan fought
for survival, its warring tribes shedders of generation upon
generation of civil blood. To the southwest lay Iran, cradle of
civilization, its inhabitants the ancestors and brothers of the
Tajik people. To the west and northwest the great and an-
cient Tajik cities of Bukhara and Samarkand yet remained,
their fading glories giving voice to the height of Tajik culture
and civilization, the seat of their poets, heroes, and kings.
Those cities, because of the maneuverings of modern Soviet
politics, now rested in the domain of the Uzbeks who are of
Turkish stock. And to the east, beyond the treacherous passes
of the Pamir and Tian Shan ranges, ultimately rising to the
Himalayas, the very roof of the world, lay China, descending
from the world's greatest mountains to its abundant fertility.

Tajikistan is an abundant headwaters. The heavy snows high in
the glacial mountains partake in a constant melt sending powerful
streams flowing down between hills the country over, creating a verdant Dushanbe instead of a dusty Kabul. Evidently the Soviets saw
some potential. They forcibly relocated the traditionally mountain-
dwelling Tajiks to the sweltering valleys, diverting the waters and
filling the virgin fields with cotton and newly established towns
such as Sovietski and Moskovski.

My favorite Soviet-inspired Tajikistan place name is probably the
regional name Leninabad, an interesting blend of the Russian leaders' name and the Tajik verb "to establish" that one will recognize in
the names of other Muslim cities such as the Islamabad of Pakistan
or the Faizabad of northern Afghanistan. *Faiz* means grace. I think
the name Faizabad symbolizes our greatest hopes for Tajikistan.
We spend our lives here trying to redefine their concept of faiz and
explain what it would mean for the Tajiks to be established in it.

We drove over a decaying cement bridge that spanned across a broad *sang-ob*. Sang-ob literally means "rock water" which, consistent with the general thrust of the Tajik language, gets right to the point without any meanderings through the roots of other languages. Sang-ob is a refreshingly frugal way of describing the broad, rocky, dry beds that lie throughout the country awaiting the next flash-flood-inducing melt of mountain snows. There was a small channel under the bridge, its swift, clear current reminding me of a Colorado stream. Looking back downstream as we crossed, I could see the last of the cotton fields disappearing. Good riddance?

Cotton seems to have a knack for enslaving people and inducing suffering. I have heard the stories of the forcibly resettled ancestors of my Tajik friends coming in from the newly established cotton fields. But it was not all bad. The men learned to read and soon education spread to the women and children as well. I can picture it from the way my Tajik friends have described those days. The men, from the graying elders with their long beards and *toki* (traditional hat) covered heads, to the youths capable of picking many kilos of cotton a day, walked together through the evening light to the newly built schools where the Soviets taught them to read and write.

It was an incredible time, a whole culture's men becoming literate together, taking the distinction away from the village mullah who had studied in the great Tajik cities' *madrasas* (schools) and come home to the mountains able to read his Arabic Qur'an and Persian classics. In those days the mullahs, the villagers' link to their culture's greatest days, would read the centuries-old Persian poetry. And as I understand it, at those village readings the listeners would slowly begin to commit what they heard to memory.

Granted, Soviet cotton brought suffering as much of Tajik freedom was stripped away. But the coerced migration to the thirsty cotton fields also brought the liberty born of education. Of course it was not a perfect intellectual liberty as, among other things, it legislated the abandonment of the Tajik/Persian alphabet.

The Giant Saint

As with so many other languages that the Soviet Union engulfed, the Tajik language found new expression forcibly paired with the Russian Cyrillic script. A new era of Tajik poetry began, a poetry praising the beauty of the Soviet machine. And fittingly, due to the widely imposed Cyrillic forms on many languages, the poetic art praising the machine, regardless of the native tongue being expressed, took on a common, machine-like form from Dushanbe to Moscow. Art certainly seemed to be reflecting the communist reality, but interestingly, the ever-increasing number of literate Tajiks began to convert their history and culture from Persian to Cyrillic. The new education tapped the culture's deeper roots, providing the greatest numbers of literate Tajiks in history the ability to read their own people's works.

I find it ironic that the Tajiks' literacy revolution, that would finally allow the common people accessibility to the full gamut of their culture's abundant literary past, would be ushered in with the decreed abandonment of the alphabet all of those books were written in. As the Tajiks were moving closer to their great poets than ever before, the ancient poets themselves wouldn't have been able to read their own works. Classic Tajik literature looked Soviet, and contemporary Tajik literature was about Soviets. But from what I have seen and heard in Tajikistan, those Tajik poems praising the Soviet dream were probably sincere. To the Tajiks, picking cotton wasn't so bad, especially if they could enjoy a good book when they got home from the fields.

After the bridge and the cotton fields had fallen away behind us, we found ourselves laboring up a road that had seen no repairs for quite some time. We thumped along sharing a fresh-baked *non* (Tajik round bread) between us as small villages of simple mud houses passed regularly on either side. We slowed as we came to a military checkpoint. The guard didn't know any of us, so we had to stop while he checked our papers. As he finished and waved us on, Alisher began telling a fascinating story about how he had accompanied his grandfather to this same mazor some fifteen years before. They had come in the back of one of their new cities' Soviet collective farm trucks, about forty of them jammed into the bed.

I could imagine the scene, the work truck crawling along the primitive road, bearing the throng of mostly elderly, gray-bearded cotton workers, sitting on their provisions and sleeping mats as the pair of sacrificial sheep jittered wide eyed among them. Using the equipment of their atheistic infrastructure to aid them in their pilgrimage, it must have been quite an experience for Alisher to squat beside his grandfather, having him point out the slowly rising mountains and the villages that were the birthplaces of the old men he was sitting with. For most of these men of limited means, this would be their pilgrimage, the Mecca of their lives. Hopefully Allah would understand. Alisher, decades from a gray beard, was alive to the earth, to the possibilities of a few days and nights at a fascinating place in the mountains. The old men, being old, were alive to the heavens, to the gravity of impressing Allah.

Today, just a decade and a half later, the Soviet system is no more. Jets shuttle wealthy Tajiks across an entire continent to Saudi Arabian hajj (pilgrimage to Mecca) in a fraction of the time that Alisher's great-grandfather had been able to make it to this regional mazor, setting off across the mountains on horseback, packed donkey in tow. The jet might even take less time than his grandfather, and he had been able to make the trip in the back of that old collective farm truck.

Poverty still keeps the majority of Tajiks isolated, unable to venture far from their street or keep their cell phone service up and running. However, modern isolation is easily shattered. Scrounge up a couple of somoni to put on that cell phone account, find a high hill to climb, and your father working construction in Moscow is only a few numbers away. Saudi Arabia and Allah are further.

After awhile, the hills receded into a small valley. Our driver, who had made this pilgrimage before, told us that we should soon pass a huge pile of rocks with a fascinating history. Tamerlane, the brutal Central Asian ruler, known to the Tajiks as Timurmalik, is remembered for making massive piles of human skulls, so a pile of rocks was a pretty tame pile for the man. Sure enough, even as our driver related the history behind the rock monument, the pile appeared out in a field before us just off to the left of the road. We stopped the car. I grabbed my camera, snapping a few shots as we walked over.

According to local legend, Tamerlane, driving his army on a major military campaign, stopped in this small valley of what is now southern Tajikistan and commanded each soldier to pick up a single stone from the stream and place it in a pile. Tamerlane and his army came back to the same valley on their return from war, and each of the surviving soldiers was instructed to take one stone off the pile and return it to the stream. If the legend is true, this monument to Tamerlane's dead soldiers would have been erected around AD 1370, give or take twenty years. The rocks are small and the pile massive. It must have been a bloody war. Tamerlane is thought to have killed millions of people in his conquests, so I wonder if there are piles of rocks scattered in forgotten fields throughout Central Asia. And knowing some historians suggest that it was Tamerlane who largely wiped out Christianity from Central Asia, I wonder at God's sovereignty behind the rock monument's commemoration.

As we resumed our journey we inched past a couple of shepherds who were doing a poor job of keeping their flocks off the road. As I looked at them I wondered if Esau might be coming to meet us just around the next curve. I reflected on how the patriarchs made their monuments the same way throughout the book of Genesis. Men like Joshua followed suit. When God spoke to him, Jacob made a pillar of stone. The patriarchs knew that nothing lasts like rock. Tamerlane, wrestling with God in an entirely different manner, thousands of years later, marked his great events the same way.

Presently, I put my writings and family pictures on round disks called CDs. Hopefully the reader has heard of them. I doubt my grandchildren will recognize one. I'd say it's just slightly unlikely that my great-grandchildren will have Microsoft Word and CD-ROM capability. They probably won't even know that poem about Ozymandias. Note to self: Print out family pictures, buy sturdy ammunition box from Army surplus, bury box under big pile of rocks in form of an "X."

I never realized there could be such a great difference between piles of rocks. When Tamerlane or Shelly's Ozymandias build monuments to themselves or their troops, I find a certain sadness in the stones. There is such a difference of tone between Shelly's poem of a proud king's deserted monument boasting in a barren place and Joshua's words in Joshua chapter six when he says to the nation:

> When your children ask their fathers in time to come,
> saying, 'What are these stones' then you shall inform your
> children, saying, 'Israel crossed this Jordan on dry ground.'
> For the LORD your God dried up the waters of the Jordan
> before you until you had crossed, just as the LORD your God
> had done to the Red Sea, which He dried up before us until
> we had crossed; that all the peoples of the earth may know
> that the hand of the Lord is mighty, so that you may fear the
> Lord your God forever. (Josh 4:21–24, NASB)

As we sped on towards pilgrimage to the mystically powerful bones of a Muslim saint, I reflected on how an altar built for the worship of the One who is worthy of that worship sets an entirely different tone. In front of such stones, wonder replaces despair. I think the fundamental difference in tone is encapsulated well in Joshua's last word above, "forever." As I place my rock, and figuratively I believe every human places one, I want it to be firmly on the monument to the living God. I'm reminded of Peter's words, "you also, like living stones, are being built into a spiritual house to be a holy priesthood, offering spiritual sacrifices acceptable to God through Jesus Christ"(1 Pet 2:5). There is a difference between laying your cold stone in tribute to some forgotten demigod and being a living stone in the house of the eternal God.

In the distance I could see the distinct tuft of dense trees that everyone in the car was excitedly saying marked the mazor. As we grew closer I could see the massive trees, so inviting in the heat. We pulled into the parking lot. As we got out and grabbed our things from the back, the first thing I noticed was a huge billboard about halfway up the mountain directly across the valley from the mazor's gravel parking lot. The large billboard, a close-up of President Emomali Rahmon's face, looked so out of place, a strange intrusion to the virgin landscape. Was he advertising himself to the pilgrims? Was he getting an early start campaigning for a third consecutive, seven-year term hoping to get out of the political doldrums and finally grab over 97 percent of the vote? Was he threatening to the pilgrims, "Don't you even think about becoming extremists!"

Imagine summiting a Colorado fourteener and as you round the last timeless boulder, there's a massive glamour shot of George W. Bush welcoming you to the top. Or imagine finding him peering out at your family from the dim floodlighting between the stalactites of a dark recess of Carlsbad Caverns. "Daddy, is that man following us?" your daughter asks as you quickly cover her eyes. Creepy comes to mind. It would make me wonder what he was up to, trying to invade the whole country with his presence. So, filled with a healthy amount of the creepy as Emomali loomed behind, we turned and hurried across the parking lot toward the mazor's entrance.

My heebie-jeebies were kept in check a bit knowing that, unlike another Central Asian president, Emomali had not yet begun naming months of the year after himself or his family members, though I doubted his children would object. I also felt a little better knowing that the United States had yet to see FedEx Carlsbad Caverns.

Just a heartbeat ago in Central Asia, it was looking like Tajiks would be dating things anno Lenin. But as it turns out, humans and their kingdoms are mortal.

Abiding

> *For everyone who has these three loves, hell is closer to him*
> *than the veins in his neck; first, eating good food, second,*
> *wearing nice clothes, and third, sitting with the wealthy.*[1]

An Arabic-inscribed brick arch lined in intricate blue and yellow tiles marked the entrance to the mazor. The arch was topped with a familiar verdant dome, peaked with the crescent moon of Islam. Through the arch I could see streams running along the path and winding between massive trees that looked as if they must have been here when the saint's bones were first buried. The natural springs created an unusual lushness that stood as an island of forest amid the regions' thirsty scarcity. I wondered if this was similar to Abraham's experience of the Oaks of Mamre, though I could already tell that many of the giants were sycamores and walnuts. The cool air hit me as we stood out in the parking gravel staring up at the arched entrance. It certainly felt spiritual as my soul longed to dash from the sun deep into the coolness.

Off to the side of the arch I noticed several large, hand-written placards. A steady hand had mapped out the mazor grounds for the pilgrims. My eyes fell on the word *kushtorgoh*, which means "killing place." I felt happy that sacrificing was regulated as to area. I wondered if I might see one. Regardless, it seemed that meat would likely be a part of lunch.

Another sign stated the rules. I couldn't figure out all of them, but the ones I could fully understand seemed to follow standard legalistic concerns. I was glad I was not a woman as then I would not be able to go inside the mazor to see the grave of the saint. Evidently, an unbelieving American man's presence was preferable to a Muslim woman's. If there had been a religiously pluralistic feminist woman present with me in front of the placard I wondered which of her conflicting philosophies her emotions would follow.

It also appeared that there would be no smoking, chewing *noss* (Tajik tobacco), or washing the car with spring water during our visit. We were to be quiet and respectful at all times. The "No kissing" rule tickled me a bit. It seemed like the caretakers were doing a solid pharisaical job of ferreting the joy out. Our crew entered smiling and chattering away. Tajiks are not big readers. Still, there were no obnoxious noss-chewing men washing their cars in the parking lot, and the inner sanctum of the mazor was certainly free of women, so the mood seemed as solemn as the cool air that enveloped us as we entered in under the arch.

We wound our way towards the famous Muslim saint's mazor, his resting place. The landscaping was superb as the caretakers had harnessed the delta of diverging natural springs among the ancient trees and channeled them to water new rows of sapling pines planted neatly between the paths and streams. But I had to wonder if the young trees would get enough sunlight beneath these giants.

Climbing some broad brick steps, we stood together staring at Mazori Sulton Uvais. The great Uvais' bones were housed in this quaint brick building. I immediately began admiring the mazor's beautiful hand-carved wooden windows. A golden, crescent-mooned dome rested above the entrance. A young mullah, dressed traditionally with a toki skull cap and long *joma* coat sat on a bench, hands outstretched, palms heavenward waiting to receive Allah's blessing as he led a group of pilgrims in prayer. We stopped our chattering and listened to the Arabic mantra. I knew none of our party understood. We stared up at the sycamore trees towering above the dome as we listened to the water rhythms gurgling from the spring. In the low place beside the mazor, pilgrims were gathered along the spring's banks engaged in the rites surrounding the holy water.

In the absence of a golden scoop with a diamond-studded handle, the pilgrims passed along a sun-faded, pinkish plastic ladle sipping the clear water as they prayed along the bank. It was definitely a more organic scene than I have observed in the Catholicism of Europe. I only hoped that regarding actual fingers on display, this mazor would be considerably less organic.

Women drank down in the stream beside the men. This would be the closest they would come to the holy bones. Many filled RC Cola bottles with holy water to bring home to neighbors or drink themselves later on. Perhaps they hoped the water would battle against a lingering illness. Having been briefed by Suhrob on Tajik beliefs about the efficacy of the water, I wondered if some of the men might be bottling it up in hopes that perhaps this potion would finally bring fertility to their bed.

Since some Tajiks believe that you must eat "hot foods," like sheep meat, to get a boy and "cold foods," like goat, to get a girl, I wondered if they'd be heating their water or adding oil to it or something. Though I didn't understand much of what I was seeing, it was clear to me that deep desires were visibly, often with manifest desperation, bubbling up all along the bank.

Suhrob, Safar, and Alisher, along with our driver, joined the action near the source and were soon passing the scoop among them. I snapped their pictures. As an unbeliever and nonparticipant I had become the pilgrimage's designated documenter. I was fine with the role until the part, days later, when I knew I'd be feeding paper into my printer and, some details of my education not having stuck sufficiently, asking my wife to please cut the pictures out. In our marriage we have learned that it's best that Ann wield the scissors. I should have seen that coming from my elementary report cards with penmanship grades constantly threatening my future.

As they drank and bottled I noticed an ornate wood pavilion behind us. I imagined that would probably be the next picture-taking site. The pavilion's wooden posts probably originated from the northwestern area of Tajikistan. The area is famous for its incredible carving.

I looked down at Alisher as he kneeled beside the spring drinking from the scoop. I noticed no evidence of internal spiritual tension in his expression. Did he not understand the implications? Was he an exceptionally adept syncretist? Perhaps he was not as serious about the gospel as he had let on. He had never said he believed in Christ, but he had been so interested that sometimes I wondered if he was a secret believer. Was he drinking defensively, functionally, or ritualistically?

After finishing up at the spring and snapping a few shots under the pavilion, we moved on to the entrance of the mazor. We removed our shoes at the door and placed them beside those of the pilgrims presently inside. Upon entering, it took me a little while to figure out what I was looking at. A narrow protrusion ran the length of the long room. It was draped in thick green cloth embroidered with stylized Arabic letters. At first it reminded me of a formal dining table.

Because of its excessive length it didn't register for a few moments that I was looking at a coffin. It must have been around fifteen feet long. Suhrob set my mind on track more or less when he leaned over and whispered, "Look how tall he was!" I realized then what I was looking at. I hadn't yet learned that according to the Hadith (the recorded sayings and actions of the Prophet Muhammad), God created Adam sixty cubits (around ninety feet) tall and man has been slowly decreasing in stature ever since.

That Suhrob immediately and unhesitatingly believed this local saint must have been one of the tallest men ever to walk the earth—even though the literature provided made no mention of his stature—sent a wave of impertinence over me. I found it difficult to control my urge to follow the example of Mark Twain abroad and ask all present in the most unimpressed tone I could muster, "Is, is he dead?" Thankfully I refrained, though I probably exuded an impressive plethora of nonverbal clues as to the anger I was actively suppressing.

I purchased a copy of the mazor's little white booklet containing the legends about Sulton Uvais. I would spend the next couple weeks of my language lessons pouring over the legends. With the guidance of my perpetually even-keeled language coach, Safar, helping me wade through the literary Tajik and frequent jaunts into mysterious Arabic, I would try to piece together the stories surrounding this place.

When reading the Bible in Tajik I find my mind decoding rapidly, making intelligent guesses in a single bound because of my familiarity with the text. But with this booklet, my anticipation abilities were sucked into a black hole, and I regularly found myself wistfully ruminating on the gift of tongues.

I found nothing about Uvais being a sultan. It must be more of an honorary title since he was such a devoted Muslim hermit. It is said that because the Prophet Mohammed lost all his teeth in wars, Uvais reverently broke out all of his own teeth. Another time, he went and drew water for his blind mother only to find her asleep when he returned. So he stood next to her holding the water all through the watches of the night until his hands froze to the pitcher. He was ready with the ice water when his mother woke up. I think that story is supposed to be inspiring or convicting or something, but I'm not sure.

Uvais was always praying, going above and beyond Islam's scheduled five daily times. He would fast for days at a time out in the secluded desserts of Yemen, counting his prayers out on his rosary-like string of beads (known as a *tasbih* in Tajik). Sometimes children would find him and mockingly throw rocks at him for his etherealness. He would only reply asking them to please throw small rocks so that he would not bleed and thus break his *taorat* (his ritual purity required for prayer).

If he found the seeds of the fruits of heaven on the ground he would pick them up and put them on higher ground. According to my friend Suhrob the fruits of heaven include pomegranates, watermelon, and cantaloupe.

It's difficult from the booklet to get a feel for where Uvais lived. Supposedly from Yemen he seems to have traveled the world over, grazing his sheep and camels in seclusion, away from all men, and taking care of his blind mother. Legend has it that he grazed his cattle from Yemen all the way northeast to this site of his burial in southern Tajikistan, returning to his homeland again later. Having common pilgrims as well as famous Muslim saints and kings such as Omar and Ali miraculously teleported into his nomadic life to beg his wisdom only adds to the sense of erratic drifting.

The story goes that before his passing, Uvais told the people of Yemen that upon his death a white camel would appear. They were to put his body upon it and follow along behind. The mystic camel would stop seven times in its wanderings. They were to bury his body at the camel's final stop.

When, upon his death, the foretold white camel appeared, the people of Yemen remembered his prophecy and obeyed. They set the body atop the camel and followed it from Yemen until it finally came to its seventh rest at this spring in Tajikistan. When they unloaded his body, the white camel disappeared. The people of Yemen buried Uvais here, the spot of the present mazor, a place where, the legends tell, Uvais had shepherded his flocks while he was alive.

The other legends in the booklet speak a great deal about fear, slavery to Allah, intense awareness of impending death as close as the beating veins in one's own neck, and the great merit found in living the strict eremitic life. There is precious little of love and relationship and nothing of founded, unbounded grace.

Often when singing worship songs here in Tajikistan I look around at the Tajik believers and seekers and am struck by the uniqueness of the activity. I have several times observed an interesting dynamic in the lives of my Muslim friends when they, through our friendship, observe Christian worship for the first time, especially in song. The experience often sparks a similar response in them. Not infrequently after such an exposure I find them moving towards the Sufi channel of Islam, which is the charismatic stream of the faith. Whether the sudden interest in Sufi poetry and energetic worship is a defensive maneuver or a searching prompted by a new awareness of relational void, I do not know. I suspect an interplay between the two.

Witnessing Christian worship for the first time, seeing Christian community singing from the heart on themes of grace, joy, and love is certainly a thing my Tajik friends have never before imagined. They must wonder if perhaps they have only missed this joy, this relationship within Islam, and they set about exploring. As I watch them seek I pray they move back toward the worship that sparked the search.

The guys spent a few more minutes mulling around the mazor soaking in the spiritual ambiance. I sat down at a shady spot along a brick wall. A branch of the spring babbled behind me. A Tajik man walked by wearing a Messiah volleyball T-shirt. I wondered if that counted as getting the gospel out. The middle-aged man looked like he was in the mazor's groundskeeping division, and I had my doubts as to whether he was a big Messiah volleyball fan since Tajiks typically have never even heard of Michael Jordan, baseball, football, or, well, you name it.

Sometimes they ask me if I can drive to America from Tajikistan, and I find myself in yet another conversation about the inconvenient presence of the Atlantic Ocean. However, I've also gotten thumped by one of my Tajik students in an impromptu geography contest. So it seems that in the Central Asia of the information age extremes coexist.

I remember asking a Tajik boy one time if he liked Shaquille O'Neal. I thought this was a reasonable question since he was wearing Shaq's jersey. His blank stare cleared things up. I'm beginning to doubt whether there are really as many Green Bay Packers fans here as I first thought. The Packers must have printed Favre's number backwards or something, a fortunate NFL mistake that provided warm coats to countless cold souls in southern Tajikistan.

I shouldn't be surprised by this lack of knowledge though, because I have lived in Tajikistan a few years now and would not be able to name a single great *buzkashi* (goat pull) champion or his goat-carcass toting exploits, though I do know stories of memorable tramplings. Tramplings seem to be the longest-living highlight. Let me just say horses make linebackers look tame. It would definitely be several hundred pounds better to be floored by Brian Urlacher than to find oneself under the hooves of a stallion.

I almost had a chance to become one of those trampling highlights when I attended my first buzkashi tournament insufficiently informed on the sport. Let's just say that when a hundred men on horseback are racing towards the fleeing crowd, concentrating on the scrum for the decapitated goat instead of the fans among and below them, the best place to hide is definitely, and I feel strongly about this, on top of or underneath a bus in the parking lot. In retrospect, it would have been great to know that the parking lot was in bounds.

In my opinion, fan trampling should at the very least make the rider ineligible to win the carpet and livestock prizes. I should add that, as some of our foreign friends found out the hard way, a buzkashi tournament is not the proper setting for a family picnic unless you enjoy sheer panic after potato salad. Tip: Just leave the Tupperware. I am well aware you can't get it in Central Asia, but it's still not worth it.

Such Tajik sports as buzkashi got me to reconsider the societal benefits of suing. Even though I find our American liability culture idiotic and don't know how to respond reading cautions like, "Warning! Do not stick toys in mouth. May cause choking," seeing

Tajik children packed in well beyond seating capacity and literally hanging off the front end of a moving roller coaster as the operator kicks it into high gear makes me homesick for a little more law and a little less fatalism.

Trying their best to renegotiate their fate, a few pilgrims near the spring were down to their elbows in water, attempting to gather holy pebbles. Perhaps they were hoping to overcome infertility or disease. Perhaps the gathering of real pebbles could somehow bring hope as a physical embodiment of their good works. The eternal scale of judgment is such a powerful metaphor in the Tajik mind. Tajiks believe your life can be represented by that scale. Your good works, like these pebbles, are placed on one side, your evil works on the other. You wait until the end to see which way your life scale will tip, determining your eternal destiny or severity of purgatory.

Soon everyone in our group was finished, and we decided it was time for lunch. We walked along the paths toward the kushtorgoh (killing place), which didn't exactly sound like the most pleasant place for a picnic. Fortunately, the Tajik cots were set up among the great trees and ever-diverging streams, a fair distance from the kushtorgoh. A few women were busy boiling water for tea using a huge metal cauldron. I didn't see any sacrifices going on presently. Other groups of pilgrims had taken the choice cots carved elaborately from beautiful wood, but we found ourselves an empty, metal-framed cot set against a steep hill. We put our lunch provisions out on the simple tablecloth provided and settled in.

Cots hold a prominent place in Tajik culture. Much of the year Tajikistan is intensely hot. Families will spend the hottest part of a summer afternoon sleeping inside. Thick mud walls provide a moderately cool place of relief. The cot, traditionally wood, but increasingly constructed of metal, is a big square frame a few feet off the ground with wood slats forming a platform. Often the cot is placed in the yard under grapevines overlooking the almost universal family garden. In the cool of the evening, the women emerge from the home, throw a simple carpet over the slats and line the edges with *korpachas* (mattresses for sitting) and pillows. The cot is thus prepared for the evening meal.

Often in the summers, following *xuroki shom* (dinner), when the dry heat begins to fade into the night, the women, gathering the pieces of non in a table cloth and clearing the tea, will retire to the house with the children while the household's men sleep out on the cot, looking up at the moon through the leaves and ripening grape clusters as they drift off. I like to imagine one of the families' elders singing the old legends accompanied by his *dumbra* (two stringed guitar) as the surrounding neighbors and animals listen in. But unfortunately, a more likely scenario would be a stereo thumping out Russian pop with more power and a great deal less charm.

Our taxi driver found a deep pool in the spring channel running beside our cot. He placed our watermelon there in the cool water. It bobbed beside two other nice melons belonging to fellow pilgrims. I envied the melons and their swim as they bumped and rolled in the pool, their mottled rinds of such healthy green hues, joyfully floating on the clear waters in the dappled shade. It amazes me how a few melons, sunlight, shade, and a spring-fed pool can put the world's best art to shame.

In his classic book, *Orthodoxy*, G. K. Chesterton, speaking on the human experience of wonder, says, "A child of seven is excited being told that Tommy opened a door and saw a dragon. But a child of three is excited by being told that Tommy opened a door. Boys like romantic tales; but babies like realistic tales—because they find them romantic."[2]

This passage has always stayed in my mind. Perhaps that is because in this postmodern, post-attention span, post-appreciation age, I feel that most people, especially in the West, would not even be impressed with the dragon behind the door. It would have to be tap dancing, violently swallowing another dragon whole, or selling cheap car insurance to invoke wonder. Our culture's desires seem to be in a state of mature decadence. It appears that peace has clearly passed our civilization's understanding and seems unattainable through all the decay. I hope I am wrong.

Tajikistan's simplicity has been a balm to my old and infirm fascination. It has revived my ability to wonder, which has been an incredible gift because I feel that this lack of attention, reflection, and therefore wonder is also a struggle in my spiritual walk with God. I find myself drawn repeatedly to Ephesians 3:18–19, with a hunger to awaken to the true dimensions of Christ's love. How wide, how deep! I'm reminded of Jesus' injunction to become like children. Surely our appreciation and capacity for wonder, a wonder we so often abundantly see in children, is something that God desires to revive and sanctify in us since we are created to worship Him. Not simply to believe, but to delight. It is quite difficult for worship to happen with a dead or distracted sense of wonder. I am so thankful for Tajikistan and how it has revived in me the ability to take joy in watermelons. I have been reminded that they are miraculous. I think a long time ago I used to know that.

We all removed our shoes and clamored up onto the cot. The taxi driver and I, as the oldest two in our party, sat in the places of honor along the backside of the cot. Having grown up in America where I would not be surprised if I was to see footage of one of our presidents—maybe "W"—hanging out with his buddies in a tank top perhaps to show off his "guns" or insisting someone else take the best seat in the house, I'm uncomfortable with such formality and social ranking. The honor thing is uncharted territory since I've been culturally well trained to take potshots at all authority. I have often resisted such strict seating arrangements, but have learned it's better just to sit down where I'm put as Tajiks feel dishonored if they're denied the chance to honor.

As Suhrob, Safar, and Alisher sat down along the two sides, honored to give us the best seats, I was reminded of a story another of my Tajik friends had told me. My friend Habib was a good wrestler from a family of good wrestlers. Every spring our town hosts the biggest of its wrestling tournaments around Idi Navruz (Persian New Year). A few years back, Habib and his older brother found themselves easily moving through the competitors out in the open field until it came down to a semifinal between the two brothers. Habib immediately forfeited allowing his older brother to move on to the final, where he lost.

When I listened to Habib tell the story it was clear that he does wonder if he could have won the greatest wrestling tournament in his region of Tajikistan, but it is equally clear that his dominant emotion is joy. He is so proud to have had the opportunity to honor his older brother. To my American mind, accustomed to universal competition from markets down to siblings, distrust of tradition, incessant free and increasingly destructive speech, and an aggressive individualism morbidly awaiting a misstep by God, parents, presidents and, most importantly, movie stars, it was hard for me to even begin to understand Habib's actions. Though I can't remember what I said when Habib finished his story, I think my main thought was basically, "What the heck?"

We opened my backpack and their plastic bags and proceeded to place our lunch provisions out on the tablecloth. On such a hot day, forsaking superstitions, they even braved my ice-cold filtered water. We passed around the RC Cola bottles and a couple of *peolas* (Tajik teacups). A woman passed by and took our order for a *choinik* (teapot) of black tea and another of green. We reclined against the cot railings eating sausage and cookies as we waited for her to bring our tea. The cookies I had brought were a big hit as tasty desserts seem to have passed Central Asia by. Safar asked for the recipe. I wondered how I would explain fractions, because even if Safar could grasp them, it would certainly be his wife who would be making the cookies and I doubted she'd understand what a third of a peola meant.

My wife, Ann, is always running into the fraction problem when Tajik ladies, raving about her desserts, are pressing her to give them the secrets of her divine goodies, the likes of which they have never experienced before. Ann took advantage of this desire and started a baking class as a way to meet neighbor women and hopefully find opportunities to share the gospel. Lesson one in her classes is always fractions.

I have glanced in before to see Ann sitting on the floor around the low Tajik table in our living room, surrounded by Tajik ladies in their twenties, thirties, and forties, as she holds up the classic construction paper pie chart to illustrate halves, thirds, and fourths. It is an amazing sight. But certainly the way a Tajik woman can design and make a dress or prepare just about anything from scratch impresses in the other direction.

This talk of competency and food preparation reminds me of when Ann and I first arrived in Tajikistan and our coworkers showed us our "stocked" kitchen, which they had been nice enough to prepare. After they left we looked at the potatoes, onions, carrots, milk, and chunk of some kind of meat, wondering what in the world we were going to do. Even if I could have spoken a word of Tajik I could have dialed Pizza Hut's 648-8888 until my fingers bled and nothing, nothing would have come hot and ready, our calls' futility sounding out into the oppressive, food-chainless, Central Asian night.

Didn't cooking mean adding water and butter followed by stirring? We had brought the book *Where There is No Doctor*, but we had forgotten the essential American companion volume, *Where There is No McDonald's*. That's when Ann and I knew, in spite of all our mad microwaving skills, we were in deep.

Suhrob's cell phone rang, snapping me back to the moment. I smiled as he proceeded to have the characteristic phone conversation composed of ten-second increments. The Tajik cell phone provider, Babylon T's system, was set up so that calls under ten seconds are free which rapidly led to the changing of an entire nation's phone etiquette. After using the first ten-second call to hastily establish who you both are, it is imperative that you skip the asalom formalities and get right down to ten-second dense bits of content from then on out. It's even becoming common to answer the phone now, "*Gap za!*" (Talk!), which saves a call I suppose. It's funny that the bluntness seems both characteristically Tajik and yet an affront to their social ways at the same time.

Even we in the rich foreigner community find ourselves phoning each other in ten-second increments, which is ridiculous but understandable. Living long enough in another economic setting pushes one's thinking toward the local norm, especially when one wants to be sensitive and reach out in love.

Evidence of our foreign community's gradual shift in economic outlook is seen in the return of conversations over who owes whom twenty-five cents for last week's taxi ride. Such conversations have risen from the dead of my preemployment high school days when my friends and I would rake each other over the coals for the debts of unpaid shared gas from five weekends ago.

After incessant ringing and loud "*Gap zas!*" that tested our endurance, Suhrob finally put the torturous cell phone away, and we returned to a more peaceful state that lasted for more than two seconds at a time. The waitress returned to our table with a few more peolas and the two teapots we had ordered. All the guys were eager to serve our party, but Alisher got to it first and was soon busily preparing the teapots in the traditional manner before serving.

I have been told that the way the Tajiks fill a peola three times, each time pouring the cup of tea back into the pot and then letting the tea sit for a few minutes, is not only functionally helpful as it mixes and settles the leaves, but also has superstitious portent, which I have unfortunately forgotten. But forgetting the meaning of superstitions is probably fine as many Tajiks themselves only have the vaguest of ideas as to why they fear what they fear and do what they do.

As we waited for the tea leaves to settle, a shriveled old man hobbled up. Instantly our taxi driver jumped up and helped the man shake his way to a comfortable position up onto the edge of our cot. He looked too weak to try to scoot to a place of honor along the backside, so no one suggested it. Sometimes, jadedly, I have thought that Tajik hospitality and instant inclusion is perhaps fueled by fear and selfish desire to be rewarded for good works. But more often than not I believe it to be a sincere health and beauty in the culture. Tajikistan is not about activity. There are no to-do lists, but there are plenty of relationships. And the old stranger, welcomed instantly among us as we chatted, was indeed a beautiful thing.

He never spoke, and he nodded off at least once, but he seemed happy and proud when I snapped his picture. It would not be ridiculous to think that perhaps this might be one of maybe just a couple of times in his life that he'd had his picture taken. He looked like the stereotypical Tajik elder; a round toki skull cap sitting atop his ancient, shriveled face and a long grey beard hanging down onto his flowing red-striped joma coat. His joma coat looked about like the coat that Jacob gave to Joseph as I imagined it. The old man loved our watermelon which, fortunately for him, was soft enough to eat without the help of many teeth. As we sipped our tea together I looked at him and wondered if he was alone in the world, sort of wandering around the mazor grounds, eating from the pilgrims' bounty.

A generous pilgrim came over with a large wooden *tabak* (bowl) filled with soup. Tajiks say that sharing a meal with others from a tabak makes the food taste better than eating from your own bowl by yourself. Though I love the idea of community and can see the truth in the increase of joy found in sharing a common bowl, after seeing five pairs of hands using flat bread to sop up the broth, licking their fingers after every bite, my appetite disappeared, and I found myself picking at the edge of the bowl just to be polite.

They looked happy and perfectly in their element as they shared the generous portion their fellow pilgrim had provided. Alisher removed the chunk of sacrificial mutton and set it aside. The meat is usually removed like this and then cut into small strips more easily eaten by hand. This is a convenient way to prepare the roast for everyone as the typical Tajik family may very well own only one or two knives. I could see clearly the ornate black decorations that had been carved and somehow permanently engraved into the wood. It was a beautiful bowl. If it was oiled from time to time to keep it from cracking it would be a solid tabak for many years.

The men continued tearing the chapatti-thin bread and mashing it down into the thin broth with their fingers. I stayed with my spot along the edge where other fingers were not being too sloppy. I picked quickly because I knew from experience the longer I waited the less I was going to want to eat from the tabak.

I can handle eating from a tabak with my wife and cute little kiddos, Grace and Silas, but hearing the slurping as the taxi driver and my buddies cleaned their digits, holding their right hands carefully at an angle so that the oil would not roll down their arms was just not appetizing. As I felt some broth run down my arm I was reminded that I wasn't even good at this.

Making matters worse, as I tried my best to politely eat, I knew that Tajiks hardly ever use soap. I knew this tabak had probably only been rinsed off quickly in the spring the last five hundred times it had been eaten off of by pilgrims. I would be surprised if there was soap on the premises.

I also knew how Tajiks wash their hands. I had just seen my bowlmates give an example of the method. To the Tajik, washing hands seems to have more to do with ritual and a sort of formal tradition than the functional aspect of killing germs, germs which Ann and I have had to argue over the existence of with trained nurses here.

At the beginning of a meal, Tajiks sit down and start in on the raisins, nuts, bits of bread, and other finger foods, which they wash down with tea. Right before the main course is brought out, in a manner reminiscent of ancient foot washing, the host will take a pitcher of water, a basin, and a towel around to each guest. The guest will hold his hands out above the basin as the host pours the water over them for a quick rinse. It is a beautiful ritual, but I have never seen soap in the proceedings, and if the meal never gets past finger foods then evidently there is no need to wash at all.

I do so enjoy soap and have grown to love it more here in Tajikistan. Constant bouts with giardia during the hot months test Ann's and my resolve to show our love for the Tajiks by faking an enthusiastic joy in eating the food they provide us. We are thankful when the flies die away as it grows cold so we can eat more heartily in the homes of our friends without the constant fear that there is a pretty high risk that the food set before us is going to make us very sick for the next few days.

I fear we Americans might slowly be forgetting that there is something powerful in sharing a meal with others. So this half-hearted appetite we so often try to conceal from our Tajik friends breaks our hearts. We desperately want to show our love, because Christ so unbelievably first loved us. It is discouraging when, repeatedly, a bowl of soup, spiritlessly picked, gets in the way. In Tajikistan, perhaps incarnational ministry, perhaps letting nothing hinder the gospel, means to eat everything with abandon and willingly suffer the consequences. Would Paul agree that we should be willing to get giardia so that by all means possible we might save some? Unfortunately, I think we know the answer.

Soon the tabak was empty and the strips of roast eaten. The old man led us in enjoying more slices of our spring-cooled watermelon. I was hoping this Tajik elder would be a fount of poetry and traditional stories. Often his generation is the last great source of oral tradition, the remnant displaying the incredible powers of human memorization. The Soviet Union ushered in new times, and it is increasingly difficult to find men of the old ways.

Tajikistan still displays the evidence of an oral culture. Tajiks still have the traditional contests in poetry memorization. I heard an example of this in the famous story of how a poor village boy with a great mind is challenged to one such contest by a boy from the great schools in the city. The rules are simple. Whatever letter the last line of the quoted poem ends with, the other person must search his memory to find a poem that begins with that letter. The contest goes on and on until one of the duelers cannot think of a poem beginning with that letter, or a new one of that letter if the letter has been previously used. In the story, of course, the village boy shockingly wins.

To see the way the present generation of Tajiks' eyes sparkle when they tell such stories of dueling poets reveals deep veneration. As long as there is such esteem, the past is not totally gone but it is an appreciation largely void of imitation. Young Tajiks marvel at the storehouse of their grandfather's knowledge, but they wonder more intensely at television, music, and to a lesser extent, books.

It has been interesting to see the last stand of an oral culture. Sometimes as illiteracy rates increase, especially in the villages, or when I on occasion meet a Soviet-educated father who can read sitting beside his children who cannot, I wonder if perhaps pockets of oral culture will remain.

But as electricity lines reach ever further out into the country-side, I think even if illiteracy rates rise, traditional Tajik oral culture is gone. Not that I even remotely think that literacy is a bad thing. Absolutely not! It is an incredible gift. But while holding a deep, unshakeable appreciation for literacy, I believe it is still possible to appreciate the aspects of beauty in an oral culture. It is a culture steadily drifting away before us like the dozing old man beside me, the visible manifestation of his dying kind.

Returning

If, except for Allah, you know nobody, it is better for you.[3]

After lunch I actually drifted off myself for a few minutes. The old man and I napped on the shaded cot out of the heat while the other four took a last look around the mazor grounds. When I awoke, we packed up and took a leisurely stroll, admiring the impressive girth of the sycamore and walnut trunks. We snapped a few more group pictures before heading back to the parking lot.

As we sleepily piled back into the car in the dusty midafternoon heat, I thought back on what I had seen. Leaving Mazori Sulton Uvais behind us, I looked out at the cotton fields and their simple irrigation systems. The monotonous sky lacked the slightest trace of a cloud. I knew it would not be surprising if I did not see a cloudy sky until September.

Coming from the Midwest, I miss the volatility of weather, the passion of thunderstorms, the melancholy of a cloudy day, and the relief of rain. I miss Missouri where trees spring up unattended and acorns hit the ground growing. I miss land where shade from neighboring trees is a bigger threat than the unrelenting sun. But as I glanced at my contentedly napping buddies in the back seat I knew I was experiencing this geographic shock alone. Tajiks love their land.

We have a coffee-table picture book that has large colorful pages showing beautiful nature scenes from every part of America. I love to sit down with our Tajik guests and point out the incredible foliage of Maine in the fall, the deep green pines of the Pacific Northwest, or the mystery of a southern swamp.

I find myself flipping the pages quickly trying to show my guest the most magnificent shots. Perhaps this action proceeds from a deep desire to share what's important to me. I want them to appreciate what I find to be beautiful. But I've learned that if I want to impress them all I have to do is turn to the pages of the Southwest and let them gaze at shots of the Grand Canyon, an Arizona sunset, or the rock formations of Monument Valley; basically, to show them a bit of familiar home on a grander scale. This reminds me that appreciation must be developed.

I know it does not matter if they ever appreciate an ocean view. But it matters more than the whole world that they grow to appreciate, to worship our unfathomably gracious God who loved us so much that He sent His Son.

I thought back again to the mazor. It is a vaguely spiritual place. In conversation with my friends while we were walking the mazor grounds, it became clear to me that most of the pilgrims do not know who this giant saint was, what he believed, where he came from, or what he did. My Tajik friends, outside of the Arabic-speaking world and taught that the Qur'an is not the Qur'an if it is not in Arabic, do not even know their own source or much of what it says of Allah.

The man, the site, the faith all seemed awash in a great haze. It didn't seem to bother them though it bothered me a great deal. Today I had seen the mazor's attempts to be a mediator between Allah and man. I had seen my friends as they made their approach to the saint's bones, hoping to somehow appeal through them, through the merit of bones, for Allah's favor. It is an anxious, fearful approach.

I looked out ahead into the pounding heat as we bumped along towards home. The sweltering haze curled the very air, rising up from the asphalt road, encrypting the world before us. The air frothed in uncertainty as if the mazor possessed fingers of obscurity physically reaching out, rippling along the countryside, opiating the whole land.

I looked out at mazor-laden Tajikistan all around me. I must grow to understand the Tajiks better, to know what they appreciate and how they love. Sulton Uvais advised that if we know no one other than Allah it is better for us. First John chapter four speaks against Uvais' wisdom concerning relationships, speaking right into my soul that I must love the Tajiks for God is love. It reminds, if I do not love others, I do not know God. I prayed for more love. I prayed for more understanding. I prayed that the presence of the Holy Spirit in Tajikistan would prove the God of Abraham, Isaac, and Jacob to be infinitely taller than fifteen feet.

IV
NORMAL LIFE

However new and astonishing one's surroundings, the tendency is to become a part of them so soon that almost from the first the power to see them objectively and fully measure their strangeness is lost.[1]

There are those people like Erma Bombeck who have a talent for seeing the ludicrous situations of daily life surrounding them. Some people might only see your run-of-the-mill Tajik woman out in front of our building, half-boiled teapot in hand, frantically trying to start a small brush-fire under a couple of bricks, while others see a golden farce in the making. It doesn't matter what it is, they find the absurdity. Most of the time life's humor eludes our notice even though that humor is constantly crashing right into the middle of our experience.

And often we slowly seem to lose the ability or desire to observe the entertaining din as time goes by. I have a great-aunt who, realizing this, instructed me the first time we came out to Tajikistan to be sure to journal right away. I thought that it might be better to wait until I understood at least a miniscule amount of what I was observing before I attempted to write some observations. But I did understand her point, which is why I've taken the time to record this bit about our "normal" Tajik life before we lose the ability to notice it. It seems like every five minutes Ann and I are having a communal guffaw over some peculiarity or cultural difference, so I would hope material won't be a problem, although at the moment nothing is coming to mind.

Perhaps it would be best to begin with some burning questions I have. Why, for instance, does this certain boy collecting scrap food for his cow continue to come to our house every night even though every night I tell him we have a solid alliance with a rival cow-food collector? And why is the live electricity line running into our building low enough to bump my head on? And why did our neighbors on the floor above us rewire our floor's stairwell light so that now only the switch inside their apartment can turn it on? Why does our house helper insist on putting a sopping wet rag right at the entrance to our home so everyone either tracks more mud onto the entryway carpet or gets wet socks? Why do our neighbors insist on keeping the courtyard water pump going full blast 24/7 when we live in a country where the government infuriatingly regularly feels the need to ration water? If they would turn it off, maybe water pressure would improve to the point of reaching the second- and third-floor apartments thereby negating the pressing need for the courtyard pump. Why do Tajiks mummify themselves in warm weather and then go about in light blazers or sleeveless sweater vests right about the time I'm thinking it's time to break the winter coat out of storage? And if they believe that evil spirits inhabit trash dumps, then why are we making one in our courtyard?

But lest this become one-sided, let's examine a typical visit our family might make to a Tajik friend's home. Our stealthless, often mufflerless taxi announces our arrival, initiating a negotiation over price because I failed to negotiate beforehand yet again. Incidentally, negotiations are my favorite way of publicly displaying my incompetence.

I know our Tajik friends must be amusedly looking out the window at us by this time as we attempt to get out of the taxi without sustaining any back injuries due to our overpacking. We have with us what to them must look like enough stuff to move in for at least half a year. We exit anxiously, glancing at our watches. Why? Because we only have two hours before Grace must be home and safely napping in her Pack 'N Play in a perfect symbiotic environment maintained by the sound of a gentle, yet sustained, South American rain. Regrettably, Grace will not sleep in the absence of a South American rainstorm. Fortuitously, this rain has been most accurately recorded onto our white noise sleep machine. Needless to say, we have become big fans of naturalists who record South American rainstorms. Our baby's eccentric sleep needs are not easy to explain to our Tajik friends.

We pass a Tajik child on our way up. He is happily snoozing in his apartment entryway, ball in hand, as if he had passed out suddenly during play. Only five and already a veritable master of such a power nap as would make most military field personnel envious. We labor up to the fourth floor under the weight of a diaper bag containing roughly the contents of a Babies "R" Us store.

Arriving at our Tajik friend's door, we knock. Their completely naked, two-year-old boy answers. No worries, he has been potty trained for roughly four years. Grace meanwhile has had an accident on the way up prompting us, once seated next to the Tajik snack trays, to begin an intricate search through her diaper bag that, at least to Daddy, seems cruelly without a table of contents. Desitin diaper-rash cream, check; Turkish diaper with evil eye logo for baby protection, check; portable plastic changing station, check; imported Austrian wipes, check; Purell for 99.9 percent hand sanitation, check. And there is the vague hope that sometime just before it's time to go, we'll be settled.

As an aside, I think we're six months away from Grace being able to say something scholarly like, "Mother, Father, I am going to go to the bathroom in my pants now, for I do not at this time, wish to use the toilet." I believe there should be a parenting law stating that in a child's first two years, grammatical understanding must never surpass toileting skills. In the absence of diapers, Tajiks know this law quite well. Americans, on the other hand, have invented another phase after diapers called Pull-Ups in order to prevent potty training from taking place for the maximum amount of time.

Our hosts bring out a pitcher of water and a basin to wash our hands. A slight pour, a dab dry from the communal cloth and we're "clean." When they withdraw, we lather on the Purell and reminisce about the good ol' days of washing our hands with soap in the restroom.

Tajiks find it inappropriate if anyone asks to use the restroom in mixed company. Ann had fun with this once and told her friends the horrifying true story of the time back in the States when she stood in a coed line waiting to use a very busy bathroom during a party. A gentleman insisted she cut in front of him due to her pregnancy. Tajiks also believe pregnancy should never be acknowledged and absolutely never discussed in front of any person even slightly resembling a man. Relating this story, a crushing combo of pregnancy and bathroom etiquette nightmares, produced upon her audience very near the effects of the climax of a Hollywood thriller. And my shock returns the favor every time I go to a Tajik restroom and realize soap is not one of the items they feel the need to stock.

Though we could go on forever, perhaps we should just skip the stories of the midnight flower plantings and crosswalk additions that precipitously occur on the main road in the wee hours of the morning before every trip President Emomali Rahman makes to our town. And I should not even mention my ever-present question, "What if, upon the President's arrival, he was to drive down a different road?" And I won't even ask how high electricity has to be to actually blow an extension cord into small pieces.

Instead we will return to our run-of-the-mill harried young Tajik woman trying to make that fire in order to boil that tea. As she squats there beside her two bricks encouraging the small pile of straw and twigs to stay lit, she is aided in her secluded plight by a lone, gallantly shining BMW parked just behind her and her forlorn fire.

Besides its primary function of being an off-the-charts prestige item, the Beemer has the secondary benefit of being a great wind buffer which is good because the owner of this car is waiting in a dark room upstairs for his relative to bring him his tea. Though he is a powerful man with a car probably worth more than the cumulative worldly possessions of the entire stairwell he is visiting, he has not been able to provide electricity. So he sits in the slightly chilled room hoping the fire outside will catch and that tea will be brought. And perhaps, at least until he gets back home to his generator, perhaps he wishes he ran the power plant a little differently.

V

100% UNNATURAL

Floating Over the Atlantic

We were about halfway back in coach. Ann and I sat as bookends for Grace and Silas, strategically placed in an attempt to contain their enthusiasm from being excessively unleashed upon our unsuspecting neighbors. It was to be a twelve-hour flight from Istanbul to Chicago. Fortunately, Turks seem to love and appreciate children more than any other people group we have come into contact with. I especially remember a green-mohawked, pierced, Turkish chainsmoker who suddenly transformed into Raffi as he cooed through his piercings and pinched our children's cheeks.

Thankfully, the Turkish Air flight hadn't sold out. We had an extra seat to put Silas in next to Grace. Our ongoing science experiment on how many hours an adult can sit motionless, acting as a cradle without going insane, would have to wait for other transatlantic flights. One tip though: sitting on your entire family's flight pillows adds at least an hour and could very likely help you set a new personal record. As Grace and Silas explored the new fascinations of shoehorns, sleeping masks, and baby-blue traction socks, Ann and I put our trays down and gave our drink orders to the friendly Turkish flight attendant.

Since we had come directly from Tajikistan, her tiny cart seemed to be just about as magical as Santa's bag. Wish for anything, close your eyes, reach in, and pull it out! It appeared there were more options in this fantastic, compact rolling cart than in all of Central Asia. I was so impressed by the cart that I briefly thought about asking for golden waters drawn from the fountain of youth. I decided on a 7UP instead. I think I could recall what it tasted like.

Not wanting to be confused with Tajik Airlines, which is magical in sort of a dark-side-of-the-force or sucked-into-a-vortex sort of way, Turkish Airlines gave me an entire can all to myself. Tajik Air, on the other hand, gives you the choice of a tiny paper cup of tepid fizzy water or off-brand Central Asian cola. It is hard to express how off off-brand cola can become in Central Asia. Additionally, unlike Tajik Air, the engines actually had sufficient "umph" to propel our plane to cruising altitude before our descent. So we were feeling quite at our leisure as we released our seat belts and popped open our drinks.

I spun the can around noticing it advertised itself to be some new form of 7UP with real lemon. In bold letters across the top it said confidently, "100 percent natural!" I showed the ridiculous declaration to Ann and we enjoyed a good laugh together. Whether it referred to the lemon alone didn't matter. We couldn't stop giggling. It was clear to us that either we were now absurd or America was. We hoped we would soon be enjoying organic Twinkies too.

The can seemed symbolic of our lives. We felt about as normal as a 100 percent natural 7UP. Even though we would be returning to Kansas City tomorrow we could not help but echo Dorothy in saying to ourselves, "We're not in Kansas anymore." I think we've lived in Oz too long to ever return to Kansas in the same way again. And increasingly, we have the feeling that whether we tap ruby slippers together or not, there is truly no place on this earth that is like home.

Take Grace's reaction to the news of our upcoming flight, for example. Ann told Grace we would be flying back to Kansas City on Turkish Airlines. Having been to Turkey a few times already, Grace

paused at this news and after some reflection asked in all seriousness, "Should, should, um, should I wear a belly dancing outfit on
the plane?" By the look in her eyes we knew what she really wanted
to ask was, "Please, oh please, can I wear a belly dancing outfit on
the plane!!?"

What first occurs to our nearly five-year-old daughter is probably
not normal for Kansas kindergartners. And, English-competency
ready or not, Grace would be exactly that in a few weeks. It was nice
to know at least she'd be ahead of her class in Tajik proficiency and
belly dancing.

And how many other little girls' favorite game is "packing my
carry-on"? Ann grew up normal enough, instilling the fear of fail-
ure in her little sister by playing countless hours of perfectionistic
teacher. And I grew up relatively normal with the neighbor boys and
myself turning all objects in our vicinity into imaginary weapons to
turn on one another. It never occurred to either of us to play "packing my carry-on."

At first it was a sad game. When we arrived back in Tajikistan
with three-year-old Grace and seven-month-old Silas, there was a
wild insecurity driving Grace's incessant need to pack, unpack, and
repack all of her very favorite toys in her imaginary carry-on every
day. Remembering our family history, she knew she must be ready
to go "home" at any moment. Continental moves often come without warning. Grace wouldn't settle into her new life.

Making matters worse, in our last stint back stateside, she had
gone from quite competent in Tajik to not even understanding the
Tajik words for "hello" and "bread" on our return. Silas expressed
his upheaval by stopping naps completely for a few weeks, which
isn't normal behavior for a seven month old. Evidently he noticed
things were different. It was a mess deep enough to break a par-
ent's heart.

But six months later, praise God, Silas was napping happily
again and Grace had found a gaggle of little Tajik neighbors to visit

and ecstatically run around with every day. With three or four hours of linguistic immersion daily it didn't take a genius to see that it was only a matter of time before her Tajik expression would sound flawless compared to ours.

Yet every time the gaggle found its way into our apartment, it didn't take long to recognize the chasm again. We thought Grace and Silas' toy stash was fairly modest, but to Tajiks it seems like our children reside in a children's palace and vacation away to fantastic America somewhere over the rainbow. The chasm might be obscured for happy moments but it is still there, always.

For better or worse we have our limits as to how far we will go to fit in. Perhaps Grace will find herself a bit of an outsider as the sole girl toddler around without a shaved head, but we've decided against shaving her bald. Call it a family rule—an addendum since it never really came up in America. And so it will, yet again, be a bit harder for her to fit in with all the neighbor girls whose mothers are passionately pursuing thicker hair for their daughters with razors and drastic action.

We also have no plans for arranging our children's marriages. Though, depending on their choices, we might regret the lost opportunity. Upon returning stateside, our children might not fare much better at fully joining the crowd, which actually doesn't sound like a bad thing now that I think about it. Fortunately, Americans value individualism as opposed to Tajiks where the mentality feels stiflingly something like, "All together now, on three, shave your daughters bald or else! One, two, three!"

Yet even with the cultural depth that will help our children when they return to America, we still worry sometimes. I'm reminded of an amazing story a man who grew up as a missionary kid in Africa told me. I can't remember whether it was his group of missionary kid college friends or another group of missionary kids at college. But the story went that every weekend these globe-trotting, rootless students would find each other, go down to the airport near their college and hang out there playing cards, studying, and doing all the things that college students do on weekends. It just happened to be that their favorite place to do the normal college things was the airport.

These kids were drawn to the airport. It was where they felt most comfortable, most at home. So when it comes time for our Grace and Silas to choose a college, perhaps it would be wise to check to make sure the local airport is a comfortable, accommodating spot. How are the restrooms? Do the gates have good study surfaces? I'd say we'd probably be the only prospective family checking out the airport for study and socializing potential, though if we're lucky perhaps we'll meet some upperclassmen missionary kids there who could show them the ropes, security checks, and perhaps their favorite terminal. I wonder if they'd only be able to bring three-ounce bottles of Mountain Dew to their all-nighters.

But I suppose hanging out at airports isn't so bad compared to other missionary-kid horror stories I've heard. For example, I heard about a family who emerged from years in the jungle and checked in at a big city hotel only to have one of their children run right through a glass window in the lobby. It is fortunate most children in our society get a good feel for the properties of glass before they attain the capability of high speeds.

To the Tajiks, I know we must constantly seem to be shattering through the glass windows of culture, language, and daily life with power and speed that babies should not possess. In so many ways in Tajikistan we are newborns trapped in the bodies of adults as we reminisce on the glory days of full competence. The glass shards can certainly fly as we smash our way through the subtlety of taboos and faux pas like an ostrich obliviously barreling through a patio door. I hope we are not judged as fully functional adults, but being seen as ostriches isn't very appealing either.

Even though we are now fluent, often a simple question can throw us for quite a loop. For example, when one of my neighbors asks me, "How much is a *korpacha* of *ord* in America?" my thought process as I try to come up with the answer goes something ridiculously like the following:

"Okay, one korpacha of ord. That's fifty kilos of flour I think. One kilo is, um. What is it again? Two point two pounds? Okay, so basically how much is like a ton of flour? How much is a pound of flour? Flour, flour, do we still even have that for sale back home? Man, I bet they'd give a discount if I bought over one hundred pounds of flour with my shopper card. Well, maybe not, but I might get on television or shopper-of-the-month status or something."

So after rigorous mental deliberations I usually respond, *name-donam* (I don't know). I realize that sounds to my neighbor about the same as that US politician who missed the price of a gallon of milk by like 400 percent or something. To Tajiks, not knowing the price of fifty kilos of flour off the top of your head is like not knowing what town you live in or that we need air to breathe.

Though we've yet to buy an entire korpacha of flour and though we were presently sitting on an airplane, sipping 7UP while flying across Europe and over the North Atlantic Ocean towards the United States, in some ways we have begun to adjust our thinking to align more properly with Tajik home economics.

For example, Ann and I are now quite the connoisseurs of plastic bags. Before coming to Tajikistan we had no refinement in this art. But now, compared to most of our American countrymen, we would be considered experts in the field.

By way of explanation as to how we developed this sophisticated skill, it is necessary to know that Tajiks carry almost everything concealed in a plastic bag. Whenever Tajiks carry a new purchase from the store or take anything outside their home for any reason, they are vigilantly careful to conceal the item in a thick plastic bag. A repairman bags his hammer. A pair of women will carefully wrap their box of tea leaves as they head out for a visit.

In an impoverished society of harsh scarcity, it seems an absolute essential to hide the knowledge of your material possessions
as much as possible from your neighbors, especially since the "evil
eye," with its ability to curse your life and destroy your success, mysteriously feeds off the envy in your neighbor's heart. As that envy
grows, somehow fate itself can align against you. It is not a totally
foreign idea. Poe assigns similar power to the winged seraphs' covet-
ousness in his poem Annabel Lee:

> The Angels, not half so happy in heaven,
> Went envying her and me—
> Yes!—that was the reason (as all men know,
> In this kingdom by the sea)
> That the wind came out of the cloud by night,
> Chilling and killing my Annabel Lee.[1]

So in Tajikistan a plastic bag defends well against your neighbors' knowledge of your material success and therefore against
jealousy and its spiritually ominous results.

As an aside, this evil eye conjecture is why Tajiks will not com-
pliment someone on a beautiful baby. That would be like wishing
for something awful to happen. And if a woman wants to acclaim a
friend on a nice dress she is wearing, she would never say something
suspiciously envious like, "You look beautiful in that dress." Rather,
she would say something less dangerous and more evil-eye resistant
such as, "That dress suits you."

We've been the ostrich running through the glass realm of com-
pliments more than once. I imagine we've caused a mess of alarm
around the neighborhood. Is it our imagination or can we hear them
whispering on our approach, "Hide the babies; the foreigners are coming!" Now we can try saying, "That baby suits you." This probably isn't
right either but at least it's not dangerous.

Oddly, even though wealthy Tajiks know they can't throw a
plastic bag around their new BMW or two-story mansion with

Russian-inspired Cinderella turrets, they flock to the prestige items while continuing to ignore indoor plumbing and utilities. Maybe they think they are more powerful than fate. But small things among the weaker folk remain hidden in plastic bags.

Now, when choosing the perfect plastic bag to conceal one's goods before hitting the street, one wants to find something edgy but not trashy. As a general rule, Russian plastic bags are trashy. Avoid them if possible. I wish elderly Tajik women did. It is curious to see respectable old ladies, too modest and protected to have often left a three-street radius of their homes since the day they were given as brides decades ago, carrying around their homemade bread wrapped in a near-naked Russian model smoking suggestively. These ladies wrap themselves so carefully in deep concealing headscarves and proceed to parade about with flirtatious bread. But better them than you. You must make a better choice.

One could go with a trendy plastic bag like say Britney Spears or that Gabriella girl from *High School Musical*, but going that route one runs the risk of being in advance of the star's local fame. And it's hard to be trendy when you're the only one who knows you're being trendy. We have no confidence in our trendy criterion here as the top of the non-Russian, non-Hindi pop world seems to be a strange time-warp mix of Michael Jackson, 50 Cent, Shakira, Mike Tyson, and of course all things Van Damme.

My Tajik English students here actually introduced me to 50 Cent, which left me quite happy I have not done a better job in teaching them the English language. Rap seems to be a lot more uplifting if you don't know the rapping medium. It would probably be a societal move in the right direction if American young people started to listen exclusively to Portuguese rap. So at any rate, trendy plastic bags are a big risk. Better not until I learn my Bollywood stars sufficiently.

One could go cheap, red, Chinese plastic, but what would the neighbors think? Your plastic bag helps rank you socially and cheap Chinese plastic is not conducive to upward mobility. Plus, there are durability issues, especially with public transport. One does not want the bottom falling out of one's bag spilling kilos of carrots, potatoes, and onions all over the floor of a jammed mashrutka while riding back from the bazaar. This is a very real possibility. Very little glue seals the Chinese plastic bags since most of the glue was released directly into the atmosphere over Beijing. Best to save the Chinese plastic for trips to the trash dump.

Now a nice floral pattern is a good choice for either guys or girls. Guys get flowers on holidays in Tajikistan, so there is no threat to masculinity by going floral. But I must admit I have had trouble adjusting to the sight of bulky guys hulking off to the boxing center with their sparring clothes wrapped in floral-design plastic bags tucked neatly under their arms. It's even weirder when they are holding hands. It's normal for guys to hold hands here, but I definitely doubt their idols Tyson and Van Damme would approve.

Every week when my Tajik buddies and I get together to play soccer or ultimate Frisbee in the valley on the outskirts of town, they always come dressed in style, their sports clothes folded neatly in a plastic bag, often a floral. And in the dying light, drenched in sweat when we decide it's time to call it quits and begin the walk back towards town, they all whip out their bags and change back into their nice duds and dress shoes before beginning our slosh back across the river valley towards home.

It is well understood that I'm the weirdo as we walk together. With my clinging shirt and dusty backpack slung over my sweaty shoulder in the twilight, I'm the guy who just can't figure out respectability. To their credit, they resist the urge to walk a few meters ahead. Plastic bags neatly folded under their arms, they walk loyally by my side across the marshes and into town. Risking association with me in the full bloom of my grubby glory gives me reason to reflect on the true nature of friendship. And among the peer pressure of my longsuffering friends, I begin to wonder if perhaps I'm the strange one for not wanting to wear dress shoes across the marshes.

We actually have two collections of plastic bags on our apartment balcony. The cheap ones are wadded together in a big ball beside the publicly presentable ones. Those are folded neatly in a stack to prevent wrinkles. It's not a good idea to iron plastic bags, yet transporting your tools to your buddy in a wrinkly bag would be tacky, so better keep the supply tidy.

There are a plethora of occasions when we put a bag from the tidy stack to good use. For example, when we want to regift nonedible edibles it is imperative to have a classy bag to prepare the gift. Or when going to summer camp it is nice to have a presentable plastic bag to pack.

Unfortunately, there is not a plastic bag in the world built strong enough to hold our camp supplies. Back before we had kids, I will never forget waiting for the mashrutka to arrive and drive us off into the mountains for the summer camp our organization was running. As we stood beside our Tajik staff, Ann and I couldn't help but compare our supplies with theirs.

Ann and I had just brought the essentials—complex water filtration systems, massive amounts of snacks to keep us alive, toilet paper rolls, five pounds of medicine each, a book for every day of the week, insecticides, and about two sets of clothes per day to name a few items. We had been proud of how light we had packed, sauntering buoyantly along to our pick-up point ever so slightly hunched under the weight of our backpacks, and our lone suitcase busting at the seams between us. Then we saw our Tajik staff waiting there chatting, each holding a single sturdy plastic bag.

What!? What could possibly fit in there? One change of clothes? A toothbrush perhaps? Their bags weren't even bulging! We looked for rocks to hide under as we realized we were like the stereotypical British couple who insisted on bringing their hundred-piece silver and lace set into the jungle so they could have proper tea times on the big game hunt. But doggone it, we were going to bring more than two pairs of underwear to camp even if it killed us!

If we were ever going to attend camp with all of our supplies in a single plastic bag, which we absolutely weren't, but if we were, it would have to be an extraordinary plastic bag. This brings us to the pride and joy of our collection. The crème brulee, the choice Chianti wine of our stock are a few bags of such a magnificently high-grade, indestructible plastic that they hold a special place in our hearts. We have a pair of near mint-condition, circa 2003, special-edition Target bags and a handful of fine international airport-grade plastics that prove to the neighbors that we are serious about our upward mobility. We only show these bags to our most trusted friends. These are not to be gifted. These are by all means to be saved for special occasions, conspicuous outings, or perhaps Grace's dowry.

Sometimes when Ann and I find ourselves reverently fingering an especially fine plastic or admiringly discussing the craftsmanship of a sturdy design, we realize how far we have progressed in our art. Though back stateside, when we find ourselves hording Target bags in Ann's closet, filling the cupboard with tinfoil scraps the size of a cookie, and wondering about the feasibility of putting a Ziploc through the dishwasher, it feels more like regression. It feels like we've overshot being fashionably green and are now environmentally neon.

But even as we advance in our conformity to Tajik home economics we are aware we have new weaknesses cropping up. For example, every day we live here we know that our chances of ever again winning Trivial Pursuit diminish. You simply can't go for years at a time without watching a single news broadcast or sporting event in English and expect to get those pieces of pie. Although, if there are any questions that inquire about Russian Olympic target shooting, skeet shooting, arrow shooting, shot gun shooting, really any type of Russian shooting be it male, female, or mixed synchronized doubles shooting, we should be ready. Endless hours of Russian Olympic coverage are of course devoted to what they are medaling in, and the Russians sure seem to be able to shoot stuff. If Russians could run and jump better instead of having steady digits and such infernally brilliant eyesight, the Olympics would have been a lot less excruciating.

We should have seen our pieless, trivia-deficient future coming though. The first time we met our team leader at a seminar in the States, he had already spent many years abroad. I'll never forget sitting down with him in the lobby in front of the television. In the middle of an ancient Seinfeld rerun he looked over at Ann and me and said, "Is this that Seinfeld show? I think I've heard about this." Ann and I looked at each other and our brainwaves met panicking, "No knowledge of Jerry! Where in the world are we moving to? What have we done!?"

And we have certainly done some stupid things in our new Central Asian home. But we're learning. We have learned not to scream at our Muslim guests, "No! Stop! Don't eat those! They have pork in them!" We have learned not to serve little old Tajik ladies, who have never used a fork or sat at a table before, spaghetti unless they are wearing a red korta dress to begin with. "Scoot your seat up closer and twist the fork like this." Not worth it.

We have learned that buffets are always a bad idea. We have learned it's embarrassing to say during a quiet moment at a funeral meal, "In America we eat cow manure." We have learned the subtle but important linguistic difference between the words for "cow meat" and "cow manure." We have learned what the expression, "You stick both fingers up your nose and come as a guest" means and to bring a gift with us when we visit in order to prevent it being said of us. We have learned to ask why our babysitter wants a salary advance and to say no if it is because a fortune-teller has told her she must immediately sacrifice a black chicken.

It's all just so bizarre. I remember our 9/11 experience, which was far from the typical American experience. This was before we had children. First off, we didn't even find out about it until September 12, which puts us solidly in the minority of Americans. I remember I jumped into the back of our driver's car to head to the office on the twelfth. He turned to me and said something in hasty Tajik about being very sorry about buildings blowing up in America at which point I decided it would be good to check my email. My in-box was full of messages from friends and family back home. Some said we needed to come home now. Passions were high. An hour from the Afghanistan border I looked out the office window toward the southern Central Asian hills and wondered why things seemed so calm.

As Americans, it was interesting to find ourselves on September 12 surrounded by a population that is nearly 100 percent Muslim. But we knew most of the time that Tajiks seem more freaked out by Afghan extremists than Americans do, like the time there was a drug-czar-related shootout in our town. Amid the distant gunfire we could hear coming from the neighborhood just past the park, we heard all the whisperings from our neighbors about how the drug czar had brought a truckload of Afghans with him and therefore even with hundreds of Tajik policemen all hope was lost.

After September 12 and 13 passed with polite condolences from the neighbors, no one was even mentioning the American tragedy at all. It was just another far-off disaster to be treated by Tajiks as Americans treat a genocide in Africa, with ten lines on page A-15 of the newspaper. The talk was back to local weddings and the best wrestlers in town.

In pre-internet southern Tajikistan, playing endless cards as we sifted through the situation, Ann and I waited for news from an e-mail we could download at a snail's pace. No convenient long-distance calling capability. Then as the staff of other foreign NGOs (nongovernmental organizations) began evacuating the area, it was to the suitcases to stuff our hasty piles in as quickly as possible as if we would never return. The neighbors stared incomprehensibly as we said some rushed goodbyes, loaded the rough equivalent of a thousand plastic bags into the mashrutka, and raced off to the capital in a whirlwind.

From there it was frequent visits to foreigners' homes to watch BBC's take on the situation. Word finally came from headquarters that we were to evacuate. Then it was a blur of buying tickets, saying goodbye to all the foreigners who were staying, and flying swiftly home.

But it wasn't until arriving home and connecting to twenty-four-hour cable news with the endless discussion of random apocalyptic possibilities that we really began to feel afraid. The world seemed a much scarier place from CNN-illuminated Kansas than it had an hour from the Afghanistan border. So after a quick evacuation conference with our mission board, we fled back to Tajikistan and continued our lives.

We were back well before Christmas although the suitcase containing our gifts to each other didn't reach us until May. Our flight back in was filled with reporters and journalists of all stripes. The usually sparse Tajik Air flight from Munich was filled to the brim. Or so I thought.

I painfully remember most of the flight stuffed in basically a fetal position with three carry-ons variously attached to my person. Halfway through the flight I decided that the plane wasn't actually going to make it to cruising altitude and I couldn't sit and panic over the sound of the struggling engines forever so using strength of heroic proportions where I think I might have actually performed an inverted iron cross with two carry-ons in my fight to the aisle, I escaped my sardine row and headed slightly downhill toward the restroom.

Unbelievably, two Tajik Air employees were sound asleep, sprawled comfortably across three empty seats apiece, using bunches of blankets, which they evidently had forgotten to distribute in their haste toward cozy hibernation. My jaw dropped and though I don't often guffaw, I think I might have let out one or two. Fortunately, the flight attendants were too deeply asleep to notice or I might have had to sit on the wing or something.

After an arrival where we had to let the passport control officer borrow our pen—not the first time—so he could fill out the items necessary to let us enter his country, we found ourselves in an angry mob of reporters and cameramen at the baggage check. Evidently they had lost expensive equipment. Suddenly we didn't feel so bad that one of our suitcases went missing. Unfortunately there would be no Christmas presents.

Unlike the reporters who were there for just a moment then whisked away to large media conglomerates to recoup their losses, I kept going back to the airport on trips to the capital over the next few months to ask if our suitcase had showed yet. Probably due to this persistence, in May our NGO's driver, who no one without unusual inside information should have been able to connect with us, got a mysterious call at his home hours from the capital from a guy evidently representing the pirating division at the international airport. The mystery man said to our NGO driver, "I have the suitcase. If no one investigates or complains it will be dropped off at your house tomorrow." At least it wasn't swimming with the fishes so we were happy to get the suitcase and have a bit of Christmas in May to wrap up our atypical 9/11 experience at threat-level rainbow bright.

Circling Chicago

After an inordinate amount of time arching southwest across the vast reaches of Canada, we finally began our approach into Chicago. Mercifully, Grace and Silas were dozing. Ann and I were still alive as air traffic control allowed us to begin our circling descent toward home.

"Home," yes, we still use the word for what awaited us below. We've noticed though that some of our teammates who have been in Tajikistan a few years longer than us have made the momentous switch and now use the word in reference to Tajikistan.

Even though we still use the word "home" for our US of A, our America seems a little less homelike every time we land. But many ties and allegiances remain strong. Consider our unbridled affections toward fast food for example.

I remember after a significant stretch of month upon weary month of glum hamburgerless existence, sitting down with Ann at Munich airport's Burger King to enjoy our hot treasures. I knew it was going to be a special moment as Ann almost religiously unwrapped her Whopper, careful not to let a single onion or tomato fall away.

I prepared the camera and had her pose, mouth open, an inch from her first bite. I captured the moment and was putting the camera away as Ann took that bite. Ann actually burst into joyful tears! So I quickly whipped out the camera again and took the passionate picture for posterity. Her heart had escaped the oppression of Whopperless Central Asia and had been transported home. I made a mental note to send the picture to Mr. King.

Among the varied elations of our times back stateside, we face the increasing feeling that we don't truly belong in either place. Early on in trips back, this feeling is noticed intensely when walking into a grocery store. I swear the Muzak track must always be playing the *Hallelujah Chorus* at high-decibel levels as we stand mesmerized by endless glistening aisles of choice that we can't even reach the top of without a ladder and store assistance. And if we partook in all the choices on those aisles we'd need even more assistance, probably permanent.

In Tajikistan we often cook with a Mennonite cookbook but usually find it to be too flashy to follow with what we find at the local bazaar. We have to use a substitution guide to creatively wade our way through the superfluous extravagances of lavish Mennonite cuisine. So the grocery store just about knocks us unconscious the first couple of times as we drown in the mix of vague guilt and palatable joy.

On one of our trips back stateside I attempted to have a little fun with sorting out my feelings by writing a little piece. I imagined the conversation that might ensue over breakfast if one of my Tajik friends came to visit us here in suburban America. I titled it *A Tajik in My Kitchen* and have included it below:

Alisher: Asalom, Akai David.

Me: Morning, Alisher. Man, I'm tired. I thought we'd take it easy today since we've had a couple full sightseeing days already. We could stay home and I could show you the many joys of cable.

Alisher: Should I go buy bread?

Me: Oh, no, we've still got some frozen. I'll zap it.

Alisher: How often do your women make bread?

Me: Um, I think my Grandma used to make it. I think I heard that. And we got a bread machine for our wedding. Pretty sure it's in my parents' basement somewhere. Oh, and Alisher, try not to use the phrase "your women."

Alisher: So none of your neighbors bake bread!? Akai David, do you really have neighbors?

Me: Of course we have neighbors.

Alisher: Then where are they?

Me: Work and soccer mostly. They drive there. It's really far away.

Alisher: All of them?

Me: Yeah, and everybody's got their own car.

Alisher: I can't believe women can drive! What if the car breaks? Who will fix it?

Me: I know what you mean. That's why Ann and I both carry cell phones.

Alisher: So if she calls you, you can go find her and fix her car?

Me: No, no, crazy. It's so we can call the tow truck quickly. Don't look at me like that. Our cars don't break anyway. Probably because I was born before my car was.

Alisher: Unlike my car?

Me: Exactly. In America cars are not family heirlooms.

Alisher: What's an heirloom?

Me: In your car's case it's a testament to the fact that your ancestors were mechanical geniuses. I never knew you could put a gas tank in the passenger seat.

Alisher: Depends on the tube.

Me: I believe I speak for most Americans when I say we prefer not to experiment. You want some water?

Alisher: Are you going to have ice in your water!?

Me: You can close your eyes if you want. It hasn't killed me yet. And brace yourself, I also like it when a fan is blowing directly on me. You know how insane we are. We even have a thing called iced tea and our population is still increasing.

Alisher: You keep telling me that ice is okay, but you do get sick sometimes.

Me: There might be other factors besides fans and ice, don't you think?

Alisher: *(Long pause, staring blankly.)*

Me: All right, fine. Let's not have that conversation again. Bread's done. It's got a few cooler damp spots, but the other spots are so hot it'll even things out.

Alisher: Your bread is gross.

Me: True. But it's impossible to disrespect it. I mean look at this perfect slice here. Can you tell which side is the top?

Alisher: No.

Me: Exactly, so it's impossible to knowingly flip it upside down. So you don't have to worry about disrespecting your bread. Sliced bread, it can still be holy without the fear of desecration!

Alisher: I don't think your bread is holy. Why do Americans eat it? They have enough money to eat anything!

Me: Well, we've found that food is best in bulk and in boxes. It never goes bad or if it does it's not until like 2025 so then you basically never have to go shopping. It's great!

Alisher: *(Again with the staring blankly.)*

Me: No, really, it's great. You'll just have to take my word for it.

Alisher: But where do you get your fruits and vegetables? I never see any fruit trees or gardens. All I see is lots of green grass and trees that serve no purpose.

Me: It's called aesthetics. And if you have grass you eliminate the need to sweep your dust every day. We'll have to Google "lawns in the state of Arizona" so you can see how much better even rocks would be for a yard than dust. They paint the rocks green sometimes and I'm going to hesitantly guess that's for aesthetics too. You can probably even use the Russian Google site if you want to see them.

Alisher: But where are your fruit trees?!

Me: They're so messy and time consuming. Besides, we don't need any fruit trees here because there is a magical land where everything grows forever. I can have a strawberry on New Year's just as good as the strawberries we had last night. There are no seasons in this magical place and every year the fruit is bigger, brighter, and cheaper than the last! And sometimes they even come up with new fruits that never existed before or at least new colors for the old ones. That's so we don't get bored with our produce. Plus marketing has discovered that brand-new kinds of fruit sell better. And "year round" means no canning. I didn't even know that food had seasons until we went to Tajikistan!

Alisher: Stop it.

Me: No, seriously, look here on the strawberry carton. Here, read.

Alisher: "Ca-li-forn-ia?"

Me: Absolutely!

Alisher: Is that where the bread comes from, too?

Me: Why not!

Alisher: I want to go to this California!

Me: We all do. We all do.

Alisher: Tajiks must run it.

Me: What's that supposed to mean? Is this about the potato thing again? Look, just because I don't know how to plant a potato doesn't mean no one does. We can probably even program machines to plant our potatoes. I bet we don't even need dirt to grow them anymore. So stop making fun of me.

Alisher: America is so different.

Me: Just wait till we've watched a few hours of cable.

Alisher: And is this, this, um, strawberry-banana yogurt tube also from California?

Me: Actually, no one knows what it is or where it's from. I can see you're not buying all of this. Look, if we were in Tajikistan all the women in your family would have to wake up way before dawn to begin to make the dough and start the fire for the oven. It takes them like five hours to make breakfast! How long did it take us? Like five minutes and no women required, which is good because they're all out driving around. It's all about time, see. Now we've got time today, extra time to watch television. Okay, today is a bad example. Well, actually most days are a bad example, come to think of it. But you see don't you? We're saving time.

Alisher: Then why are Americans so busy?

Me: Just eat your yogurt tube.

Alisher: I do miss fresh bread.

Me: Yeah, absolutely. Tajikistan beats us there. But I saw a movie about fresh bread a while back called "The Bread, My Sweet." So possibly we are definitely maybe sitting on the cusp of a movement towards fresh bread and away from Rice Krispie treats here.

Alisher: People will start baking bread again?

Me: Or at least we'll import more bread from Italy or have more Italian bakeries close by.

Alisher: That you have to drive to.

Me: But fortunately for us everyone can drive. So your little brother can go get that bread while you do other things.

Alisher: It still seems strange to me. Could I have some warmer water please? This is too cold even without the ice.

Me: Suit yourself but I'm telling you there is nothing like cold drinks in the summer.

Alisher: Perhaps.

Me: Okay, here you go. Hot enough?

Alisher: Yes. Thank you. Akai David?

Me: Yeah?

Alisher: Akai David, every time I go to your bathroom I am very afraid.

Me: What? What are you talking about?

Alisher: Those books in there. They say such scary things! I am trying not to forget anything so I can be sure to tell all my family and neighbors when I go back to Tajikistan.

Me: Alisher, maybe you shouldn't read *Reader's Digest* anymore. It can be scary for the uninitiated. They just want to sell magazines so they put things on the cover like, "Ten ways you'll probably die before you finish reading this article" or "Believe it! Your children are building bombs in the basement!" It makes you want to read it. Fortunately in Tajikistan you don't have basements. That was a joke.

Alisher: I don't understand.

Me: Just don't read *Reader's Digest* anymore.

Alisher: Yes, I think you are right. I should not read it anymore. I think the hot spots in this bread just burned my mouth.

Me: Yeah, sorry about that. And yet you still don't want something cold to drink? So Alisher, what else have you been thinking about what you've seen here the last couple of days?

Alisher: Well, Akai David, yesterday I noticed something. Why don't you fill up every seat in the car with neighbors before you go somewhere? You say there are neighbors, right? So why don't you fill all the seats? It seems like every car I see only has one person in it!

Me: Remember that crazy van ride we took together from the bazaar that brutally hot day in Kadimobod? After we got out we couldn't feel our legs or stop laughing. So yeah our driving habits must be hard for you to understand since Tajiks have discovered that fifteen adults, five children, three fifty-pound grain sacks, and one or two assorted livestock can all fit in a minivan with only minimal structural damage to the vehicle, themselves, and the livestock. Just wait until you see the raw potential of a Hummer! You could carry a whole village! We test it at a place called Sam's Club.

Alisher: But, Akai David, if each person gave you fifty cents, you could make maybe three dollars every time! Or why not have car stands on all the main streets like we do where people can wait until the car fills up before they drive?

Me: You mean with strangers? They might kill you!

Alisher: What?

Me: Look, any American who has ever watched the local news would be opposed to your idea. And there is such a thing as a seat belt law here so at the most I could only make two dollars every time. But, really, we can't do that, just waiting in the mall parking lot until we get three other people who want to head north. There are really too many reasons why this is a bad idea. Good for Tajikistan, bad for here. Besides, you'd probably have to get a taxi license or something. And what about insurance? You'd definitely have to get insurance to be picking up strangers all the time.

Alisher: What's insurance?

Me: It's the reason Americans must have a job at all times no matter what!

Alisher: Do I need insurance now? I am a guest.

Me: You probably do need insurance and that guest thing doesn't mean much here, so don't hurt yourself. If someone else hurts you, you'll be fine though. In fact, you might only be a coffee burn away from going home as the richest man in all of Tajikistan! But if you got hurt on your own and we had to call an ambulance or something we could end up paying a few thousand dollars!

Alisher: My people work for years in Russia to save up that much money so they can come back home and get married!

Me: So you are beginning to see why insurance is so important.

Alisher: I guess I see.

Me: Sorry to shoot down your business venture there. Any more ideas on how to make some money? Maybe you might see an opportunity I'm missing.

Alisher: Well, Akai David, I know how to give shots. My aunt is a nurse and she showed me how. So could we go door to door and give shots to your neighbors whenever they are sick? If they paid for the medicine, I would only need maybe fifty cents for each visit I made. We do it like this in Tajikistan so we don't have to go to hospitals to pay more. So if things are so expensive to even go to the hospital at all like you say, then Americans will want this!

Me: But see, what you just said scares us more than insurance. You'll have to just take my word on this too. Besides, you're forgetting again that Americans prefer to swallow medicine. I don't know of a single person who injects their multivitamin here so you'd have less business than you think.

Alisher: Then I would do it for twenty-five-cents profit a visit!

Me: You're missing the point. Good breakfast?

Alisher: Yes! *Rahmat*, Akai David that was a very, um, interesting breakfast. I was hoping to go outside for a minute. If I see another person, what should I do?

Me: It's Tuesday, so that's doubtful. If you do see anyone, either ignore them or make an extremely noncommittal nod like this. Just do what they do, which will probably be nothing. Remember what we talked about, if you're yourself, you'll make the neighbors very nervous. And stay out of people's yards. That makes them nervous too.

Alisher: Why?

Me: Because of suing.

Alisher: What's suing?

Me: It's many American's hope of realizing the American dream. So stay on the sidewalk.

Alisher: Why is the sidewalk different?

Me: Because it's not private prop . . . Oh, why don't I just go
        with you?
Alisher: No, outside sounds scary. Let's just watch TV.
Me: Now that's the spirit.

I remember how therapeutic it was to be back home in America
writing that piece. Except for the reverse culture shock mental haze
hanging over me, I remember how empowered and alive I felt.
Finally English again. Finally I could at least attempt to be funny!
Finally I could understand other people's jokes. In Tajikistan I
greatly miss being able to tell a joke, to feel like I have a sense of
humor. If, as Shakespeare affirmed through Polonius, brevity is the
soul of wit then circumlocution is the soul of botched jokes and
blank stares. Trust me.

I had a language teacher our second year in Tajikistan who had
quite a sense of humor. He'd tell a joke, laugh by himself a while,
then spend ten minutes explaining the cultural background, the
politics, the new vocabulary, or whatever it was I was missing.
Good times.

Years have passed and now I get some of the jokes. But there is
still a separation. I'll be standing with a group of my Tajik friends
and one of them will start in on a joke saying, "A Cuban, an Italian,
a Russian, and a Tajik are on a train. The Cuban smokes half a fine
cigar then tosses the rest out the window. The others yell, "What are
you doing? That's a fine cigar!" The Cuban says, "Oh, we have too
many where I come from." The Italian opens a fine bottle of wine,
pours a bit into a glass and tosses the rest of the bottle out the window. The others yell, "What are you doing? That's a fine wine!" The
Italian replies, "Oh, where I come from we have so much of that." A
little while later the Russian grabs the Tajik and throws him out the
window. The other two yell, "What are you doing? You just threw
him out the window!" The Russian says, "Oh, where I come from we
have tons of them."

All the Tajiks burst into laughter and slap each other on the back as I smile awkwardly. I don't really feel I can fully join in. As a foreigner it doesn't seem right. I can listen and smile and perhaps even laugh a bit if it's not too boisterous, but I can feel a distance. Insider self-effacing mockery is much different than outsider.

But although we are outsiders, we constantly seek to bond with them, to share our true hearts in common. That is why we have come. We realize our love for them in Christ, that compels us to look for every opportunity to share the gospel, puts us in perpetual risk of losing our Tajik friends so close to our hearts. And we have lost many. We pray it is only for a season. But nothing, nothing, nothing compares to the bond we sometimes graciously find in Christ. The unity we feel powerfully present between ourselves and a Tajik believer amazes us.

In our experience, the unity found in our faith effortlessly supersedes the most diverse elements of culture. We have become brothers, sisters, everlasting family, and I realize that the joy and hope found in that unity will take the rest of my spiritual journey to plumb the heights of.

Approaching Customs

We landed at O'Hare. Predictably, we were soon far behind the other passengers. We struggled down an endless hall dedicated to Michael Jordan, toward baggage claim and customs wishing our drowsy children could handle their own carry-on bags or at least themselves. After loading a couple of luggage carts far beyond capacity at baggage claim we inched along painfully. We finally arrived at the very back of a long and boisterous customs line. Surrounded by Americans for the first time in well over a year, Ann and I smiled at each other as we navigated slowly back and forth through the switchbacks toward the front of the line.

We couldn't believe our ears. All around us total strangers were joking away with each other in tennis shoes and grubby clothes like they hadn't a care in the world, not even when entering a country. Standing in that line was truly like a breath of fresh air. In the absence of fear that there might be an angry machine-gun-toting officer with a penchant for corruption around the next pole, the freedom of the mood was clearly reflected in the conversation. Too few airports in the world are like this. This was wonderful.

Every time back to the States I find I am both more patriotic and less patriotic than before I left. I appreciate certain things deeply now upon my returns that I hardly even noticed before such as this ease in conversation with strangers, the unpretentiousness reflected in everyone's attire, the freedom to drive from the Atlantic to the Pacific without a single checkpoint, the liberty to head south without having to pack a burka for Ann, the joy in worshiping openly, and the hope of having a vote that could actually make a difference. As we stood there a great number of other wonders about this country came to my mind. I felt good about taking my family to the front of this line and on into this place we still called home.

But as we struggled to move our luggage carts around another turn in line, I reflected on aspects of home that I have become less patriotic about. Overseas sharing the light of Christ, it has become so much clearer that I must, I must, be first and foremost a Christian and not, absolutely not, primarily an American. So often I am embarrassed over where I come from as I try to share Christ. To many Muslims, the West is synonymous with Christianity. Therefore, whatever the West does and is represents Christ. The pursuit of freedom for greater and greater personal power to indulge in morally reprehensible behavior is not something I am proud to come home to or to try to explain to my Tajik friends.

But at least most of the time it is easier to explain the awful weight of my own sinfulness and the joy of the forgiveness I have found in Christ with a Tajik Muslim than with a typical American. At least the Tajik will engage, with a rational discussion being a very real possibility. A response of anger is so absolutely wonderful compared to the indifference and death of meaningful conversation that I so often meet with in increasingly postmodern America. For all our society's advances, in comparison to my American countrymen, I find Tajiks to be refreshingly rational beings when it comes to the matters of greatest significance.

At the common level where I live, work, and think as largely an outcast in both societies, I have felt a great difference. Being a social outcast in Tajikistan feels much more human to me than being a social outcast in America. When in Tajikistan, as Hebrews admonishes, I go to Christ outside the camp, even though they might despise the place I go, the Tajik community does not strip me of the dignity of being a human being as I feel American society increasingly attempts to strip everyone of with its vacuous humanistic, relativistic outlook.

I realize the oxymoronic gospel of absolute relativism that pervades our nation is not something I can ever get remotely behind. My heart, my soul, my strength, my mind, my hope, my joy, my peace, my love, and my worldview are already worlds away from mainstream America and still heading in opposite directions. As we approached customs, I felt a familiar melancholy mingling with my excitement as I prepared to enter this place, my country.

There is a passage in Exodus I have grown to love. Speaking of the first Passover in Exodus chapter 12, God instructs the Israelites, "This is how you are to eat it: with your cloak tucked into your belt, your sandals on your feet and your staff in your hand. Eat it in haste; it is the LORD's Passover" (Ex 12:11). Throughout Scripture God has gone to great pains to show how different we are to be, to instill in our hearts the reality that we are pilgrims, sojourners. As followers of Christ we are all pilgrims. In Tajikistan, it is so easy for me to remember this. In America, often I struggle to recall it, with all the shiny distractions and ease with which I can fit in if I want to.

Now at the front of the customs line I passed our passports to the officer. He glanced at them, leaning over the desk to see Grace and Silas sleepily fussing at our feet among the luggage. As he passed them back and motioned us to enter this new land once again, I felt the urge to tighten up the belt on my spiritual sojourning cloak, tighten and hold on to the reality that we are supposed to feel unnatural. Not to stand outside the camp in bitterness or fear but in love to have the overflowing joy, peace, and hope of the Lord be the aroma of our separateness as we look for opportunities to engage.

A mature Christian sojourning stance can be so elusive. I prayed for maturity. I prayed that my children would hold tight the great blessing of their foreignness. I prayed that they would discover that Christ would use the lessons of their otherness to burn deep into their hearts the reality that neither America nor Tajikistan is truly home.

VI
THIS OLD TAJIK HOUSE

I have heard that becoming a homeowner puts one in a special club that only members can fully appreciate. I absolutely agree. I remember when my friends began to purchase their first homes, precipitating about a year of droning conversations on the many joys of mortgages, interest rates, insurance, tiling, painting, drywall, building codes, foundation support beams, and the stupefaction to be experienced at Home Depot every Saturday morning. By means of this story, I will submit my application to join this club. However, I fear membership will be denied on account of the fact that the homeowners' code on Earth reads a bit different than the one on Mars.

To buy a house in Tajikistan, one must be well below reproach, masochistic, or simply an unfortunate soul. For the pure of heart, a successful trip to the notary alone could take over a year and require a team of determined lawyers to fix the situation afterwards. The pure of heart in Tajikistan are usually blessed to fruitlessly see government officials 100,000 times. In Tajikistan there are ample opportunities to participate in an unofficial Bible study toward understanding King David's ragings on injustice. Therefore, it is with joy as unfathomable as the Pacific Ocean's Challenger Deep Gorge that Ann and I are going to purchase our family's Tajik house from our team leader, our team leader who already has all the proper paperwork finished with the exception of one house certificate. So I might only have to visit the government officials a thousand times.

Though the final house certificate is pending, we have already begun remodeling. We're ripping out some water-damaged floors and stripping the walls down to ancient unfired mud bricks and sand. Might I just say a homeowner's heart experiences a sudden downward sensation when he sees great similarities between the typical archaeological dig and his daughter's bedroom? I'm tempted to date the potshards. Perhaps BC shards could help with refinancing?

Alabaster, by the way, does not stick to crumbling dirt and sand. So in came the *shakatur* crew to shakatur our archaeological site. Shakatur is comprised of bags and bags of sand mixed with white pasty stuff bubbling up in a big cauldron, which I really hope won't stick permanently to our driveway. "Really sticks well to old dirt though," I was told. I promise from the bottom of that very same plunging heart to never again complain about drywall.

Another crew recently finished their exterior project. They tore down and replaced the collapsing exterior dirt wall that acts as a friendly fortress between us and our neighbors. Tajiks have told me many times before that they are an honest people. Then why the standard, impenetrable, ten-foot-high walls and steel cages on all windows?

The project proved a bit challenging as the neighbors had nearly everything imaginable leaning up against their side of the wall. They had to remove their makeshift barn, shed, firewood storage hut, and pit toilet so the workmen could stack mud brick upon mud brick—cemented with mud of course—up and up a good few feet past the height of the previous wall. Increasing the wall's height was a stratagem born of my wall crew's wisdom and experience in such matters. They knew that when the neighbors put their roofs back, they would be forced to have the slants go down towards their yard instead of draining, as had previously been the case, right into the mud foundation on our side of the wall. Who needs *People's Court*?

The neighbors on that side haven't been easy to love lately. I thought perhaps they would say thank you for my covering all costs to replace the mutual wall. Instead they seem to have been content to send their oldest boy over periodically to yell at the workmen to hurry up and finish before it rains and their firewood gets wet. At least we are providing more firewood for them. Out in front of the house, lining the street, are three extremely large trees. Or, rather, I should say, *were* three extremely large trees. Now, there are two big trees and a massive stump.

According to the witnesses, when we were gone in the capital, Dushanbe, a few weeks back, a big important-looking man showed up in front of the house with trucks and equipment. After getting a good amount of money from the buyer, which exchanged hands right there in front of our house, the important person proceeded to oversee the felling of the big tree. Reportedly during the process, he was repeatedly urging the crew to hurry up. Makes you wonder.

So the other day when I strolled over to spend some quality time with the neighbors as they were chopping away at our stump they told me, with little gentility, that this happened because I had been gone. In my defense, I had no idea my trees were in immediate danger. The neighbor on the other side of our house gave me the obvious solution to the danger of having large, neighborhood-benefiting shade trees in our front yard. "Cut the other two down and chop them into firewood in your backyard before they come and get the other ones." An interesting solution.

I'm beginning to see that the home association has different goals here. I might even be able to keep a camper outside our home! I could park it right beside our friendly front garden so quaintly fenced with, I kid you not, barbed wire. Evidently our garden was fenced with barbed wire as a subtle deterrent so neighborhood children and passersby would stop chopping down and making off with or setting fire to—both have happened—the surviving battle-scarred pine trees lining the inside of our garden. If you haven't guessed, liability is different here. I'm reminded of this fact every time the neighbors' babies toddle past on the sidewalk, inches from our barbed wire.

I have certainly learned a fair amount about the remodeling processes here. For example I know that our courtyard wall waits ready now for *andovar*, which is hay mixed with mud. This will be slathered on to protect the mud bricks. Then we'll whitewash over that and the security of our northern front will be complete. Even Tom Sawyer couldn't get someone to help with this.

I have also learned and relearned some of the rules regarding Tajik repairmen, the most important of which is that if you want them to work after lunch, then they must eat on the job site. Feed them there or risk a lonely afternoon. Still, the standard pay rates are so low that a homeowner can hardly complain. Sometimes I have estimated that I have had six men working on the house—half of them high-end skilled tradesmen—from sunrise to sunset, fed all of them lunch, and still spent less than ninety dollars for the day! Believe it or not, prices here are a great deal higher than they used to be.

Also hard to believe is the fact that the country of Tajikistan has one main bazaar called Sultoni Kabir, which appears to me to serve the remodeling needs of the entire country. Even to find things as simple as a nice broom or red dye to add to paint, a multiple hour trip to the capital's famous bazaar is often in order. Though I don't have any numbers, my gut tells me that a single Home Depot probably does more business per day than Sultoni Kabir bazaar. How is it possible that one bazaar, which seems to be similar in size to your average Lowe's, serves as headquarters for all things home improvement for all of Tajikistan? I suppose it must be because with dirt so readily available who needs a hardware store?

I was imagining the other day how much fun it would be to have *Trading Spaces: Tajikistan*. Given twenty-four hours, a light blue room, and a budget of one hundred dollars, what could you do? You could go crazy, drive up to the capital and buy paint, a brush, red paint coloring and a red broom, drive back down and paint the once blue room a light red—dark red would have blown the budget combined with transportation costs to and from the capital—set the broom against the wall and just wait for the shock of the returning owner!

Or maybe if we sent Oprah some footage of our mud-brick walls, she'd send out a crew that spoke Farsi and/or Russian to hit Sultani Kabir bazaar before coming down and making Oprah magic with sand and whitewash. They could call the episode, "Shakatur to impress!" And while they were here maybe they could find a way to get that sticky white stuff off the driveway. Good times for a new member of the homeowner's club.

VII
A WINTER'S NIGHT

Seven o'clock

There are no ordinary people. You have never talked to a mere mortal. Nations, cultures, arts, civilizations—these are mortal, and their life is to ours as the life of a gnat.[1]

Ann and I could see through the cracked door out into our living room. The lights suddenly grew bright and intense and we knew we were about to be in cold darkness. A moment later our entire city's electricity thumped off and we were once again enveloped in a familiar Kadimobod night. We knew the drill by heart, the candlelight flickering into our children's room as we finished our songs, prayers, and kisses, showing Grace her flashlight still worked, and laying Silas down in his crib.

We made our hasty retreat from the room. As we withdrew we were careful to unplug the two space heaters, not trusting our children's bedroom to the possible electrical surges and common explosions of Kadimobod's duct-taped power grid. We shut the door tight in hopes that the heat we had so carefully tried to fill their small room with would remain long enough to give them a cozy sleep. We were thankful for the two hours of rationed electricity we had been given that evening.

We blew the candles out in the living room as we walked past the low Tajik table and ancient Soviet heating coils lifelessly lining the wall, invoking the memory of better winters past. Ann led the way out into the hall she had already lit candles for, wisely anticipating the nightly plunge into darkness. I followed, shutting the door behind us as another barrier against the cold we tried to banish to certain areas of our apartment, areas away from where our children slept.

I grabbed an extra candle, a solidly cemented red nub waxed into its teacup holder, as I shivered my way into the kitchen. I wondered if it would be better to just unplug the refrigerator and open the door. It had to be colder in the kitchen than in the fridge and unplugging it would ensure its safety better than the surge protector sitting idle on the shelf beside our drip-bucket water filter.

If you put your tongue on a piece of metal in your kitchen and the fire department has to be called to assist, in my opinion, something has gone dreadfully wrong. Fortunately, our kitchen was not in that immediate danger. But so many others, we were aware, were not so lucky. Our teammates' kitchen flooded their apartment when the indoor pipes burst. And more ominously, the freezing waters filling their apartment complex's cavernous communal basement were slowly climbing the stairs toward the first floor. I wondered how many Tajiks were out there thinking, "Enough with this democracy idea! Where is the Soviet Union when you need them?"

Ann lit our portable propane heater in the family room while I opened our other propane tank and lit the stove. I was careful to put the pale-yellow kettle on the gas knowing that it—unlike the white kettle—contained filtered water. Since we didn't have to boil away potential disease first, filtered water would get us our hot cocoa a lot sooner.

Ann had carefully laid a packet of Swiss Miss cocoa on the counter. Tonight was our weekly Friday night date, so we had decided to splurge on cocoa that Ann's mom had sent us in a package that we had picked up in the capital a month previous. I went to the cupboard and did my best in the candlelight to count how many cocoa packets we had left.

I considered the length of the remaining winter and estimated that we could each have our own packet tonight. But I decided it would be better to split one tonight and defer the joy we'd find in the special treat of splitting the additional packet sometime on a Tuesday or a Wednesday. Besides, most of the joy, we had learned, was found in thankful anticipation.

As the kettle heated, I zipped my coat and adjusted my stocking cap. I opened the door and went out onto the frigid balcony of our second-floor apartment. Ducking under our lamentable laundry that had been in various states of drying for over a week now, I found my way to the window. I looked out on our town immersed in a night of overcast winter blackness. My hair hurt a bit in that vague itchy way, the familiar result of wearing a cap entirely too often.

Water pressure had not been strong enough lately to force the water through the tiny hot-water heater that hung above our toilet. But even if pressure had been high enough when water happened to be on, it wouldn't have mattered, as the two hours of anemic electricity each morning and again each night would have failed to heat the water sufficiently for showers. No, when we were feeling brave we filled our blue plastic basin with a couple of kettles of hot water and stood ankle deep in rapidly cooling water spasmodically ladling as if we were in a time trial to qualify for the new Winter Olympic sport of bucket bathing. Perhaps we had finally found a way to represent the USA. Though I have a feeling many countries would wipe the floor with America in that event.

Often on nights such as this I'm reminded of a passage from *Little House on the Prairie* that my mom read to me all those years ago on a prairie that has changed a lot faster than our Kadimobod. Kadimobod, after all, recently celebrated its 2,700-year anniversary.

I remember Mr. Edwards had just braved the flooding creek and made the Christmas trip with special presents for Mary and Laura. Pa and Ma scold him for being so reckless as he tells of his journey to Independence where he happened to run into Santa Claus. Ma instructs the girls to close their wide eyes as Mr. Edwards stuffs their stockings.

The girls are overjoyed when they open their eyes and get to look through their bulging socks to find their presents. When Laura finds a special cake made with pure white flour and sweetened white sugar in hers, she takes a tiny nibble from the bottom so it would not show. As always, Mary was not so greedy. The passage concludes:

> And in the very toe of each stocking was a shining bright new penny! They had never even thought of such a thing as having a penny. Think of having a whole penny for your very own. Think of having a cup and a cake and a stick of candy and a penny! There never had been such a Christmas.[2]

Even before coming here to live our modern version of *Little House*, that passage deeply affected me. It stayed in my mind all these years. As I looked out at the night, I considered how little I understand true thankfulness in order "to grasp how wide and long and high and deep is the love of Christ" (Eph 13:18). As I looked back at the cocoa packet on the kitchen counter I felt I grasped a little better what Paul prayed the Ephesians would comprehend. We have finally stopped shaking the snow globe of our lives long enough to set it down on the table and reflect on the beauty of the falling snow.

I returned to the kitchen, grabbed the kettle, poured the steaming water into our mugs and carefully divided the cocoa between them. I grabbed the mugs and followed the flickering to the family room. I shut the warped wooden door behind me as tight as I could manage. Ann was bundled, quietly sitting on the couch in the candlelight. She took her mug of cocoa as we snuggled in. I joined her in staring into the warm hope born of the propane flames lapping up against the grill as they heated our tiny family room.

We knew when we moved here from the States that we were in for dark times. That's why we painted the walls yellow. And even though we could hardly make out the color at the moment, I think the room felt warmer to us knowing we had golden walls surrounding, resiliently jubilant in the dark like flower bulbs poised just below a snowy surface.

We sat close together for a while staring at the radiating flames. It was a long night. There was no hurry and no electricity to fuel the many technological advances that incessantly free me and save me time. I felt happy to be fully with my wife.

That is something I love about Tajikistan, that it moves slow enough to give a culture a fighting chance at community. I remember visiting my grandma in the nursing home a few years ago. She was sitting with her new friends in the dining area. I pulled up a chair and tried to help Grandma eat as one of her friends sitting across the table started in on a story.

She spoke of a very hot summer in Kansas City back in the days before air conditioning. After dark, her family joined the other families of the neighborhood in the cool park where they laid out blankets on the lawn. Whole families curled up together right beside their neighbors as they drifted off to sleep, a peaceful community upon the grass.

I came across a passage in one of Garrison Keillor's books that describes a nearly identical scene he witnessed on a summer night as a boy when his father and he were visiting Brooklyn. I can't imagine taking my family to sleep for the night in a Brooklyn park today even if I sat vigilantly awake. Our society has certainly changed, though I'd be hesitant to label the change progress.

Earlier tonight I remember looking out from our balcony at the familiar scene of our Tajik neighbors huddled together in the gathering darkness of wintry dusk. A group of old men had stood backs to the wind in their long joma coats and toki caps. Perhaps they spoke of how they preferred sitting outside their apartments beside the newly planted courtyard trees every night of the summer. Women stood together and gossiped of this and that, the countless children dashing recklessly among them in the dimness smacking around their communal half-flat ball. Unmarried daughters and newly acquired daughters-in-law hurriedly wrapped fresh-baked bread in blankets, reaching in to grab the last ones from the sides of the earthen oven before putting the fire out for the night.

We have lived here long enough, watched this courtyard winter scene unfold so many times before that we too can feel the anticipation growing as the groups chat together waiting. We can sense the excitement. When the groups have nearly disappeared from before my eyes in the growing darkness, their voices seem to grow crisp and louder as my ears tune in and take the lead in my observation.

And then it happens. The government flips the magical switch and the communal joyful whoop goes up all around. From the streets on every side to the furthest reaches of the city the echoes of the synchronized cheer hang for a moment on the wintery air. And then the communal expression disappears into the night as completely as the warm breath that voiced the sounds. The irresistible glow of modernity fills the silence. Immediately the cold crowds disperse in pursuit of hot bread, Russian news, and perhaps, if the government is feeling generous, a late-night Bollywood movie.

Ironically the most enthusiastic communal expression, the joyful whoop that arises from each and every neighbor in one accord, is made in celebration of the very thing that ends the nightly community. I'm reminded of Neil Postman books I've read and how he constantly warns in them that technology takes away as well as gives. Often it takes much more. As he once said in a speech, "Technological change is not additive. It is ecological."[3] Our neighborhood is proof that Postman was right. When Kadimobod flips on the electrical grid, it is not that the culture goes on as before simply with the addition of electricity. No, all activity changes. The instant the stairwell's light hits our gathered neighbors, they dissolve into nothing as if they were never there at all. And almost before my pupils have had time to adjust to the sudden light, I am left to stare into only a deserted lot.

For Americans, sleeping in the park among the neighbors is a dreamy, impressionistic memory of our grandparents. In the full-flickering glory of our deficient, disordered attention, we listen to them speak about such things. Every once in a while in a brief, still moment we wonder why we feel so lonely. Snapping out of that, we resolve to avoid brief, still moments in the future. For America, community was generations ago. For Tajiks, it was yesterday, today, and tomorrow, but I do not know for how many tomorrows.

I was so enjoying the peace and stillness, or at least enjoying the idea of trying to find joy in it, that I felt a healthy amount of familiar internal conflict when, perhaps much to Mr. Postman's disappointment, Ann and I grew impatient with the whole peace thing. I returned to the balcony to see if we had enough juice to jump-start the television.

Stepping out I noticed that the mazor's (Muslim saint's burial building) electrical line across the street had been switched back on. The holy site was all aglow. I looked out over the city and was glad to see most of it was still dark. I took that as a good sign. The worst feeling is when you have been sitting in the dark for hours believing that the whole world is experiencing this along with you only to take a look out of the balcony window to discover that it is your house alone, dark within the effervescent, glowing world. You feel the revelation settle into the pit of your stomach. The city is not being stingy. No, something in your immediate vicinity that you are probably personally responsible for has exploded or melted yet again.

A few neighbors' houses glowed, evidence to the fact that they had illegally tapped into the mazor's line. It was not a bad line to tap into, though there were better lines to be pirated. Other neighbors, in a joint venture, had strung hundreds of feet of cheap electrical line to tap into the line running to the government building sector. That was usually a winning strategy perhaps only trumped by tapping into a usually generous hospital line or the line of some important general, mysteriously wealthy beyond compare.

As I stood there, I wished hospital lines were even more reliable than they are and I wished that Tajiks would not adore their friendly neighborhood drug runner just because he gives them fifty kilos of flour on Muslim holidays, sparkles when he walks, and has a reliable electric line to tap.

We try to obey the "no tapping" rules, which I think most of the neighbors think is a ridiculous decision. So we are in the dark a little more often than most. I think the common attitude in Tajikistan that has been well taught to the citizens by the government is, "Rules? What rules?" Still, we give honesty a go most of the time.

I bent over our little electricity accumulator. I had recently bought it in Dushanbe along with its attached car battery. Whenever the electricity comes on Ann and I race, often nearly knocking each other down in our enthusiastic haste, to plug in and flip the accumulator on to store every second of electricity we can. From the balcony I had hung two makeshift light bulbs, one to the kitchen and one to the family room. Long black extension cords that I had duct taped to the balcony wall and floor to keep them out of our way marked their balcony exit trails.

I read recently a man writing passionately that poetry is absolutely the best thing on the planet. That man has clearly never lived in Central Asia. We've got plenty of poetry here, but clearly duct tape is the single greatest thing in the whole wide world. It gives people who haven't a clue, like us, a decent shot at fixing anything!

Duct tape the window. Duct tape the leak. Duct tape the baby's wound. Wonderful stuff.

Using the electricity accumulator, we have found we are usually able to store enough electricity in the car battery for a few hours of light to both rooms. But we are hesitant to use our power charge in this way for two reasons. First, for the same reason I usually take our trash out late at night to avoid the neighbor kids rooting through it and spreading tales of canned corn and conspicuous juice and yogurt consumption. We are a bit embarrassed that the neighbors will see our light and know we are not only able to afford to fill propane tanks but also to buy some fantastic system to create our own light.

We try to pull the curtains but we know they can still see us living the electric high life. It is a constant internal struggle as we sit drinking RC Cola in generated light knowing the gospel is worth infinitely more than this, but afraid of burning out and exhausted by always fighting to hide so much of who we are.

The second reason is probably just a tad less important. We have found that if we save every volt or watt or whatever it is we are saving, then we usually have enough of a charge to flip both the television and DVD player on. If we have the juice to get it going then it will usually run for a couple of hours. But did we presently have the necessary power to start them up was always the question.

I skipped over the jealousy-inducing light bulb extension cords, grabbed and plugged in the cord for the television and DVD player. This ran through a convenient, duct-taped hole in the glass window between the family room and the balcony. I put my finger on the switch, yelled "Ready!" to Ann, crossed my fingers, tried not to let my hopes get too high, and flipped.

"Yes! Yes! All right!" Ann cheered from the family room as the accumulator inverted a sufficient stream of power from the battery. Bang the drums! Hurdle the mountains! Quote Tajik poetry! There would be television tonight! Hopefully the neighbors could not see the faint familiar glow through the drawn curtains. We sat down to continue the *West Wing* saga. Our Scottish friends in the capital are kind enough to act as our Tajikistan Blockbuster. We were presently engrossed in season seven.

President Bartlett prepares to step down as his second term comes to a close, shifting the focus of the show onto the race of new candidates for the presidency. We sat in the dark Central Asian night bundled up close to the small propane heater and watched intently as the Republican and Democratic presidential candidates desperately fought to win over the restless masses. Each state's people rose up over various issues in frantic protest for change, seeking the candidate most likely to get them what they needed before everything fell apart. Which candidate would promise them more? Which candidate could pull America out of its dire state?

I am aware that suffering is universal, that everyone's life no matter how wealthy or insulated ends in the tragedy of death. I even agree that America is in a desperate state, though for different reasons than dealt with on *West Wing* or solvable by any political party. Yet from our seats in Tajikistan the show seemed more like satire than drama. Or perhaps farce is the better word to describe the effect of the show on a Central Asian audience. Episode by episode as the election nears, the Americans become increasingly panicked over this and that, whipped up into a frenzy evidently because they are the richest nation in the world by a smaller margin than a few years before. Surely this must be farce.

Exempting the true tragedies of international crises and societal moral decline, often I have felt that watching the show here has much the same effect on the audience that Jane Austen novels do. Her characters are constantly embroiled in conflicts that are entertainingly lighthearted because when it boils right down to it, her readers know subconsciously that even if the other young ladies out in society are more accomplished or the heroine's family has to downgrade to a country mansion, they are really going to be alright in the end. Compared to Tajikistan, nearly every material sacrifice in America seems like moving to a country mansion.

Ann and I have discovered that Tajiks never speak of being pregnant. It is a private, even secret subject. Even when a woman is clearly showing, it is usually not mentioned. And if this were not strange enough, often a newborn child has no name for weeks. We used to think of this as inexplicable behavior, but we wonder now if this is simply a form of self-defense. Babies die so often here. Perhaps there are too many memories of pain to risk joy and hope. I know it is stoic Tajikistan outside our door, a world where mothers are afraid to attach themselves to their own babies.

I know when things in the United States are not going well there is suddenly a lot of talk about 401(k)s. When things in Tajikistan are not going well there is suddenly a lot of talk about what household items to burn. And there have been so many stories of people dying of carbon monoxide poisoning this winter that evidently there should have been more discussion.

I met a British doctor in Dushanbe who has spent many years in the high mountains of Northern Afghanistan with his wife and small children trying to help the people. When they arrived and settled in, they were the only family in the whole area that had a car. Apricots were the only fruit their neighbors had. Meat was for holidays. As we talked and as I began to understand what life was like there it became apparent that Kadimobod seemed like heaven comparatively so I asked him, "Do the young men in your area have an almost complete desperation to leave their home and get to Kabul or Russia or America like the Tajiks in Kadimobod do?" When he replied "no" I was reminded of my Tajik friend's grandma who is constantly telling her miserable grandsons, who dream of one day making it to the West, that they live like kings in these modern days of Kadimobod with water pipes, electricity, television, and candy.

Yet droves of young Tajiks dream of the salvation plane to the West. As a walking college application resource center, I'm reminded of this almost daily. And Westerners dream of the salvation program to bigger and better self-indulgence. Being a Westerner, I am reminded of this almost daily as well. I often think of the Israelites in the desert angering God by complaining about having to eat God's manna every day, month after month, and it scares me because I know I would have been complaining too. Is it surprising that joy and thankfulness are elusive when we are constantly trying to find and define them using geographic and materialistic terms?

The world should see America's desperation and know that our ways are not the answer. But the world does not see this. So often the salvation it seeks comes in the form of a plane ticket and a visa. Many here in Tajikistan will tolerate me babbling about God loving them so much that He sent His only Son to die for them only until the application process is completed. Have mercy on our souls.

Eight o'clock

> *From where I'm lying, through the window I can see a branch blowing in the wind and it makes me cry. I can only see the branch. Nothing else. It's moving in the wind and since the wind never blows here it reminds me of home.*[4]

West Wing ended, initiating our nightly bedtime routine. I closed the propane tank and rolled the heater into the corner of the room. A rush of cold air pressed in from the hallway as Ann unjammed the door and disappeared into the dark kitchen with the mugs and a candle. I followed, my senses startled to heightened awareness as the cold hit my face. Passing Ann as she finished off a few kitchen preparations for morning, I popped the balcony door open and stepped out, closing the door behind me. I bent over the stove's propane tank and gave it a good turn to make sure it was closed tightly before going over to the accumulator to unplug the extension cords and switch off the system. Ducking under the mildewing laundry again, I returned to my spot at the window.

A Winter's Night

The Muslim saint's mazor grounds were no longer shining. Looking out south over the city, my eyes found no light to focus on. The night was so dark that I heard the cold drizzle before I saw it. My heart sunk. As my eyes adjusted I could just make out the cold rain falling down into the courtyard. The drops were beginning to accumulate and streak along the glass. In America I used to love rain, but so often here it means harsher electricity rationing and more calls to repairmen. Drizzles are not supposed to fell electric lines, but in Tajikistan they do. A lone man passed, moving quickly along the main road by the light of a small flashlight. I wondered if he was going home or perhaps on a vodka run to the candlelit corner store. Or maybe he was one of the rare devout and on his way to the mosque for nightly prayers.

A few weeks ago during Ramadan (the Islamic month of fasting) the night streets were teeming with groups of men on their way to nightly prayers. Every year we have been here, the Ramadan crowds have increased. Tajiks are rediscovering Islam, searching what the Soviet Union said they must not explore. The growing interest is almost palpable, the increasing community pressure building in the way common to Islam.

A few years ago even the women were intrigued enough to gather together near the mosques and listen in at the windows. The mullahs (religious leaders) found this unacceptable and announced that women should stay home. It was not a surprising decision. Tajik women always seem to be circling around the perimeter of religious life like dogs grasping at the scraps left by the men.

From what we have been able to gather, it is the local women's understanding that their reward of heaven will be to join, not Allah, but a Muslim man's ninety-nine-virgin harem. Astonishingly, devotion still grows among the women. They have explained this to us before saying that in heaven there will be no jealousy. Yet I would think the parable of the good shepherd leaving the ninety-nine sheep in search of them would stunningly capture their hearts.

During the nights of Ramadan, the streets burst with the nominal briefly transformed to devout. Every year more flow toward the mosque than the year before. And every year the ranks of the devout increase as more continue attending prayers after the fast has ended.

I have heard that many in Iran grow weary of Islam. They have seen the reality created by their faith's theocracy these past decades and grow restless with the results. If what I have heard is true, then the youth turn in droves to drugs, Western pop culture, and sometimes Christ. Perhaps the proposed law in Iran that would make the death sentence mandatory for any Iranian who converts from Islam to another faith reflects the growing atmosphere of desperation on the part of the government as they attempt to control the drift of their nation's heart.

But Tajikistan's heart does not appear to have reached such a drifting state. Having been deprived of the full experience of Islam for so long by the Soviet's long rule, there is the sense that now, finally now, they can fully be Muslims. And so every year during the nights of Ramadan, there are more men on the streets than the year before.

I joined Ann in the bathroom for the important tasks of brushing and flossing, important since we usually go years at a time without a trip to a dentist. And making it more important still is the fact that a dental problem might mean an international flight.

During the sweltering months, our tiny bathroom is the bane of our existence as we can hardly both fit in it at the same time. But during the freezing winter we become aware that blessings certainly come in the diminutive. I squeezed in beside her at the rusty sink. The rinsing bottle of filtered water on the cracked tile floor under the sink was empty so I was soon on my way back to the kitchen for a refill.

As the filtered water rose, I stared at the countless bottles on the floor containing straight tap water. It is important that Ann and I are on the same page with which bottles contain filtered water and which ones hold tap. Our system used to be that RC Cola bottles were for filtered water while Upper Ten and RC Orange bottles were for the unclean stuff. But thanks to duct tape and a Sharpie, now any new bottle can be redeemed as a container for the pure. Wonderful stuff, duct tape.

Finishing up brushing and flossing with a confident clean rinse we took turns ladling freezing water from a bucket onto our hands to give them a hasty, unpleasant wash. I thanked God I was not a poor washerwoman slopping around freezing water on the floors of depressing places all winter for a living. Every morning I pass these widows and *partoft* (thrown away) women in the freezing cold halls of our windowless, unheated, decaying Soviet office building.

I know the women's names and say hello when I pass. It's so unusual here to treat them as valuable equals and I can see it warms the hearts of *Apai* (older sister) Parvina, Apai Sulhiya, and Apai Nozanin when I greet them by name. Perhaps for a moment each day they forget about their cracked, swollen hands, their income of roughly seven dollars per month, and the cold house they must return to.

Ann, following her motherly instincts, looked our apartment over in detail once more before heading to bed with a candle she would use to read. In the absolute stillness, it felt like 2 a.m., but it was only approaching 9 p.m. Not yet sleepy or feeling like reading on this particular, perpetual night, I sat down at the kitchen table that is jammed snugly into the corner of our family room. I took to staring at the candle playfully illuminating the yellow wall beside it.

The candle on the table glowed in the same place where our tiny Christmas tree, with its dollhouse-sized ornaments and matchstick-slender candy canes, had sat a few weeks before. As I remember, we received our miniature tree in a package from home the fall before our first Christmas here. That was before we had children. It was so important to have it on our table reminding us every day that our Savior's birthday was approaching.

In Tajikistan there is, of course, nothing to remind one that Christmas approaches. While it is beautiful to experience the deep sacredness of the season without the slightest sounds of commercialism or triviality, and while it is nice to finally have a Christmastime without being in a mental state of information and sensory overload where nothing worth considering can truly be considered, it is predominantly sad because as Christmas nears and there is not the slightest inclination of the forthcoming holy night, we have an overwhelmingly solemn sense of why we are here. Our Christmas outreaches, our tiny kindnesses to the poor, our sowing of gospel seed upon the frozen soil seem so small against the backdrop of the nation.

Just as our Christmastimes in the Muslim world experience a purification, so does our patriotism. We examine our American roots so that as much as possible they will not stand in the way of Tajiks coming to Christ. A few years ago I remember reading in *WORLD* magazine:

> *The radical Islamic hatred of the West is motivated partly by their revulsion at the cultural decadence of the West. The cultural influence of America overseas is no longer democratic ideals, political freedom, and economic prosperity as it was formerly, but rather sexual permissiveness, pornographic entertainment, legalized abortion, and an anti-cultural hedonism.*[5]

I have thought a lot about this quote over the years as we have lived among Muslims overseas. I have found that most Tajiks, when not in circles where they are trying to act religious, seem to love the West in all its immoral exporting glory. Anyone who has a Christian view of human nature should not be surprised by that. The men especially seem to enjoy the new opportunities to revel in the filth of it all.

In this environment, I have found that when I talk about God, try to share Christ, it is imperative that I distance myself from my roots because most Muslims that I have met take the culture that they see represented in Western entertainment as the natural out-flow of the Christian faith. This perception that Muslims have is of course strengthened by the fact that so many in the West profess to be Christians.

And no doubt this association between society's creeds and fruits in the Muslim's mind is bolstered all the more by the fact that Islam and *sharia* (Islamic) law often take over nearly every facet of a culture where Islam is professed. Muslims often have difficulty with the idea of the separation of church and state. From what I have observed, most Muslim cultures can't wrap their minds around the West's blatant hypocrisy. With sharia law directing traffic, they are trained to be more subtle.

Often I find it wise to make a firm declaration that my nation is not Christian. I find that is often an important place to begin if my Muslim friends are to begin to warm to discussing Christ. As long as my friend thinks America or the West is Christ's kingdom, I haven't a chance in the world to show the beauty of my Savior.

America is not a Christian country. That must be my starting point. I learned this truth in my first conversations with Muslims while in New Jersey. They would say, "Just look around us at New York and New Jersey! I want nothing to do with Christianity." So we try to return together to Jesus' many statements, "The kingdom of God is like . . ." and away from "The democracy of America is like . . ." The kingdom of God is booming in South Korea, in Africa, in China, and South America. Upending their assumptions about the identity of Jesus' followers gives us a better chance to start anew as well.

Our candle had burned low. I grabbed the holder and returned to the kitchen by its waning light. As I took a slender new one from the shelf, I made a mental note to buy another package of candles tomorrow. I knew our little neighbor girls would be out front sitting by their rickety tables, hunched and bundled against the cold, on their short rusty-legged stools. They'd sit hour after hour selling a box of matches to the passing smoker, a dried yogurt ball, apricot, or Iranian hard candy to the wealthy child on his way home from school or perhaps a box of tea leaves to an old woman expecting guests.

It would, of course, be cheaper to buy my candles in bulk from the bazaar. But I knew the few-*diram* (cent) profit my neighbors would make when I bought my candles would be important to them. Perhaps they'd put it toward that new school notebook or bag of flour for next month's bread.

There are usually three or four of our poorer neighbor families whose children work the small tables—their eternal, survival "lemonade" stands. They sit outside our building beside the road. In especially desperate times, I see them out there, late into the night, well after the time when the crowds have disappeared, and I wonder what future there will be for these little girls and boys selling for penny profits twelve or fourteen hours a day every day of the year.

I usually buy my small boxes of chalky Iranian cookies and packages of cheap Chinese candles from a little girl whose family lives on the first floor of the next stairwell. Often she has a little English book shivering on her lap as I walk by. She is a sweet girl and her family seems especially poor. I decided I would buy my candles from her tomorrow. She could keep the change. A familiar feeling washed over me as, once again forgetting the power in the Holy Spirit, I thought, "I am so weak. What can I possibly do here?"

Using the last of the candle's flame, I held it to the bottom of my new candle and let the crimson drops of wax fall into a new teacup until a hot pool had formed sufficient to secure my new light. I lit the wick and wandered out to the balcony for a last look at the electricity situation before bed. All was darkness save the candle-illuminated drizzle of rain rolling down the freezing panes.

It appeared that all power lines had been shut off sending the entire city into a forced dormancy.

Perhaps the villagers are the most fortunate this winter. Out in the simplicity of the countryside they still prepare for winter just as their great-great grandparents did. The new growth of every tree had been chopped and stacked. The manure from the family cow and its calf had been gathered, shaped, and dried month after month in preparation for winter cooking and heating. Vegetables and apples had been buried in the cool, dry ground within their sheds.

In every direction from our town the villages, deep in hibernation, wait out there in the black among the rolling mountains. The villagers lie quietly in their mud homes, eating their carefully prepared provisions and waiting patiently for spring. In spring the soil will be tilled, the gardens prepared, and the new saplings planted. Perhaps they slumber dreaming of the celebration on spring's first day, of Navruz (Persian New Year) when vibrantly colored, heirloom *chakand* dresses and the joyful braids of youthful exuberance will grace the women as they carry plates of *sumanak* (green wheat, newly sprouted). The women will use the sumanak sprouts to fill their freshly washed tablecloths. They will lay them on the ground and prepare for a feast while the men test their vigor wrestling upon the new spring fields. And throughout the country, the Tajiks will sing again as we have heard them sing each year,

> *Bahor omad! Bahor omad! Guli Savsan kator omad!*
> (Spring came! Spring came! The Lily flower came in rows!)[6]

As I looked out at the coldest winter Central Asia had seen in decades, I hoped all souls out there were warm, or at least warm enough, for only the survivors would sing together on Navruz.

Nine o'clock

> For behold, darkness will cover the earth
> And deep darkness the peoples;
>   But the LORD will rise upon you
> And His glory will appear upon you.
>   Nations will come to your light,
> And kings to the brightness of your rising.
> (Isa 60:2–3 NASB)

In Tajikistan, winter has not yet lost its power to slow, to encourage reflection and searching. Sometimes I feel that in the more stable regions of our world, winter only retains its God-given contemplative powers outside our doors and away from our technology. But step outside and watch your breath disappear into the endless sky and no matter what your country, a winter walk is, I think, still the walk of every man, whether Adam Jones or Abdulloh Juraxon.

Euro news may speak of faster download rates with higher resolutions to fantastic new devices even as the ancient Soviet pipes of Dushanbe burst, pouring layer upon layer of ice over a thousand alleys. But a winter night is a powerful leveler. There is something about the dark cold that encourages reflection on all humanity has in common, and the differences of culture that I once thought insurmountable suddenly seem insignificant set against our kindred struggles. There might be jumbo jets above the thick, snowy clouds floating over a thousand mud-hut villages, but they fade to distant white noise in the frozen stillness.

And there has been great suffering in the stillness. There has been death in Tajikistan this winter. In one of Aesop's Fables, the grasshopper plays while the ant prepares for winter. In Tajikistan, the grasshoppers have played aggressively and thievingly for so long that it appears to me that the ants no longer have a will toward preparation. Corruption may yield imported sedans for a few, but for the majority it yields stagnancy and brutal pain.

A Winter's Night

As I look out the balcony window, I can see in my fresh memories, the Tajik women bundled against the cold dragging along in all directions, hauling their water back across town. They are returning from the rare working water pump. In the park a crowd has gathered. Word has spread. Near the pump, not frozen over or burst just beneath the surface, hundreds of women stand in a mob stolidly waiting their turn to fill their buckets and begin the slosh toward home.

South at the lonely Panj River, marking the border with Afghanistan, guards in thick military coats check the duffel bags of incoming travelers for heroin and Arabic books hoping to curb the degeneration of society caused by drugs and radical Islam. The guards recognize heroin, but not knowing their own holy language, they confiscate all books written in Arabic, obeying their government's orders. The government fears their own faith might grow too strong. In neighboring countries there is precedent for that.

Poor mountain Afghans see their sheep and goats die in droves, watch their hopes freeze to death. None but the old have ever seen such a winter.

Recycled Aeroflot planes full of anxious Tajiks fly to Russia every day from every airport the country over. Thousands upon thousands leave to join the millions of their countrymen already there. They hope they can band together to avoid the police and racist roving gangs, find a shared room not too squalid, and discover a boss who will not abuse them or lock them in a closet until he can sell them to another boss without paying them. It is a desperate nation, usually a nation at war, which sends the best of its young men north to unfriendly foreign soil in waves as winter descends.

Schools cancel classes because there is no heat. The government orders all restaurants, stores, and nonessential entities in the capital to close their doors and go home to wait in order to save the country's dwindling power supply. Whole regions of the country experience utter darkness, not a second of electricity for months at a time. The suave attendants at the Turkish furniture store off Rudaki Street, Tajikistan's equivalent to Chicago's Michigan Avenue, are reduced to greeting their elite patrons by prying the automatic doors open, digging in their finger nails, and contorting their faces under the strain as their legendary escalator lies dormant just behind them.

The weak lose their fights with hepatitis and tuberculosis in freezing hospital wings. Newborn babies die unable to handle the harshness of their new world. Whole families are found dead of carbon-monoxide poisoning, lying together on mats in forgotten, cold apartments. The sick buy a little medicine with their precious saved money, knowing there is a very good chance it is not real.

The people, meal after meal, day after day, week after week, monotonously eat non and tea, non and tea, non and tea with perhaps a potato, an onion, a glass of precious milk, or an egg thrown in a few times a week for a cherished treat.

People desperately try to tap into the electricity lines of the rich. They scrounge up a little cash, a couple somoni, to pay off the electrical station man who found out. My students' homes hover around freezing as they huddle together in one small room, daily gathering sticks as best they can, unable to afford propane or coal.

Bereft trees line the streets stripped of limbs and twigs, most new growth. Their barren trunks look forlorn as if they too mourn the desperation that led to the loss of their shaded splendor. Crowds run instantly from every direction toward the hopeful sound of a chain saw, preparing to fight over the scraps of wood deemed of insufficient girth by the government crew. My neighbors, grown men, fight before my eyes over who had their hand on the sycamore limb first when the tree came down. Small children race off with twigs, repeatedly glancing behind nervously to make sure no one follows to challenge their acquisition. The watching old men exchange stories about last winter when an overly anxious neighbor, too zealous for branches, was crushed to death as the tree came down.

Our house helper, returning to work in our home after a break, responds to our questions of how her break went with a shrug of her shoulders and tears she tries to suppress as she looks away.

The remaining young, not forced to Russia, dream of Aeroflot planes heading west toward education and opportunity as they see their country despair within the rotting remnants of the Soviet system. It is as if the system were an organ transplant the country is rejecting. The Soviet doctors who performed the systematic transplant are long gone as the host lies dying. Ask a Tajik professional, an architect for example, to explain to you what he is doing in Tajik. He cannot. There is no language for it. There are only Russian words and the decay of an imported civilization whose makers and sustainers have gone back home.

Those who do not look to the West or to Russia, China, and Iran for their salvation, look back into their ancient past and rename all their streets. Slowly the taxi drivers stop using the old street names; names of Russian poets, politicians, cosmonauts, and wrestlers. We make more lefts onto streets named for their most famous ancient kings, like Somoni. It is as if the nation is desperate to remind itself how great it once was.

And with the advent of new technology, the new transplants of internet, cell phone, and satellite, combined with age-old human nature, there seems to have come an intensified desperation produced by comparison. The glory of the old is the Soviet Union. The glory of the nation is the ancient past. The glory of the future is despaired of. The nation looks back as the young look abroad.

The KGB constantly harasses us, taking us to court, dragging our students in, threatening them, and closing our youth center and all our operations with false accusations flying because we are Christians, because we will not be silent. We will continue proclaiming hope is found in Jesus Christ. There are many written confessions and betrayals being gathered. Some are forced confessions, others volunteered by our Tajik friends, friends we hold close to our broken hearts. We pray against bitterness.

As I stare at the surrounding despair out my window, I feel I can almost see Dr. Zhivago walking down our road. Wherever he was forced, whatever army pressed him into miserable servitude, however cold and dark his surroundings, he retained his resilient wonder. The infinite glory of God reflected in the most common patterns of frost cannot be suppressed for those who have eyes to see. And what is frost compared to the gospel?

I turned away from the blackness and, holding the candle before me, went back into the kitchen. I closed the balcony door, the kitchen door, and finally the family room door tight as I retreated to bed. Ann was reading there under the covers of our full-sized mattress on the floor. Shedding a layer or two but keeping my hat, I blew out my candle and slipped under the thick stack of covers. Ann, ready for sleep as well, set her book down, settled in, and blew out her candle. Immersed in total darkness we said quick prayers, kissed goodnight, and did our best to cocoon ourselves against the growing cold.

There in the deep darkness I wondered when the nations would come to His light. Lying there I wished I could reach up into the cold air, grab hold of His light and pull it down to our Tajikistan, to His Tajikistan. Yes, it is His Tajikistan. My heart echoed Isaiah the prophet beating, "Oh, that You would rend the heavens and come down" (Isa 64:1 NASB). Yet the frost remained all around us. But what is frost compared to the gospel? What is frost compared to the gospel? What!?

VIII
BAHRIDDIN'S WEDDING

Two New Brides

Orzu dorad dilam.
Kai yoram paido meshavad?
Dar gulistoni irom
Sairu tamosho meshavad.

It has hope, my heart.
When will my lover appear?
In the flower garden of paradise
There will be strolling and gazing.[1]

The green, Russian Lada, circa 1975, rolled to a dusty halt on the shoulder of the road. There, a packed dirt road led off toward the small mountain town of Kuizamin. Grabbing my backpack as I got out, I waved my thanks. I watched as my fellow taxi travelers puttered back onto the blacktop and on down the road that would lead them the rest of the way to their destination. I turned to take in the view where I had been dropped. I was about an hour out from Kadimobod now, well into the foothills of the Pamir Mountains. In the distance I could make out the region's famous mountain and pilgrimage site, Kui Imom Islamjon. Bahriddin's wedding was tomorrow. If I walked three or four villages up this dusty side road in the direction of the famous mountain, I hoped to eventually find my way to his family's farm. As the sun began to set I told myself that even in the dark I should be able to find it since I'd been there twice before.

It was a privilege to be coming the day before the wedding. I had known Bahriddin a few years now and we had grown pretty close. I met him our first year in Tajikistan when he was a volunteer at our organization's summer camp for orphans and poor children. A year or two later he had earned a position at our NGO (nongovernmental organization) and had been a great employee for us ever since. I was honored to have been invited to come out, spend the night, and observe all the preparations for the big day. Tomorrow Ann and Grace would be coming for the *tui* (wedding) along with some of our teammates and Tajik coworkers. But for now, I was alone as I set out down the road.

Behind me I could still make out a large village. A wealth of trees rose up from it making it appear like a tiny Eden in a valley tucked among the parched October hills. Bahriddin had pointed the village out to me on my prior trips telling of how it had been settled by Uzbeks long ago. The Uzbeks had fled to the area to escape one political persecution or another, now ancient history. There were a few such Uzbek villages here and there among this rolling, rising brown land. Most villages were Tajik, though of course over the generations there had been much intermarriage. I've heard that a few of these Uzbek areas, resisting Russian and Tajik influences, still have a school or two that teach in their mother tongue.

Soon I was weaving my way through the mud-brick-wall labyrinth of the first small village I came across. The usual aggressive hospitality of the Tajiks was shocked out of them by the sight of a lone backpacking foreigner walking through their remote village unannounced. I wondered if I was the first American they had ever seen. I wondered if they all thought I was Russian. I wasn't as pale as the typical Russian, but it was probably hard for them to tell that

in the dimness. Passing small groups in the twilight, we exchanged
a few hesitant "*asaloms.*" Near the village spring, the children ceased
their play and the women their evening gossip to watch the strange
creature pass.

Three young boys, piled upon a donkey, clopped along behind
me with a lethargy conducive to the mood of the rapidly cooling fall
air. We steadily advanced together toward the creeping, setting sun.
It felt as if the whole world was going to sleep, perhaps until March.
I turned back for their reassurance as I pointed at the path I thought
might lead me out of the village. A few nods in the dim light put a
renewed confidence in my steps. Without a word, we all knew I was
only passing through.

Emerging from the first village, I quickened the pace a bit,
knowing I wasn't going to make it through to Bahriddin's village
before complete darkness set in. The curious ones at my heels faded
away, staring after me like statues at the edge of their disappearing village. I soon found myself alone on the deeply rutted road.
It looked impassable to me, but I knew from experience that every
driver in Tajikistan would probably navigate this road without a
second thought. So what if they had worked in Russia for two years
to purchase the car. Shocks were supposed to be used strenuously.
Tajikistan certainly didn't disappoint.

Unclasping my backpack, I fished around for a small flashlight
and a bottle of filtered water. I'd brought a lot of water so my backpack was by no means light. As I took a drink, I briefly considered
pouring out a liter but thought better of it. At the bottom of my
pack, my fully charged video camera was ready to go with a pair of
blank tapes. I was eager to capture as much as I could of the cultural
wealth that this village wedding was going to provide. I crossed my
fingers for electricity to recharge.

To my right lay the massive, dormant sang-ob riverbed that the
road hugged as it slowly ascended to countless villages further up
into the foothills. I knew there was a trickling flow running along

an edge. These villages probably got their water there. Most villages had sprung up along the sang-ob because of this faithful trickle.

My adrenaline pounded in the cool, gathering darkness as I thought about the powerful flash floods that roar down from the mountains in the spring and early summer. Bahriddin told me once that his brother, even on horseback, had barely made it out of the sang-ob riverbed in time.

I made good progress as the main dirt road skirted the next couple of villages along the sang-ob, allowing me to avoid more wanderings through unknown streets among the dusty *tutho* (mulberry trees), *sebho* (apple trees), and massive gnarled *chanorho* (sycamores) in the darkness.

Dogs started in loudly somewhere off in a village on my left. Following Tajik custom, I stooped down and grabbed a couple of rocks to carry at the ready in case the dogs ventured over. The smooth rocks were already cool to the touch. The flashlight offered paltry but welcome help as I increased my pace until the barking sounded reassuringly far behind.

The light from the October night sky dimmed as I entered between rows of closely planted *safedor* (white poplar) trees lining both sides of the road. The safedors are a familiar sight in nearly every Tajik village as their straight, smooth trunks grow meters higher and inches thicker every year, providing the fastest available way to acquire timber and shade. I recognized this particular bunch and felt I should soon be entering Bahriddin's village.

Instinctively, I sensed my way back to his gate. I recognized the mud-walled farm huts that marked the beginnings of their property. Safedor poplar trunks jutted out from the farm huts' roofs revealing another element of their internal structure.

Electricity in Tajikistan had yet to start in on heavy rationings as it always did when the weather cooled. I could see the faint glow from Bahriddin's grandfather's home as I turned up the path that would lead me to his door. I hoped the family, the relatives, and neighbors—who I anticipated would all be crammed into two or three simple rooms—were enjoying the modern light. In a couple of weeks the lights could go out until spring and leave them to huddle together for a very dark winter. If they were lucky they'd get an hour of electricity in the morning and another in the evening for the next three or four months. The cities would probably only fare an hour or two better per day.

Rising up behind the house, their land rose up at a steep slope. I have learned the rhythm of Bahriddin's life well. Every summer he asks for a few weeks off to harvest his family's crops of wheat and some sort of barley. I still wasn't clear about what the barley crop was. Bahriddin says it is good for making oil. His brothers and he would be up on those hills cutting and loading the donkeys and horses week after week early in the mornings and again late into the evenings. I wondered if they, as Tajiks often do, used a makeshift tent to doze through the midday heat on the hills among their crops.

Thinking on the timeless simplicity of harvest, I felt a wave of peace and joy wash over me as an idyllic stupor. Perhaps it was because I hadn't had to bend over with a sickle, deal with a stubborn donkey, or endure the August sun myself.

Of course every network of villages has a tractor somewhere. But you have to pay the driver a few bags of grain for the gasoline and a few more for his time. And then the neighbor with the tiny electric flour mill would take a share from the crop as well. Better to do it yourself if you had the time and strength to labor.

As I passed a thickly packed pen of sheep and goats, I was surprised to see a few young goats jumping and playing on top of the woolly backs. In contrast, the young sheep were minding their manners as they tried to control their propensity to jitter. Behind the pen I could see the outhouse. Something inside snapped at the sight. It might have been my idyllic stupor. A neatly planted orchard marked the approach to the house. The rows of apple trees seemed to be the only ones still producing this late in the year. My flashlight revealed at least two varieties.

A few women washing dishes at a spigot in the yard saw me approaching and yelled for Bahriddin. He popped his head out of the house and smiled in that sincere, gentle manner I had grown to love. He searched for his shoes among the mass of black and brown dress footwear and women's work slippers surrounding the door. Slipping them on, he bounded down the stairs and through the grapevines to welcome me into his home with a characteristically Tajik embrace and a warm, "*Xush omaded! Xush omaded mehmoni aziz! Bioed! Bioed!*" ("Good coming! Good coming, dear guest. Come! Come!") We went inside.

My own shoes now among the pile outside the door, I found myself in a packed room. I surveyed the familiar scene. Bahriddin, ever the conscientious host, introduced me to the men sitting on the floor around the bountiful, celebratory *dustarxon* (Tajik tablecloth spread out on the floor). Some smiled. Others put their right hands over their hearts to reflect the sincerity of their hospitality. A couple of men even stood up respectfully. Most of them looked a little too interested. It appeared the plan B entertainment had arrived in the form of Bahriddin's American friend. I prayed for the success of the television and electricity.

Bahriddin nudged me further up to a place of honor on a korpacha along the wall furthest from the door. "*Ne. Ne. Hej gap ne,*" (No. No. Don't worry about it,) I protested at such a show of honor as I hesitantly resisted his insistent pushing. A couple of wrinkly, long-bearded elders parted to leave a small place between themselves. Yielding to the group's insistence I sat down on the korpacha cushion in the tight gap between the elders.

I looked around. Were most of these men relatives, neighbors, or friends? Well, I suppose they were all more or less related. Everyone up in these villages seems to be. I was probably the only one in the room further removed than third cousin. If they wanted to play the "find a common ancestor" game with me we might have to start talking about which son of Noah we were descended from. They'd probably enjoy that conversation. I imagined a couple of them looked a little like Shem.

A single light bulb hanging from an electrical cord a few feet above the dustarxon tablecloth illuminated sprawling heaps of fresh baked breads, bowls of walnuts, dried apricots, and chickpeas. This season's grapes and apples and newly prepared yogurts, which I knew would taste a bit too close to the farm for my taste, rounded out the spread. Yoplait French Vanilla it wasn't, unless one of the cows I had passed on the way in had recently found some highly unusual grass up on the October hills.

A middle-aged man with sun- and labor-worn hands poured me a peola (Tajik teacup) of thin black tea. "*Buxur! Buxur!*" (Eat! Eat!) The relentless hospitality to eat began to echo at me around the table from the insistent Tajik men. "*Rahmat. Rahmat. Mexuram,*" (Thank you. Thank you. I'll eat,) I answered.

Lower down the tablecloth, closer to the door, sat the young men I should have been sitting with if I had been treated like a normal Tajik. I recognized one of Bahriddin's brothers and another guy in a colorful toki skull cap who had come and played volleyball with us a few times in Kadimobod. I think he is Bahriddin's uncle, though Bahriddin looks about the same age. When the toki cap came off, that guy could play some volleyball. Bahriddin says the men play every day in his uncle's village. After swallowing a few spikes, I certainly believed him.

The tension relaxed and conversations resumed around the table as I took a sip of tea and popped a few grapes into my mouth. The guest was eating. As long as I kept eating and eating and eating and eating, everyone would be happy except me. I should make every bite count because I knew soup and a heavy dish of hot *osh* (rice pilaf) would be coming later, so I tried to eat just enough to avoid more echoing *buxurs* (eat!). Pace myself. I knew the drill.

I tore off a piece of bread from a thick round non lying near me, prompting a couple of overly attentive neighbors to push bowls of yogurt closer to me, converging from both sides. I pretended not to notice, pretended to be deeply engrossed in listening to a conversation I was really only understanding about a third of. I took a bite.

The peach preserves looked pretty good so I dipped my bread in the communal jam bowl, knowing full well there are no prohibitions against double dipping in Central Asia. Heck, double dipping wet fingers is a bit *kishlock* (village hick) in most Tajik circles, but fairly common.

The non I had chosen tasted like it had been baked a few days before. Not an unusual occurrence at weddings. I knew all of the household's women and all the women relatives nearby who could help had been baking and preparing for days. For a wedding they had to do it that way. Still, without preservatives this particular non would go better torn and mashed Tajik style into the soup coming later. I took a gulp of tea to swish around in my mouth to help break down bread remains that the peach preserves were failing to overcome.

A sturdily built man off to my left was telling a few guys about how he had just finished helping a European NGO (non-governmental organization) run a mile or so of pipe from a fresh spring higher up the mountains, providing the first fresh water source the village had ever had. Listening, I soon realized this was the talk of the room. It turned out the water pump I had seen on the way in, the one the women were squatting around rinsing off ornate Tajik wooden bowls called *degs*, was the end of the pipe. That historical spigot was a very big deal.

The men discussed running more pipe to make a couple more spigots throughout the village. Then all the women wouldn't have to come over to Bahriddin's house for fresh water. Laundry would probably still be done in the running trickle near the edge of the sang-ob. But additional pipe dreams aside, now they had clean water running to their village and the joy was evident on their faces as they spoke together.

The herb-garnished beef broth came in large wooden degs. We were instructed to eat three people to a bowl. They asked if I wanted a spoon. I declined. Refusing the spoon scored me a couple brownie points toward achieving the full rank of American Tajik, a rank to which I aspire.

As the old men on either side of me tore off pieces of bread and mashed them into our wooden bowl, soaking up enough soup to transform it into a sloshy finger food, I thought back to an American Thanksgiving meal Ann and I had hosted for my Tajik friends. One of my guests had asked me how many people should share a plate. When I answered only one person per plate, his eyes bulged. He looked down at his huge pile of turkey and other strange, but alluring foods and smiled gleefully. That time I think I scored points toward the rank of rich American, a rank far easier to achieve no matter how hard we resist.

As warm broth ran down my fingers, my arm, and onto my rolled up shirt sleeve I realized I might have lost those newly attained brownie points. The elders were slurping away with great efficiency, their long gray beards cleaner than my elbow. I left them to finish off the bowl as I found a cloth to clean up my right arm.

Between the soup course and the bringing of my favorite dish of osh, the action focused on getting the television to work. They had a satellite dish of course. They were shocked I didn't. The older generations of Tajiks recount how afraid the villagers were the first time they saw a car roll into their village. Children fled. Even some of the adults hid. Yet here we all were, a few decades later, watching a match between two European football clubs. I hoped they had ESPN. NFL highlights would have been wonderful. I was probably out of luck though. I think it was one of those satellite systems heavy on Russian and Middle Eastern stations. Not my first choice, but European football would have to do.

As we watched the clubs run up and down the stunning pitch, a pitch that appeared to have more green ground than all of Tajikistan, I looked around at the men. A few were in their twenties and thirties. Most were older. I wondered how many of this village's men were off working in Moscow or other cities up north. I wondered how many of these men around me were newly returned from Russia.

Fall is always the time when a small portion of the exodus returns. Construction, and other common work the Tajiks find in the big cities of Russia, usually slows during the winter, so if they are to come home for a couple of months to greet family and meet new children, children perhaps already a couple of years old, winter is the time to do it.

I heard a popular rhyme the other day that spoke of a child looking up at a plane in the sky and saying to himself how he wondered, how he wished this would be the plane that carried his daddy home. It seems every Tajik family has a couple of men in Russia. This is common life in Tajikistan. This reality is reflected in the folk rhymes of the children.

After our communal soup bowls were washed, Bahriddin and his brothers brought in the steaming bowls of osh. My two bearded buddies and I started in on our heaping bowl of the national dish. Osh is wonderful to eat on such a fall night. The lump of roast on top of the rice, chickpea, and carrot pilaf looked perfectly tender. Roast goat, chicken, or mutton would do but they had gone all out and prepared roast beef. Ann and I liked osh prepared with cooked raisins in it too, but we've been told osh with raisins is more of an Uzbek tradition. We hope for improved political-culinary relations between the two nations.

One of the elders tore the chunk of tender roast with his experienced fingers, placing the strips on top of our generous heap of pilaf. I restrained myself from taking more than my share of the meat. They could certainly use it more. I'd probably be the only one

in the packed room having meat again at home the day after the
wedding festivities were over.

Tajiks say that friends sharing food from the same bowl makes
the food much better. Usually I strongly disagree with this maxim,
but the osh was so good it almost seemed true as my new friends
and I pinched our fingers in unison and gleefully double-dipped
together. Cheers.

After osh and a goal by some Brit or Brit-purchased Brazilian, I
took out my video camera to record a bit of the proceedings. Across
the tablecloth from me I noticed a young guy with a deformed
eye who didn't seem too happy. He went over to the corner and
whipped out his own. At ten times the bulk of mine, his video
camera could have smashed mine into the cement floor underneath
the rugs. And the way he glared at me, I don't think he would have
minded trying.

It turned out he was the official videographer. I was on his
turf, an unwelcome usurper. Not to worry, I wasn't going to edit
and mix my footage with the latest Tajik pop songs, songs I didn't
know anyway. Plus, he actually had the boldness to go get the
good shots. He had nothing to fear. He was the true cameraman. I
avoided eye contact.

Unknowingly making the rivalry worse, Bahriddin took me over
to film a bit of the women's party going on in the adjoining room.
I stepped hesitantly over the massive pile of various women's shoes
and on into the room. Just as the shoes had led me to believe, the
room was packed. Most of the women were older, possibly the matriarchs from the surrounding villages.

The boisterous noise stopped abruptly as they all turned to stare
at us. I hid behind my camera as I panned the room, capturing the
images of the dustarxon and the *rumol-* (headscarf-) clad women.
Most had the long, flowing white rumols characteristic of older Tajik
women. The korta dresses were tucked under their legs, hiding their
bare feet as they sat on the floor upon the korpacha pads that made

a large rectangle around the dustarxon. At their ages, they were certainly an impressively flexible lot.

I have discovered that not having furniture will do wonders for a community's collective agility. In Tajikistan, I've become ashamed of my underdeveloped Achilles tendons. Before coming here I never realized that apparently Thetis had held onto both of them when she dipped me into plush America, land of chairs.

Bahriddin coaxed the women to play a traditional drum and sing. Their joy would bring him honor on this night before he was to be married. A confident old woman thumped a rhythm out beautifully on the drum, leading the ladies in energetic song as I panned the room. A few women took turns standing up in their tight spots to dance in honor of Bahriddin. The arms and hands took the expressive lead in traditional Tajik fashion. Bahriddin watched in appreciation, his right hand held permanently over his heart in the position of gratitude in order to properly honor the matriarchs' dances.

As I taped back and forth between drummer and dancers I took a moment to zoom in on an ornate carpet hanging on the wall. A picture of Bahriddin's father had somehow been worked into the fabric. Such a portrait carpet is common in Tajik homes. Usually they depict a famous Muslim saint or the family's deceased father or grandfather.

The wall hanging, the lone decoration on the whitewashed, mud-brick walls, daily reminded the family to honor the memory of their father. Bahriddin's father had died when Bahriddin and his two younger brothers were quite young. Upon his death their mother had brought the family back down the valley a couple of villages to her childhood home so they could live with her parents. I don't know if her husband's family had forced her to leave or not.

But this farm is where Bahriddin had grown up, where, as he said, Allah willing, he would now start his own family. This is Bahriddin's grandfather's home, his farm. Bahriddin's grandfather was around here somewhere. It would certainly be interesting to speak with him.

Even when the Soviets had ushered in communism, I believe this land had still been theirs to work, though I didn't understand exactly how that had played out. I had heard it was not uncommon at the time to hide some of your livestock with a shepherd up in the mountains if you knew the local communist authorities were coming. Better to not show all your wealth. Playing life in rural communist Tajikistan seemed not terribly unlike poker.

Bahriddin still spoke lovingly of the orchard his father had planted near the home they had left when he passed away. "The apple trees are still strong and wonderful there," he has told me more than once. As I finished filming his father's carpet portrait, I reflected on how the apples of carefree days are a sweet memory to my friend. I understand. Bahriddin has borne a heavy responsibility for his mother and younger brothers since he was a small boy.

"*Hazor rahmat. Hazor rahmat*" (A thousand thank-you's), we asserted profusely as the music and dancing stopped. We backed out the door, our hands over our hearts, leaving the women to their pre-wedding festivities once again. Slipping on my shoes I accompanied Bahriddin down the steps leading from the high cement platform that the small house was built upon. We walked out into the front orchard. He went about this and that, talking hurriedly with his mother and brothers as I stood quietly enjoying the cool night air near the first row of apple trees.

As I watched the fevered activity all around the yard, I wondered what Bahriddin's new wife was like. I doubted he knew. He probably knew what she looked like but that was probably about it. But I had learned such a limited relationship was often the ideal situation for a Tajik man entering marriage.

I remembered back to when I had learned this. I had been studying Tajik vocabulary out under a tree when another one of my good Tajik friends, Iskandar, sat down beside me and right away I could tell something was up. He is the kind of guy who has such an outlook on life that he doesn't quite touch the ground when he walks down the street. So by his somber look I knew something was definitely up.

He explained to me that his father was sick. This I already knew. He further explained that before he died his father had one wish, to see his youngest son married. Apparently it wasn't good enough that he had seen his other nine or ten children married.

But Iskandar had other plans. He wanted to study and work, maybe even abroad. He explained to me how his father had given him an ultimatum. Pick out a suitable girl to be his bride in the next two weeks or he would be marrying the cousin that the family had already picked out for him. This was a serious dilemma. He had two weeks. His cousin was looming. We got right to work.

Obviously I started in on the problem where any Westerner would if a Westerner ever found himself in such a situation. I tried to determine if there were girls at the university that he liked. Were there girls he respected that were close to him or that he admired from afar? Perhaps his mother could go matchmaking for one of these girls on his behalf? I even suggested a couple of university-aged peers that I knew he had a good rapport with. They were friends. They were good employees for us at camp in past summers. I suggested a couple of girls specifically that I thought would be perfect. They were smart, pretty, available, already friends with Iskandar at university, and knew how to sing the *Titanic* theme song in three languages. What more could any guy want? This was going to be easy.

As I voiced my thoughts, he squirmed, and finally verbalized his own approach. He began to talk about a girl he had seen on the road a few times near his friend's house. They had never spoken. She had crouched there at the pump mysteriously drawing water in the dusk as he hid behind a tree watching or something like that. She probably had never even noticed him. She was obviously the

perfect choice. Obviously? What, was this junior high? I looked hard
at Iskandar. Okay, apparently yes, yes, it was. But were we seriously
going to use junior-high criteria to pick a wife? I looked again at
Iskandar. Okay, yes, yes, we were. Well, I guess that's how Mowgli
fell for the big-eyed girl drawing water from the river in *The Jungle
Book* cartoon. On the other hand, Mowgli was getting his advice
from a big blue bear. At the moment, I felt Iskandar would have
been better off with Baloo as his love adviser too.

With our course soundly set toward the mysterious girl who
drew water so beautifully from the pump near his friend's house,
the question became what to do next. He did want to at least make
sure she wasn't crazy or covered with spots before his mother went
to start negotiations. More or less sound thinking, I thought. It felt
good to at least put down a few firm criteria, low a standard as they
might reflect.

He began to talk about getting some of his friends to do a bit
of spying to find out on the crazy and spotted fronts. Tajiks often
have white patches all over their skin, probably from malnutrition.
Maybe they would ask neighbor children about her. The questions
would certainly be simple enough for the children to answer. They
should know if she was insane or spotted. I decided I would not
participate in spying, and I was definitely not asking any neighbor
children if a certain girl had spots. Fortunately for Iskandar he had
other friends more loyal.

In that conversation I learned a lot about what Tajiks want and
how they go about it. Iskandar was expressing a common Tajik
desire. Tajiks often want a woman of mystery, a woman they don't
know. They want a woman they have admired from afar. More often
than not, this seems to be the ideal.

At a Tajik wedding, the groom must step on the bride's foot
three times. Between taking the bride from her father's home, putting her in a secluded room, and placing her behind a prepared
special curtain with her maid of honor at your own home, the

groom must find opportunity to step on his bride's foot these three times. It sets the tone for the marriage. If she resists, the groom is to do it harder and harder. As I think about it, Iskandar would have had a hard time going from being good friends with the girls I suggested to pounding their feet into submission.

Free-spirited Tajik girls often resist the foot-stepping ritual. Often they step back on the groom's foot or move their own foot away just in time. They know the tradition is coming and with the traditional Muslim wedding burka covering every part of their body and forcing them to stare at the ground, all they can see is their feet anyway.

If Iskandar had married one of the girls I had thought a good match, I bet he would have been in for a battle. Those girls were his friends. Perhaps he couldn't even imagine himself doing that to them. They already had an established friendship of relative equality. Perhaps there was no changing that. Perhaps Tajik guys instinctively know this. In Tajikistan, a wife is not a friend. Marriage is more of a business exchange. Perhaps these things were going through Iskandar's mind. Perhaps. Perhaps. Perhaps. As is usually the case for me in Tajikistan, I didn't really know.

But I'd have the video camera ready to capture foot stepping tomorrow. It could happen at any time. I wondered if there would be a scuffle. A big part of me hoped Bahriddin's bride would give him a good retaliatory jab to the ribs. Bahriddin was one of the nicest guys around, but he was very traditional. He would do the foot stepping. He'd do it ever so gently, but he'd do it. Could it be done in a kind way? Again, I didn't really know.

It was to be a double wedding tomorrow. That would save on costs tremendously. Only once to hire the musicians and make a wedding feast. Tomorrow Bahriddin would bring home his second bride and the middle brother, Saifuddin, his first. There was much to do. As the men and women slowly finished their meals in their respective rooms, they gathered outside and reclaimed their shoes.

In twos and threes, they wandered out into the darkness towards their villages. The drums would call them back tomorrow.

In Tajikistan when the drums begin reverberating on the cool night air announcing a wedding in a village or on a street close by, people all around commence walking towards the summoning sound. All are eager to find the music, dancing, and food they anticipate being at the source of the drums. Whether the wedding is held in a village or city, the phenomenon is the same.

Tajik weddings are outside and open. They are open to all but the annoying droves of young boys who are to be whacked on the head and driven off in the fashion of dogs when they get too close. Whack hard is the local philosophy. They are as stubborn as donkeys, though I have found they are usually more respectful in the villages than in the cities. But for all, save the boys in need of whacking, weddings are open. And since the host family has no idea how many will hear the drums and respond, it is imperative to make massive cauldrons of soup and steaming osh or play your drums quietly.

Of course playing the drums quietly is emphatically not an option. A Tajik wedding is always a show, a proud display, and a tremendous opportunity to go into some serious debt. But all that would be tomorrow night. Tonight was for the men and women closest to Bahriddin's family and the strange American in their midst.

An "Educational Girl"

> *Olucha, olucha, zardolucha*
> *Bachara kasal megand. Zikam ocha.*
> *Har gohe meram sari bolini bacha,*
> *Nolush mekunad. Tokat nadoram ocha.*
> *Nameram ocha. Ba xudo, nameram ocha.*
> *Moli mardum xurd ai.*
> *Nochor meram ocha.*

Cherry, cherry, apricot
They say the boy is sick. I am sad, mother.
Always when I go to the boy's pillow
He groans. I do not have the patience, mother.
I won't go, mother. By god, I won't go, mother.
The man's bride-price is consumed.
I am forced to go, mother.[2]

I sat against the wall watching the preparations in the now-empty men's banquet room. Bahriddin and his best man, Muslimjon, both in their late twenties, stood side by side in front of a medium-sized mirror, primping. Ties were tightened and straightened. Dress shoes were brought to a shine. Muslimjon combed the back of Bahriddin's hair so it lay just right. I smiled. Tajik men are not afraid to help each other get dressed up. Still, I prefer to comb my own hair.

Though I didn't know much about the traditional Tajik ceremonies I was soon going to be in the middle of, I knew tonight, now that all but the closest guests had departed, the important men would be climbing into some cars and heading out into the darkness toward the father of the bride's village in order to finalize tomorrow's transaction.

Bahriddin's mother had started the negotiations, started by going *xostgori* (matchmaking). She had probably started the process a few months ago. Taking a few of her closest women relatives, she had approached the young lady's family on Bahriddin's behalf. I wondered how the bride-to-be had felt that day likely standing at the door listening in on the negotiations determining her entire future. Though the son sometimes has no involvement in these arrangements whatsoever, I believe that Bahriddin had chosen or at least agreed to his mother's choice before she began the process that had led to tonight. I wondered if Bahriddin and his fiancée had ever spoken.

Bahriddin's sturdy frame filled out his suit well. Strong farm-worn hands and broad shoulders indicated to me that he was in his element out here in the mountains. A hard worker in all pursuits, he had managed to learn the English language well enough at Kadimobod University to distinguish himself above his peers and get a job at our office.

But he beamed confidence out here on his own turf. His poise surprised me. This was a confidence he absolutely did not exude on a keyboard where he was still struggling to subdue his lumbering fingers and get his typing skills up to par. It is interesting how powerful hands can be such an ally at one activity only to become your nemesis in another.

With his European facial features, maybe he could have passed as my long-lost relative who had been left out in the sun too long. Though the sun had darkened him over countless hours in the fields, he still had the remnants of the lighter complexion the Tajiks so passionately favor. When I tell Tajiks that Americans want to be dark, and that in trying to get darker they will actually pay more money than the typical Tajik makes annually, the girls especially stare at me in disbelief. I tell them people always seem to want to be what they are not, no matter what continent they live on. To Tajiks, a dark complexion is a shame. It's gypsy. It's low-class. It's mixed race and not pure Persian.

I knew Bahriddin didn't care about his complexion nearly as much as Tajik women care about his or their own. But in Tajik eyes, he was fortunate. His daughters had a good shot at being desirable if they inherited his skin tone and stayed out of the sun. Unfortunately, in the village the latter was an impossibility.

Taking a moment from his preparations at the mirror, he looked back at me and smiled his broad, sincere smile. Bahriddin was always an easy smile. He was a good friend. In spite of his frame that indicated otherwise, he was one of the gentlest, kindest Tajik men I had ever met. Once the orphans he worked with in child sponsorship saw his smile, they knew they had found a true advocate. And many had experienced enough abuse in their lives to greatly appreciate the rare ally. As I sat waiting for his friend and him to finish up at the mirror, I couldn't help but feel a great joy as I shared in his excitement.

I remembered all too vividly the only day in our friendship when I had not gotten to see a single one of Bahriddin's sincere smiles. I remember that day. He had tried to smile, tried to welcome me to his father-in-law's home, but I knew it was a smile coming out of despair. Though Tajik men, being Muslims, will sometimes take a second wife and bring her home to live alongside their first, I doubted Bahriddin would have done so, acceptable or not. No, he was only taking a new wife tomorrow because of that awful day last spring. I remembered back to his great pain.

I had known that Bahriddin's young wife had been sick for quite some time. She had even spent some time in the hospitals of Kadimobod. On that warm spring morning with the sun shining in at the office windows, a mutual friend came in to tell me that Bahriddin's wife was dying. I knew I had to go. I made the necessary preparations, stopping in at home to tell Ann what I had to do. Soon I was in a taxi heading out of town toward my friend's village. After being redirected to the nearby village of Bahriddin's father-in-law, my taxi driver and I found ourselves stepping in at the gate into an overwhelming scene.

Bahriddin met me inside the gate and offered that hollow smile now pressed deep into my memory. Always hospitable, always honoring, he had offered me a hug, as if it was his duty to comfort me, to apologize for this grief. He led me into a room filled with subdued men and dreadful silence. I picked at the soup unenthusiastically, aware that it was honoring to the family, honoring to my friend to show a lack of appetite. In the next room, Bahriddin's mother-in-law wailed with her other daughters and a few close friends around the deathbed of his wife. They would be the ones near her when she died. Bahriddin would sit here listening with the men and stare at the dirt wall.

Bahriddin's Wedding

A few weeks before this dark day, he had asked me why his life had been so hard. He had lost his father when he was only a small boy. He had married in joy only to discover that his wife was sickly and could not have children. But he had not *partoft* (thrown out or divorced) her as he was justified to do in Tajik society when it was discovered he had been strapped with an unfruitful bride. It would certainly have been easy to divorce her. In Islam, all a husband has to do to dissolve his marriage is say the word "divorce" to his wife three times in Arabic.

No, Bahriddin had honored her. He had kept her amid the growing realization he would probably have no children. I would be surprised if his relatives and perhaps even his mother had not followed Tajik custom and encouraged him to say, "*Talaq, Talaq, Talaq,*" and throw her away. He had not. But now she lay dying.

I stayed a short while. I did not speak, did not interrupt the men's silence. I did not know if this was right. In that room, surrounded by Muslims older than myself who I did not even know, in that sad room with a smattering of mullahs (religious leaders) I knew were there to perform last rites, I felt the gospel in my throat. I swallowed. And I swallowed again.

A few minutes later, Bahriddin walked me to the gate. We hugged. He looked away as he teared up. Always an honorable man, he faithfully stood at the gate with a few other men, hand over his heart to show respect and his thankfulness at my visit as our taxi bumped along the deeply channeled dirt road and out of sight.

I remember reflecting on the way back how many times I had shared the gospel with Bahriddin. He had always held it at arm's length, able to see the hope and joy of Christ, but unwilling to let the good news of forgiveness and love penetrate. Should I have shared again, shared what it is like to mourn like those who have hope? Was I wise to, by my presence, simply water the seed of the gospel Bahriddin had heard before or was I a coward? I know I am often a coward.

Back at the mirror, the memories of that spring faded quickly away as Bahriddin turned and smiled again as he finished up his preparations. He was excited. It was a new day. Maybe he would have children after all. As the three of us went outside, I felt happy to be sharing this good day with my friend. Looking sharp in their suits, Bahriddin and his best man, Muslimjon, approached the two compact cars waiting in the driveway. I lagged along behind trying to get a bit on video with my nifty night vision feature. Let's see if the territorial videographer can match that!

Not surprisingly, there seemed to have been no previous discussion as to who would be honored to make the trip to the father of the bride's home this evening with Bahriddin. As the uncles, brothers, and friends encircled the cars, I hung back and enjoyed the typical Tajik situation that necessitated vigorous discussion. There were a lot of politics going on around those two cars.

I realized the bride's village must be too far to walk to. If they sat three-across in the back seats, then the two cars had a total of ten spots. Drivers were secure. The elderly, long-bearded mullah (Muslim religious leader) had to go since he'd be performing Islamic wedding rituals in memorized Arabic. I assumed Bahriddin and Muslimjon were locks for two spots though the scene at the cars made it look like everything was up for grabs. They'd have to take the young videographer with the injured eye. Of course, as our mediator of sorts, Bahriddin's cousin had to go since he was also a close relative and next-door neighbor of the bride's family. That left three spots.

Tonight's visit was men only so I assumed the last spots would go to some combination of the uncles and brothers arguing around the car. Looks like I would be going to bed early back here at Bahriddin's. That sounded pretty good. It was nice to be an outsider. Nothing expected.

And then suddenly I was being dragged and pushed into the green car where I found myself sharing a tight back seat with

Bahriddin's Wedding

Bahriddin and Muslimjon. The mullah sat up front with a young, energetic driver. I soon found out this driver was yet another close relative of the family. Apparently he was also a lover of all Tajik music as long as it was played loud enough. Sadly he got to define "loud enough."

The moment the four doors were shut and a head-pounding beat from the speakers had been established, we spun our way out of there gaining traction as we went, leaving the crowd of men still arguing for a seat in the other car scrambling in our dust. I guess I was coming after all. I had a feeling some uncle or another had to be pretty angry with me right now. Between him and the videographer, I felt I was making enemies quite efficiently.

Though it was hard to determine what thumping emanated from the speakers and what was instigated by the deep road ruts, we soon settled into an unhealthy general upheaval going back down the road I had taken to walk in. I could make out the dry sang-ob riverbed in the moonlight as we headed toward the small highway I had come in by.

Having visited Bahriddin's house before, I knew the bride's village was actually on this side further up the sang-ob riverbed, the exact opposite direction we were traveling. So I assumed the road between the villages was no longer passable by car necessitating this back track to the highway. From the highway we could access the better-maintained road that ran through the villages on the other side of the riverbed. I hoped there was a way to cross back over. But perhaps walking would be more fun. Tajikistan and I have always seemed well fit for each other as we both appear to be insatiably drawn to doing things the hard way. Roads, bridges? A waste. Walking is more romantic.

I braced myself against the looming, hidden adventures hoping that tonight wasn't going to be a repeat of the Kui Islamjon (a famous mountain) fiasco I felt I had been tricked into. Amid the bumping and booming, I looked over at Bahriddin as if to ask if he had gotten me into another mess that would take a few days to recover from. Perhaps because of the darkness, he was not able to see the alarm and doubt in my eyes because all I got was one of those big, sincere smiles that confidently communicated, "Isn't this fun!?" I hoped so. I tried to give him the benefit of a doubt as I reflected back on our last misadventure.

As I remember, it was about two years ago that Bahriddin had invited my buddy and me for an overnight and a mountain climb out in his village. My teammate Sam—still a California surfer at heart—and I thought this sounded like a great idea. Bahriddin told us we'd wake up in the morning and then in just an hour or so we'd be able to start climbing toward the summit of the famous mountain and holy pilgrimage site of Kui Islamjon. We were promised that from the top we would have an incredible view over into the mountains of northern Afghanistan.

He was right about the fantastic view with the Panj River cutting a meandering border between the nations far down at the bottom of the ruggedness. Standing at the edge of the surrounding relatively fertile high planes of Tajikistan, looking into the barrenness of Afghanistan's northern reaches had felt like a contrast as stark as standing at the edge where rain begins and with a dry hand, reaching out across the transition line and into the soaking storm. The physical contrast between the landscapes had felt that stark.

So Sam and I had approved of the view, but Bahriddin had been a bit off with his one-hour time estimate. I began to have my doubts when Sam and I were awakened before dawn, fed a hasty and ill-advisedly heavy breakfast of bread, fresh boiled milk, and eggs and introduced to our mounts. More generally we were introduced to the idea of having mounts. Bahriddin and his brother thought it wise that the four of us take their mature horse and a donkey along with some supplies. Their year-old colt would be allowed to follow its mother. Their behavior was feeling more like "expedition" and less like "day stroll" by the minute. Though the mountain didn't look too far off in the distance as we set out, I slowly began to wonder if we'd really be back home by mid-afternoon, then rapidly began to wonder if we'd really be back home ever.

Countless, unmentionably painful hours later, Bahriddin and his little brother Abdulloh pranced along before us like otherworldly sprites as Sam and I civilly fought each other concerning who had to ride the horse. Who had to endure the hospitality, the honor of riding the infernal beast as the shooting pains throbbed down our legs? During my turns I kept my face turned away so Bahriddin wouldn't notice my rhythmic wincing. I think the contours of my legs were miraculously pounded into the bowlegged shape in a single day. It had to be a record. It sure felt like a record.

Sam and I infinitely preferred limping behind the horse, but our pride kept us from rebelling totally against our hosts' hospitality. So in ten-minute intervals we bickered back and forth, testing the limits of saving face, repeatedly mounting the horse for another dose of pain therapy. If done properly, Sam would notice gritting teeth and desperation when I spoke while Bahriddin and his brother would only notice a smile and perhaps a bit of strange enthusiasm which hopefully they'd chalk up to Americans being a bizarre lot, as usual.

Me: "You can ride the horse now, Sam." (*Through gritted teeth.*)

Sam: "Oh, no, no. I'm fine here walking."

Me: "No, I insist. I insist. It's your turn."

Sam: "No, that's okay, really. I just started walking."

Me: "No, I think surely it's your turn by now, Sam. It's your turn now. It's your turn now. Here I'll get off." (*Smiling determinedly as I attempt to dismount without losing consciousness.*)

Sam: "Well, I bet Bahriddin is tired by now. Bahriddin, you should ride the horse. You've been walking for hours."

Bahraiddin: "Oh, no, no, Akai Sam. The horse is for my guests. Your turn to ride the horse, Akai Sam."

Sam: "Oh, wonderful, Bahriddin." (*Gritting his teeth and mounting like a good sport.*)

The formalities continued at the threshold of pain tolerance until mercifully, as the sun began to go down, we arrived back in a village that had a taxi to carry us swiftly to the nearest Kadimobod medical facility.

Coming back to the present, I smiled to myself, hesitantly reflecting on the memories as I looked over at Bahriddin again. As he straightened his tie and stared out the front windshield in anticipation, I could almost feel my bowlegs throbbing. I hoped he knew what he was getting me into. I was just a fragile foreigner after all. He had learned that on our last adventure, hadn't he? It's not that I would have said no to the mountain trip if I had known a bit more going in. It's just I prefer to brace myself before significant drainings of my life force.

The taxi driver flipped the tape over, which gave me a moment to assess the severity of the ringing in my ears. Maybe the long-bearded mullah in the front seat was already deaf or surely he would have been complaining. Things had certainly changed since the days he had gone to get a bride or two.

As the music started in again, Bahriddin leaned over and yelled something in my ear.

"What?! Speak English!" I yelled at Bahriddin hoping that would give me a better shot at understanding him over the music. "Will you be my second man?!" Had I heard that right?

"You mean tonight and tomorrow for your wedding?!" I screamed hoping I had heard incorrectly.

"Yes!" Bahriddin screamed back, smiling.

"Uhhhhhh, okay!" I said.

Due to the decibel levels of the surrounding music it probably sounded more like, "AHHHHHHHH! OKAY!" as I yelled my hasty response directly into his left ear, which I might add far more accurately expressed my emotions.

"Good!" Bahriddin yelled back into my right ear. And with that bit of last-minute business settled in typical Tajik fashion, returned to staring out the front windshield.

Drat. What just happened? Was I a groomsman now? What am I wearing anyway? I looked down at my clothes. Oh well. Oh well? Oh well?! What am I doing?! I knew Muslimjon was his number-one guy and now apparently I was the guy who traditionally stood on the other side. I guess I could stand there, but if they asked for the ring or something I'd probably have to say, "Oh, you do rings here, too? I didn't know that."

I was having serious doubts that I was a good choice. I took comfort in the fact that everyone would have low expectations of me. Those expectations had to be worth a cluster of medium-sized or a pair of massive mistakes. I'd hide behind the video camera. Bahriddin would understand my camera duty keeping me from my other unknown responsibilities. Drat.

The car veered off onto a small side road and down a hill to the edge of the dry sang-ob riverbed. The large rocks, serving as a broad and seemingly endless series of natural speed bumps, brought us to a sudden halt. The driver paused and looked back at us in a way I thought was a bit on the psychotic side. Way too eager. Great. The thumping began as we headed across the dry river toward the village on the other side.

After a few minutes of off-roading, we thumped to a complete halt. The driver said something and suddenly we were all getting out of the car. I joined Bahriddin and Muslimjon behind the car.

"The rocks are too big here. The car was too low with us in it," Bahriddin explained.

I smiled as I thought about the situation. There I was, an absurdly unlikely groomsman directly from the heartland of America, in the middle of the Central Asian night. I was walking behind a thumping car in a dry sang-ob beside my buddies and a long-bearded mullah toward some dark village out there in the Tajikistan mountains somewhere to get us an "educational girl."

"Educational girl," that's what Bahriddin told me he wanted. He said that is what modern Tajik guys want nowadays. I remember when he had come to me a few months ago and asked for my advice. As I remember it, the gist of our conversation had gone something like this:

Bahriddin: "I need to pick another wife."
Me: "Oh, okay."
Bahriddin: "I don't know who to pick. My mother and my relatives want me to marry my cousin."
Me: "Yeah, that's common, right? Is this a cousin on your mother's side?"
Bahriddin: "No, it's my father's brother's daughter. Akai David, I heard that it is not good to marry your cousin."
Me: "Well, sometimes I think it can cause problems with your children. I think it makes them more likely to be born not being able to think well and things like that. Not always but sometimes."
Bahriddin: *(pensively)* "Yes, I heard that."
Me: *(ambitiously trying to expand our consideration beyond first cousins)* "Um, well, what kind of girl do you want to marry? What kind of girl do Tajik men want for a wife?"
Bahriddin: "I think most Tajik guys now want an educational girl."
Me: "An educational girl? What's that?"
Bahriddin: "A girl that has studied at university. They want a girl who knows things and not just a girl who can do work at home. My cousin is educational girl. She studies at university in Dushanbe."

As we walked along by the illumination of the car's taillights, I thought about how the cousin idea had won out easily over vague health considerations. So here we were, going to make the final arrangements with Bahriddin's uncle for his "educational girl." Maybe the fact that they were both naturally smart would offset the risk of being cousins. It should all even out. Right? The Tajik word *meshavad* came to mind. Basically, it means everything will be fine. And if I had to pick a word to sum up the Tajik philosophy of life, that's the word I'd pick. "Meshavad."

I knew the girl was lucky. Tajiks often prefer to give their daughters to first cousins because in this society where new brides can be thrown away and sent back home in lifelong shame a week or two after the wedding for as little as not doing the washing properly, having the close family ties to enforce what was right and good usually gave brides the best chance of being protected. Besides, Bahriddin was a great guy. She was lucky.

As our car, now a fair bit ahead of us, floored it to climb out on the other side of the riverbed, I looked over at Bahriddin and Muslimjon. I realized they were happy. I felt happy too. I have learned that at Tajik weddings, genuine happiness is a rare commodity. As I thought about it, I realized this might have been the first Tajik wedding I had ever been to where the mood I felt was very close to joy and hope. Usually they are such somber affairs with lots of crying on the bride's part.

Crying is so normal for brides here that there are general rules addressing the issue. Brides should cry, it is taught, because they must show they are sincerely sad to leave their family. If they do not cry it would dishonor their family. But brides must not cry too much. Losing it completely would show that she is not at all excited about getting married and that would shame the groom and his family. And if the bride shames the groom too much he might become angry and step on her foot very, very hard or even take advantage of his Islamic right as a husband and beat her when he gets her home.

Sometimes the excessive crying is sparked by something as silly as the bride's first glimpse of a depressingly long nose on the groom. But on the more serious side, most weddings, I feel, have an overarching tinge of sadness and resignation on the part of the bride. More often than not she has no idea what her husband will be like, and how he will treat her. And more importantly, she wonders how her mother-in-law, who will now rule her life, will manage her.

How many months will her mother-in-law force her to work in seclusion before she will allow the new bride to return home to visit her family and friends again? Will her mother-in-law and husband ever permit her to visit her friends again? Though thankfully not too common, some husbands are so jealous as to forbid their wife from ever visiting anyone except their own father's home ever again. Some families imprison the young woman, wearing such tight control of their sons' brides as a badge of honor.

My friend Safar told me his grandmother has never even been to the market since the day she married all those decades ago. I knew from the way he told me that within his family they are quite proud of this fact. Every Tajik woman is desperate to be married. Yet most are desperately sad, terrified by the possibilities awaiting them as it is happening. It is a strange world.

I wondered how Bahriddin's bride would react. She is an educational girl after all. Would she want to work at a job in the city? Would Bahriddin allow that? Would Bahriddin's mother allow that? Though I did not know the answers to these questions, I knew Bahriddin was a good man. Besides, somehow I had gotten the impression that his educational girl was actually quite traditional. I had a good feeling this could be a joyful experience.

The four of us climbed back into the car and started up another rutted road. The road was soon winding through the streets of Bahriddin's bride's village. Our headlights blazed the trail ahead. Eight-foot metal gates fortified the mud-brick houses on either side. Dim electricity flickered out at us from between their hinges as we passed. In a low area off to our left, we passed a small structure surrounded by massive trees. Pointing, Bahriddin leaned over and yelled over the music that it was a famous pilgrimage site, a mosque or mazor or something of the sort where many great *ashans* had come from.

"Ashan" is the word they use in this area for powerful Muslim mullahs. They have lived in this area for generations. I believe these ashans are some who try to prove they have lineage from the prophet Muhammad himself. At any rate, these ashans are proud of their lineage. Supposedly it gives them powers. The Tajiks tell legends of ashans who lived long ago, ashans who walked through fire without harm and performed many other feats.

As the mazor disappeared behind us, we came to a stop outside an open metal gate at a turn in the road. A few men immediately hustled out the gate to offer a warm welcome. Car doors popped open in haste. Hands were over hearts all around. A sea of formalities, of *asaloms, xush omadeds,* and *rahmats* were exchanged in the darkness as we made our way in through the gate and toward the house. We had arrived.

Vows in the Dark

> *Oina ba dasti rost megiram man.*
> *Mexonam. Ixtisos megiram man.*
> *Az gxaibati hamsoyam nametarsam man.*
> *Diplom ba dasti rost megiram man.*
>
> I take the mirror in my right hand.
> I will study. I will take a profession.
> The gossip of my neighbors I will not fear.
> I will take a diploma with my right hand.[3]

I took off my shoes, adding them to the great pile by the door. I tried to hide mine under a few other pairs, hoping to make them a bit more inconvenient to steal. Easy shoe accessibility is sometimes a problem at these big celebrations with neighbors and unknown children coming and going in droves. It is preferable that they do their coming and going without your shoes.

Ann sometimes carries our shoes around with us at such events just to be safe. Right about now that sounded like a great idea. I didn't want to end up wearing old Tajik house slippers to the wedding tomorrow. "Meshavad," I said to myself, finding comfort in the common Tajik philosophy of life, as I left my shoes to fend for themselves against the inevitability of what was written. Still, a guy can hope his shoes are not ill-fated, can't he?

I followed Bahriddin and the rest of our party down a short hall to the far room. The room was familiarly illuminated by a single bulb dangling from a black cord in the middle of the ceiling. I was excited. We were about to meet the "educational girl," Bahriddin's bride. Well, more or less. Probably less if tonight played out how these events typically did. There would be some playful negotiations, some prayers, some vows, and we'd probably do it all without ever seeing the bride. She'd be in another room with her friends, veiled and giggling.

Bahriddin would send his representative in to ask for her hand. I was praying hard that this job did not traditionally fall to the number-two groomsman! But regardless of who carried the message, the answer, of course, had already been determined. Well before tonight, it had been negotiated and decided by the power brokers that she would give her hand, or more accurately, that others would give it for her.

As I understood the proceedings, tomorrow would be the signing of papers, the legal portion with the Tajik state. Tonight would be the religious ceremony, the traditional Islamic vows. In Tajikistan when becoming polygamous, the marriage process skips the state portion altogether. Weddings of second wives consist solely of the Islamic vows, vows like the ones we would witness tonight. This is because the government of Tajikistan, oddly, does not technically approve of multiple wives.

Bahriddin's Wedding

Perhaps in the coming decades, America and Europe, holding high their proud banners of relativism and tolerance, will blaze the trail to the universal legalization of polygamy. With the present philosophy of the West, it would certainly be inconsistent, not to mention intolerant of others' beliefs and lifestyle choices, not to allow the practice within our societies. And perhaps such a nudge from the unmoored West will encourage countries like Tajikistan to boldly drift into more traditionally Islamic waters.

I assumed the bearded mullah we had brought from Bahriddin's village would be presiding over the ceremonies. But before all that formality, there would be a game of sorts. Sometimes this game became tense. Shanoza, one of Ann's good friends, had gleefully told us her story of the night when her Islamic wedding vows were said.

Shanoza's future groom had arrived with his entourage. They were seated in one room. Her friends and sisters were with her, gathered in another room. The groom had sent his representative to ask her to consent to marry him. She refused and the game had begun.

The representative came back to the groom with the disappointing answer. He was redeployed to the women to ask about her demands. She demanded money for all her friends. Shanoza giggled as she related the story to us. Her eyes sparkled as she told us she had asked for an exorbitant amount of money for each of her friends.

The representative spent the next few hours running back and forth between the rooms, riding the wave of Shanoza's playful negotiations. Shanoza wants this. Shanoza wants you to say that. The game went on and on. Hours passed. The groom, his fragile ego suffering, finally arose threatening to leave in a huff and end the marriage agreement before it even started. Okay, time to wrap the game up. The groom and his guests were being shamed. She loved it. But it was enough. She sent the messenger back saying she accepted. Fortunately, the groom sat back down.

This traditional game is difficult for me to understand. First of all, it does not seem to matter if the bride-to-be agrees or not since it has already been decided. The drama is an illusion. On the other hand, it is an important tradition for many Tajik women. They seem to relish the slightest hint of control and power, even if it has no real substance. Their power symbolically evaporates on the wedding day when the brides must cover themselves in a full burka. This entombing clothing allows only a woman's eyes to be seen. As far as I know, the wedding day is the only occasion when Tajik women wear a burka.

In the Tajik version of the burka, brides are covered from head to toe in such a manner that they cannot see where they are going. The symbolism is powerful. Tajik brides look down so they can see the ground for their next step. The groom will come and take his blind, often sobbing, bride by the arm and lead her home. On the way, she will have her foot stepped on three times by this man, her husband, who she has probably never spoken to before. She prays he is kind. Upon entering the groom's home, she will be led from the car to a private room where she will be put behind a concealing curtain.

The groom will leave to eat and enjoy the wedding while she sits in seclusion. She will meet her mother-in-law, her new taskmaster, who will tell her how long she must stay inside in seclusion. The mother-in-law will tell the new bride how many months it will be before she will grant the bride permission to leave their yard to make a return visit to see her parents and her family.

The new bride must work hard. She must be respectful. She must prove her womb is fruitful in the first year or two or risk being cast off and labeled barren, making it difficult to even become someone's second wife in the future. It is not hard to see, I think, why Tajik brides relish their little game. For that moment they are their own. After the moment has passed, they wait eagerly for the day when their sons grow strong and give them their turn to be the powerful matriarch. And in between come harder times.

As we entered the men's banquet room and took our honored positions at the head of the dustarxon tablecloth, I looked around the room. Ten or fifteen men, who I assumed were all part of the bride's family, respectfully stood around the bountiful dustarxon until Bahriddin's mullah found his spot and sat down. With the religious leader settled, Bahriddin and the rest of our party sat down on the floor near the head of the dustarxon.

A soup course followed by an osh course familiarly found their way to us as we sat on the floor nibbling at the specially baked breads and sipping hot tea. The second carload of men from Bahriddin's house arrived and squeezed into various nonexistent spots on the korpacha floormats. The videographer, my nemesis, set up shop in the corner filming the meal and small talk as the conversation evolved into an exploration of Islam.

The men of both families eagerly asked the deeply wrinkled mullah questions concerning religious life and practice. Our bearded mullah seemed to thoroughly enjoy speaking about this and explaining the ways of that. I focused on the conversation with all my might but the language flowed so quickly, from so many directions, that I struggled along to keep up as best I could. I needed constant clarification, but it was not the time to hinder the room for my benefit.

In my internal confusion, my mind began to wander. I began to think about Tajik marriage. I remember when my language teacher and I had done a role-play to practice my Tajik. Zikrulloh was a natural comedian, so when I told him he was the taxi driver and I was the passenger, the stage was beautifully set for his improvisation. Our role-play quickly advanced past formalities and needed locations to small talk as Zikrulloh created his fictional Tajik family, which I soon realized was his sarcastic jab at so much of Tajik society. As I remember it, the role-play had developed something like this:

Me: So are you married?

Zikrulloh: Oh yes, I have two wives.

Me: Two wives?

Z: Oh, yes! I'm a rich taxi driver, aren't I? Of course I have two wives.

Me: And do you have children?

Z: Absolutely! But so far I have only ten children. Sadly, each wife has given me just five. My good wife gave me five boys and my bad wife gave me five girls.

Me: So do you all live in one house together?

Z: Of course not! Are you crazy? It is essential to keep the wives separated. I usually live with my good wife.

Me: You mean with the one who gave you five boys?

Z: Of course.

Me: And are your children grown? What do they do?

Z: Oh, they are getting big and doing quite well. They all sell plastic bags at the bazaar so they don't really need my help anymore. They're set. How many wives do you have?

Me: One.

Z: *(shaking his head, scolding)* Ttt-ttt-ttt. You must be poor. It's good to have two wives. Then if you get in a fight you just go on over to the other house. Then everybody is happy!

Sitting there at the dustarxon beside Bahriddin, I smiled to myself remembering back to Zikrulloh's exaggerated slap at so many Tajik practices that he seemed to find ridiculous. He is a young idealistic single guy. I wondered what he'd think in five years.

As the meal was winding down and the mullah was winding up, electricity thumped off immersing us in an absolute blackness. I couldn't even see my own fingers as I waved them in front of my face. The conversation did not falter in the slightest. I could tell by their lack of reaction that they were intimately accustomed to the darkness. It was as if, like a blind community, they had honed their other senses through constant practice. Out here in the villages of Tajikistan there are almost infinite opportunities to hone.

The mullah continued on in his present discourse, his weathered voice emanating out from the pitch like a voice within a black hole. All distractions eliminated, total attention was focused on words and personalities. Though we could not see each other, truly this was face-to-face conversation. All entered fully into the moment.

In my experience, such attention no longer exists in the land of constant distraction where I was born. Such silence and focus in my home country would certainly make us as Americans nervous. After a moment I believe we would instantly spring to action to fill the peaceful silence with anything as soon as humanly possible.

In that dark moment part of me envied this opportunity to focus as a community. I do not often envy the Tajiks, their passivity or poverty, but in that moment together conversing as a group in the dark I could see the benefits. Although genuine community is incredibly more fulfilling, if given a choice, humans strangely seem to prefer isolating entertainments though I don't think we enjoy the loneliness that obviously results.

After a few moments, a couple of men flipped open their cell phones illuminating our surroundings with blue light. Modernity was here. It simply hadn't ironed out the wrinkles yet. Lit candles were brought to the dustarxon to replace the blue light. I looked over at Bahriddin and Muslimjon and then to the mullah still speaking beside them. The shadows and candlelight dancing upon the mullah's bearded face seemed to dramatize each wrinkle around his eyes as if we had been cast into a play. The flickering candle, our makeshift spotlight, focused my attention on each actor. The lead, Bahriddin, looked content at the head of the dustarxon as he waited patiently to finish the work of securing his new bride.

Surprisingly, after a short while, electricity came back on at which point the negotiations began in earnest. Bahriddin sent one of our party, perhaps a cousin, to the bride's room to ask for her hand. I realized I understood very little of what was happening around me. I did not know the nuances of the proceedings and could not anticipate anything. But the cousin came back quickly saying that she had agreed. The new bride had not seemed to want to play the game.

The mullah took the lead at this point. He was soon chanting in Arabic interspersed with Tajik questions in need of response from both Bahriddin and a middle-aged man near the far end of the room. I assumed these were the vows and I guessed that the man at the end of the room exchanging these solemn words with the mullah and Bahriddin must be the bride's father. Though I doubted that anyone, perhaps not even the mullah, understood the Arabic vows being exchanged, the chants were soon completed, sealing the contract. I was especially impressed when the vows continued on uninterrupted when the electricity went out yet again. Notably the bride had not been present at the ceremony, unless she had snuck up in the dark and escaped before the power returned. That seemed unlikely.

Soon after the vows were completed we stood up. Putting our hands over our hearts we gently bowed our way back toward the front door where I was relieved to find my shoes had enjoyed a good fate in my absence. Walking through the moonlit yard we made our way back to the car. I looked up. Amazing! I doubt there is a place on earth where the countless stars shine brighter than Central Asia.

We drove off with a great deal less enthusiasm than when we came. The driver must have grown tired. I was glad. He didn't even turn on his music. We were soon walking behind the car through the riverbed again, Bahriddin and Muslimjon discussing things together as I walked silently beside them. On the other side of the riverbed we piled back in again, our bearded mullah in the front seat with Bahriddin, Muslimjon, and me returning to the back. We drove for a while in silence.

Bahriddin's Wedding

I don't remember how the conversation started, but after a while the mullah was talking about animal sacrifice within Islam. I spoke up, eventually sharing the whole gospel as the reason why I do not sacrifice. I explained that for people who have put their faith in Christ, Idi Korbon—the Muslim holiday of sacrifice—is no longer necessary. The mullah started to heat up. I kept responding that Jesus was my sacrifice once and for all to cleanse my sins. Because his life was the perfect sacrifice—I explained echoing Hebrews—we no longer need to repeatedly shed the blood of cows and sheep year after year in a never-ending attempt to cover our sins. Jesus finished it at the cross.

The mullah continued to fume until, as has been the case so often in our relationship, Bahriddin stepped in and rescued me with some soothing comments to calm the rapidly overheating mullah in the front seat. He said that my way was good for me and the Islamic way was good for them and we needed to change the subject.

Bahriddin certainly has a gift for smoothing things over. He had rescued me enough times for me to recognize his talent. But I did not want rescuing. I wanted to speak about my rescuer whom I love and who loves them. But I could sense the opportunity had passed, if there had even been one to begin with. The car returned to silence as we finished our bumpy, midnight drive back to Bahriddin's house.

As we got out of the car at Bahriddin's, I looked up at the hills surrounding us on every side. As far as I knew, for generations these villages and even the cities interspersed had basically existed without any Christian witness. When our team leader and his family first arrived in Kadimobod a little over a decade ago, they had searched for remnants of past Christian witness. The Tajiks had spoken of one Russian Orthodox priest who had lived in Kadimobod for a little while. But all the Tajiks seemed to remember about him was that he drank a lot.

But now, a few years after our team's arrival, I was hopeful. I knew out in the hills there were a handful of villages here and there with one or two believers. Mohtobi's believing sister lived in a village out to the east, and Husniddin lived in the village of Ukob further down from here in the direction of Kadimobod. It seemed like so little, a handful of isolated believers here and there.

I thought about the house church meeting in Kadimobod and the young Tajik believers learning the importance of gathering as they fell more deeply in love with Christ together. I thought about the believers who had returned to their villages here and there, others that had gone to Russia or Dushanbe for work. I thought about this unplanned and often frustrating diaspora and wondered if God was working providentially. When, Lord, will you raise up a Tajik Paul, a Tajik Barnabas, or Timothy? Is there a Joseph being honed for service in a dark prison somewhere? Lord, glorify your name!

Walking back up the steps at Bahriddin's house, I was acutely aware that I did not know what God would do in this country. I held on to what I did know. I know He loves the Tajik people infinitely more than I do. And, though I often resist, He is teaching me to rest in His love and providence. The patriarchs often stood alone in a sea of indifference and look what the Lord accomplished through them. He orchestrated salvation, salvation freely offered to all the nations on earth. May this providential sprinkling of Tajik believers be the patriarchs and matriarchs of the miracle that is the Tajik church.

Before the "Yamaxa" Began

Shishtagi budam. Yak duxtarak paido shud.
Dasthoyash pasi pusht kutala roh bolo shud.
Guftam, "Ey duxtar, ohista rav!" Chakon shud.
Xioli dilash shukuni oson shud.

I was sitting. One young woman appeared.
Her hands behind her back, she went uphill on the road.

Bahriddin's Wedding

I said, "Hey young woman, go slowly!" She sped up.
Her heart's desire to get a husband would now
  be easily fulfilled.[4]

When I awoke the following morning, I was alone in the room.
I felt it was still very early, but I could hear feverish activity out-
side all around the house. Energetic voices yelled back and forth.
Preparations for the double wedding day were already in full swing.

I rolled over on my cotton-filled floral floor mat. The other eight
or nine men who had slept on mats all over this room the night
before had already risen. Their mats were stacked in a massive flowery pile that rose up to a great height on top of a traditional Tajik
sanduk (wedding trunk) in the corner of the room. The family would
probably be bringing home two more sanduks today, one from each
bride. Perhaps this old trunk before me was Bahriddin's mother's
wedding sanduk. As I stared blearily at the trunk, the last sleeper
and all alone, I wondered if perhaps it was time to get up.

As I rummaged around in my backpack, hurriedly getting ready,
I remembered back to being awakened late last night to the sound of
an approaching car and some shouting. I think Bahriddin had gotten up along with a couple of other men. I remember they had been
saying to each other that the musicians had arrived.

It seems the musicians had finished up another village wedding
somewhere nearby and driven over with their Yamaha keyboard,
speakers, and traditional instruments. In Tajikistan all electric
keyboards, regardless of make, are simply known as Yamaha. This
is usually pronounced *Yamaxa,* with a strong guttural "x"—think
cat with bronchitis hissing—that I can never quite get the hang of.
My daughter Grace seems to have conquered the sound effortlessly
enough though. Sometimes it sounds like she might be rabid or
something when she starts in on her street Tajik. We're very proud,
although sometimes after hearing her alarming slang we're a little
hesitant to pinch those pudgy cheeks. At any rate, the Yamaxa and

band had arrived sometime after midnight. I wondered where they had found spots to sleep.

To the older generations of Tajiks, I know the advent of the relatively new Yamaxas and speaker systems that mechanically propel the wedding singer's voice out over entire neighborhoods is a point of contention. I learned this standing next to an old *osh pover* (cook) at a wedding in Kadimobod. As I remember it, I had stood by that old osh pover as he used his massive metal spatula to turn the countless kilos of rice, oil, chick peas, and shredded carrots cooking in his intimidating black cauldron. As he worked hard on the wedding feast in the afternoon sun, sweat dripping and thick forearms ebbing, he complained to all his buddies gathered around the cauldron about how the wedding singers can't belt it out like they used to. They've grown weak and reliant on these new speaker systems. He mocked them, saying that when the electricity goes out at a wedding you'll be lucky if you can hear the singer from five yards away. The old men spoke together reverently about the famous Kadimobod singers of their day. Back then, the raw power of their own voices reverberated over the wedding crowds all the way down the streets.

These old singers and their amazing voices sounded so impressive that I found myself nostalgic for days I had never experienced, which is becoming something of a pattern for me. Every young Tajik clamors for the new Russian-inspired sounds of the latest Tajik pop coming out of Dushanbe. Down at the bazaar they roll their eyes when I ask where I can find a CD of some traditional, timeless *dumbra* (two-stringed guitar) folk singing. Well, they don't have to listen to it with me. "Just give me the CD. And by the way cool, eye-rolling Tajiks," I always want to add, "I regret to inform you that Madonna and Michael Jackson are no longer all the rage."

Now presentable, I snapped my backpack closed and stepped out into the cool fall morning. I was curious to go see the pansy, weak-crooning, modern musicians and whatever else I could

discover. Grabbing my shoes, I stepped down into the yard. The
band was already setting up in the large, packed dirt area near the
orchard at the front of the house. They didn't look like pansies to
me but evidently they were hiding weak vocal cords beneath that
macho swagger. What if electricity went out tonight? That seemed a
likely scenario to me. "Meshavad," I said to myself and immediately
felt a little better.

One of Bahriddin's cousins stood on a stool near the dusty
driveway hanging the family's best carpets as a backdrop to create an impressive dance area. I walked over to him, happy to have
something to do. He was a really nice guy. I had just met him last
night, but I thought we could be pretty good friends given time. He
looked down and informed me that after he had finished hanging
up the beautiful blue-and-red family treasures he would write out
messages on them for the wedding guests to enjoy.

Using cotton, a raw material the Soviets made all too prevalent
in Tajikistan, he would stretch it out and form it into letters that he
would artistically arch across the carpets. Then tonight as the guests
were dancing they could read things like *Xush omaded mehmoni aziz!*
("Welcome dear guest!") or perhaps, *Tui muborak!* ("Wedding con-
gratulations!"). If he got fancy, he could use that cotton to create
a couple of intertwined rings or perhaps a wedding goblet for the
carpets. The goblet motif, which I assumed was supposed to contain
wine, seemed an odd choice considering Islam's alcohol prohibition.

Tajiks largely ignore that prohibition. Well, the men do at any
rate. But out of respect for their religious law and out of a desire to
mark ourselves as religious people in a recognizable way in their society, our team has chosen to abstain from alcohol completely while
in Tajikistan, which we have learned impresses them. Ironically, as
has been the case at more than one social event, we alone, the only
non-Muslims present, decline the offered spirits.

On the pig front, except for a couple of wild boar hunters I have
met who have a jovially gluttonous time in seclusion up in the

mountains a couple of times per year, the Tajiks seem to be much more serious about the no pork rule. However, if we can find it near a Russian military base or something, we don't hesitate to have some bacon. I suppose combining the efforts of our team and the Tajiks, we do pretty well on the dietary prohibitions.

Walking over to the side yard I was able to see a handful of men working fires beneath a pair of huge cast-iron cauldrons. I was certain one was for *shorbo* (soup) and the other for osh. I would have bet five somoni on it. Next to the cauldrons, two tall, battered, metal containers sat on some rocks over another set of fires. Those must be for tea. People were running everywhere attending to their work. I'm sure there was something I could do, but I had no idea what that was. I felt confident they would not allow me to help anyway, so I stood there breathing in the morning air enjoying the surrounding din.

After a while Bahriddin found me. Since I had my video camera and Bahriddin looked as if he had a few free moments, I took advantage of the opportunity. This being a double wedding, I asked if I could interview both of the grooms for their wedding video. Bahriddin agreed, calling his younger brother Saifuddin over to join us.

As I prepared my video camera, I explained that I wanted to ask them what they thought of marriage, what their hopes and dreams for their new marriages were, and other things of that sort. Bahriddin is not exactly shy, more meek and self-effacing I would say. But his younger brother is full-fledged shy. Add to this pair of soft-spoken men a poor interviewer like myself and we had the perfect setup for a less-than-stellar interview. And that's exactly what we got. It might have actually registered negatively on the Richter scale. What did they hope for in their wives? What did they think a good husband was like? I couldn't hear Saifuddin's answers either because he was so soft-spoken or because he was too rattled. I kept panning over to Bahriddin for translation on his brother's responses.

The interview yielded no ground-breaking revelations but we did establish that an "educational girl" is better than a simple housewife. However, it sounded like a given that, upon marriage, the "educational girl" would immediately become a simple housewife. It was also stated that a husband must be kind and not harsh towards his wife. That was good. Though beating wives is permitted and even considered fairly normal behavior in Tajikistan, I hoped that their two new brides would not have to endure that.

Saifuddin added that a wife must be a hard worker and a great help to her new mother-in-law around the house. That is a Tajik nonnegotiable right up there in importance with the wife providing children early and often. Saifuddin also believed it was important that a husband be patient. It was not added that wives needed to be patient as well.

I remember my teammate John once passed along something a Tajik had told him about marriage. His Tajik friend said there are two types of marriage in Tajikistan, *mardkalon* (big man) and *zankalon* (big woman). Constant teasing about zankalon marriage is a favorite pastime among Tajik men. The terminology even has its own folklore for ammunition. For example, it is said that if your second toe is longer than your first you are, as they put it, zankalon.

I get this comment along with some playful pointing and chuckles pretty often when I wear sandals. Evidently, I naively used to like my prominent second toe. The playful teasing intensifies a bit when my neighbors see me hanging laundry on our balcony. This frustrates me. I feel an increasingly strong desire to hang up laundry in sandals.

For Tajiks, marriage is about power and control. There is little, if any, sense of servant leadership. But why would there be? As my teammate John has often explained to me, relationships, family, and marriage find their cultural forms from the worldview of the people, particularly what they believe about God. In the absence of the example of Jesus, the perfect Bridegroom who gave up his life for His bride, certain categories and definitions of love, grace, mercy, leadership, and sacrifice fail to develop in the beauty of their biblical forms. In the absence of Christ, an entirely different tone for marriage and relationship is set.

In Tajikistan I have become incredibly thankful for the example of my Savior. Though I am far from being like Him, I have learned emphatically that who you hold up as the model to which you aspire makes all the difference in the world. And things begin to come together or fall apart accordingly.

Speaking of falling apart, this interview I was attempting to conduct was making no difference whatsoever. Besides, Saifuddin looked as if this recorded questioning was causing him acute pain. Mercifully for everyone, I called it quits, put my hand over my heart and let them return to their hasty preparations. I turned to wander around the grounds, feeling like I'd probably have a few hours before we left in the cars to pick up the first bride. I think we were to pick up Bahriddin's bride first. But that was a guess. This was all uncharted water for me. Today I'd be floating with the current.

After a while I began to feel more out of place than normal, so I wandered off their property, following the dirt road towards the sang-ob riverbed. Standing on the dusty bank, I had almost three hundred and sixty degrees worth of good views. Looking out in the direction I believed would lead quickly into northern Afghanistan, the barren hills rose higher and higher until I imagine they would have to be officially called mountains.

Directly across the dry riverbed I could see hundreds of tiny animated dots about halfway up a large group of hills. From this distance I could not distinguish between cows, sheep, goats, or shepherds. I hoped they were finding enough green tufts out there among the boundless sea of withered browns. I certainly couldn't see much green from this distance.

I wondered who the shepherds for that herd were today. Bahriddin has told me that his village takes turns being shepherd.

Bahriddin's Wedding

Every morning the villagers open their pens and let their animals move out together towards the hills where they slowly merge to become a herd for the day. And every morning a different village family is responsible to go with them. So perhaps once every two weeks or so it is Bahriddin's family's turn to accompany the animals to prevent the goats from having an unduly bad influence and getting the rest of the herd's law-abiding citizens stuck or into a predicament.

Upon returning to the village in the evenings, without much help from the shepherd, the herd will gradually split off, meandering their separate ways home amid the dimming, dusty streets. They find their way back to their own homes to be penned up for the night. "Smart animals and a great system," I thought to myself as I stared out at the dots on the opposite hills until the sun spots in my eyes seemed more numerous than the livestock.

A boy around ten years old was riding toward me from the middle of the riverbed. I hadn't noticed him before. As he neared I became aware that he was singing as he poked his donkey with a stick to make slight adjustments to its course. I stood and watched him approach.

He used the stick adeptly to prod the donkey on up the steep bank where he brought him to a stop right in front of me. "*Asalom*" (hello), I greeted him. No response. I got out my video camera hoping he might repeat his song for me. "*Baroi man surud namexoned?*" ("Won't you sing a song for me?") No response. I noticed he was staring a bit open mouthed. Not so much the open-mouthed shock of seeing a foreigner or a video camera, but more like he may have had mental issues.

I tried once more asking, "*Xaraton nom dorad?*" ("Does your donkey have a name?") That was a good joke as the concept of pets is absurd here. I thought for sure I would get a smile with that one. The mouth stayed open and the eyes went to half-mast. I tried smiling broadly. Still nothing. "*Milash, xair*" ("Okay, bye"), I concluded and watched him poke his donkey on down the road.

As he rode off, I noticed a little down the bank there was a woman in a simple work korta gathering cow manure from the road with an old metal bucket. A couple of children were playing beside her as she worked. When the bucket was full, she hauled it over to the edge of the high bank where she dumped it out onto the ground beside at least one hundred other drying round cow patties. Using her hands, she formed that morning's manure into a circle. Then she rinsed her hands in the river trickle. Leaving the patties to dry in the October sun, she took her empty bucket and headed back down the road towards the village, the children bounding along beside her.

I knew the rows of patties would be an excellent heating source for her family this winter. Barren hills don't provide much lumber, and winter up in these mountains gets a lot colder than it does in Kadimobod. Even in Kadimobod I've seen my share of roofs packed with drying manure. I wondered how many of these patties the family would use during the winter. I'm sure they knew by now exactly how many they needed. They certainly couldn't count on the government giving them electricity. It is dangerous to count on electricity when working out the winter heating and cooking equation.

Further down the bank in a low spot towards the river, I saw stacks of well-formed mud bricks. I went over to examine them. The perfectly formed corners indicated the use of a mold. I assumed the straw sticking out on all sides at various angles must be to form a stronger brick. The story of Moses in Egypt came to mind. There were a lot of bricks drying in the sun. One of the village families must be building a new house or barn. I didn't think it was Bahriddin's, though they probably could have used a house addition. They only had four rooms. Now two new brides were coming to join the three-generation family later in the day. And if things went according to plan, they would be adding another generation to the house shortly.

Tajiks say mud-brick walls are strong and insulate well, keeping the house cool against the summer sun and containing the fire's warmth throughout the winter. I agree that the mud brick is a superior insulator compared to the Soviet cement-block apartment complexes that in my experience serve as giant iceboxes for most of the winter.

After a while, I turned and wound my way back toward Bahriddin's. Two men were splashing water onto the road from a tiny channel running along the side. Tajiks love to splash water over dust to keep it from clouding up and choking you when you disturb it in the slightest. It's almost a national pastime. Our national pastime, baseball, is usually a dusty affair as well, and for those of us who don't have our own grounds crew to prepare our field, we just leave it that way. I think we, as Americans, figure the sweat will eventually do the work and cake the dust billows to our body, thereby solving the problem. And to ensure maximum caking, we always schedule our games for high noon in July. Rugged. Natural. American.

But Tajiks prefer to water the dust instead of their bodies so these two were working admirably to make the immediate approach to Bahriddin's gate a little more pleasant. As I watched them carpet the road with water I felt appreciation for the pride they showed in doing every detail with excellence on this momentous occasion. Still, it is difficult to make a dusty road not dusty and I thought the three of us could have better used the time playing a little ball.

Arriving back at Bahriddin's I saw that things were moving right along. The carpets were hung as a backdrop to the water-splashed dance floor. Cotton-formed Tajik letters arching across the carpets welcomed the guests and congratulated everyone on the wedding. The speakers, drums, and headlining Yamaxa looked ready to go as the musicians sipped tea on a Tajik cot in the shade. Near the house, the cauldrons and tea cylinders were steaming into the cool October morning as the osh paz made his final feast preparations. Surely we'd be ready to go and get the first bride soon.

I took the fact that Bahriddin was already dressed and ready for his wedding as a cue that I should prepare myself. I went inside and quickly put on the best my backpack had to offer, making sure to stop for a few moments in front of a small mirror. Try to hide my bad haircut. Check. Well, meshavad at any rate. Grabbing my video camera I retrieved my shoes and walked out towards the gathering cars.

People had begun to cluster around the cars. It looked like a contingent of both men and women would be going to the father of the bride's house to get the new bride. Bahriddin and his best man looked ready to go. So it looked as if Bahriddin would be bringing his bride home first before they redeployed the four-wheeled entourage to go for his brother's bride. I noticed a few other young guys in suits and hoped I might be demoted from second man to cameraman-in-waiting.

The crowd began to pile into the numerous Russian and Korean-made cars parked haphazardly around us. The Tajik president recently passed a law that there could be no more than three or four cars in a Tajik wedding procession. An interesting law, I thought, for the president of a country to dictate and speak passionately about in a national address, an address I might add that also included new regulations for the proper way to do a funeral. But it looked like we weren't going to be obeying the wedding vehicle rule today. Evidently, the president didn't understand that the grand wedding show with its attending debt was a nonnegotiable in the ever-escalating struggle to impress for the sake of family honor.

Bahriddin found me wandering and took me under his wing again. I guessed it was going to be the same seating arrangement in our car as last night. Bahriddin scooted to the middle as I slid in beside him retaking my window seat. Grooms shouldn't have to ride in the middle enduring all the straddling issues. But what could I do? He was relentlessly gracious. He would never allow me or even Muslimjon, to straddle.

Looking across the back seat, I noticed Muslimjon seemed stoic. He was a quiet guy. I found him hard to read. Beside me, Bahriddin looked confident and excited. As for me I felt nervous and just a tad out of my comfort zone. Up in the front, our mullah sat staring out the front windshield looking a little weary. I wondered if the weddings he had officiated were well into triple digits by now. They would probably pay him mostly in food today, which should help him get his energy back up. I couldn't make out the driver's face, but as he turned the ignition and the music blared, I hoped it wasn't laced with hints of the psychotic again.

Like It or Not Here You Come

Labi chagdoni tanur
Omadai bachai zur.
"Man nameram, ocham!"
Mara mebarad ba zur.

At the edge of the earthen oven
The strong boy has come.
"I will not go, mother!"
He will carry me by force.[5]

Our impressive, president-defying wedding convoy had an uneventful late morning ride retracing our journey from the previous night. After thumping through a few villages whose mud-walled homes reminded of Barhiddin's, the cars came to a dusty halt near last night's sang-ob crossing point. I assumed the whole wedding party would be walking behind the vehicle caravan. With the ladies in elaborate korta dresses and high heels, this could prove an interesting river crossing. But Bahriddin, Muslimjon, and the mullah stayed put so I assumed I was once again misreading the situation. Perhaps we could navigate a more suitable passage in the daylight? Why then had we stopped?

A few moments later, some men and women from the other cars descended on ours with handfuls of frilly plastic flowers, red ribbon, and tape. They set to work on the hood. Suddenly it was a carnival! Our car would look good on arrival. Perhaps they had

waited to decorate until this moment in order to have the decorations look as neat and dust-free as possible when we pulled
up outside the father of the bride's home. It was a good theory.
Bahriddin, staring purposefully ahead, looked like he was in the
wedding zone so I didn't ask if my theory was correct. If only I
had brought a few smashed up cans and some string, I could have
shown them how this was done. What a dramatic clanking approach we could have made across the sang-ob. Who knows, we
might have even rustled up a wandering extremist group with all
that commotion.

With the decorations completed and the pit crew back in their
respective cars, our procession began to bump single file across the
riverbed. I wondered if it wouldn't have been better to decorate the
car after we had gotten across. At least the flowers were impervi-
ous to wilting. Well, unless the plastic was low-grade Chinese. We'd
have to wait and see on that.

Our car wound through the bride's village. Cresting the hill on
the approach to her father's gate, the car was suddenly surrounded
by a throng of villagers. We came to a halt beneath a massive tree,
somehow avoiding rolling over feet as the relatives and neighbors
pressed in on our cars. I followed as Bahriddin and Muslimjon ex-
ited boldly into the maelstrom.

A man near our car beat on a traditional tambourine. Ignoring
the jostling I took out the video camera to capture the scene. I
tried not to go into the sensory-overload-induced catatonic state
foreigners are especially susceptible to. Further up the road, the
bride's Yamaxa band began in on a pounding beat. From the
sound of it all, evidently the whole world knew we had arrived.

One of Bahriddin's cousins, who I had learned lived somewhere
on this dusty street, came over to stand beside me as I panned,
soaking in the three-hundred-and-sixty degree scene. I knew the
groom was supposed to bring a goat as a gift. I thought the goat was
supposed to be sacrificed upon arrival, so I leaned over and yelled

my question about where I could find this sacrificial goat. I wanted to record the ceremonial exchange and sacrifice. *"Bakshidem!"* (We forgave!) he screamed back at me over the incessant drumming and crowd noise. Taking that to mean there would be no goat or sacrifice to record, I spun around just in time to see Bahriddin and the rest of the wedding party disappearing in at the gate. I made haste to catch up, trying to suppress my increasingly overwhelmed feelings.

As I turned in at the metal gate and entered the yard, the decibels ratcheted up significantly. The Yamaxa was set to impress. I was glad the singer had a weak, electronically dependent voice or I was confident some eardrums would have certainly been lost in the confrontation.

A tight crowd of finely dressed women danced before Bahriddin in a proud, aloof manner that reminded me a bit of peacocks. Bahriddin stood stone faced between Muslimjon and another friend who had mercifully taken over as groomsman number two. A good choice. The new number two had a nice suit on. That certainly trumped me. Plus, he had the stolid, Tajik-wedding look down. I would have been smiling amicably at everyone, shirking somber formality and creating a massive faux pas of friendliness. Though he couldn't show it now, surely Bahriddin must have been relieved to have both flanks secure.

As I zoomed and zagged to get various shots amid the chaos, I felt relieved that all I had to worry about now was the possible revenge of my nemesis—the official videographer. He was busy at work across the yard. I kept my distance. After a while, we were shown inside to a special room where we sat for a few minutes. I hurriedly ate a bit of bread and soup as various things happened around me that I didn't understand. It was all quite tumultuous. Perhaps I wasn't the only one who was confused. Not likely, but it made me feel better to so hypothesize.

A short time later, I was back outside recording Bahriddin as he led his new bride out of the house towards the wailing band. The pressing crowd imperceptibly gave way as the couple literally inched toward the middle of the yard. She was wearing a white, Western-style wedding dress.

Strangely, the Tajiks have adopted the idea of the white wedding dress from the Russians. She would later return to her house to change into the traditional Tajik wedding burka. Picture the burka-clad Tajik bride as a Saudi Arabian woman and then replace the black sheet covering all but her eyes with flashes of color and an abundance of sequins. But she would wear this Western dress for the official government paper signing—a modern dress to fit the modern paperwork. It was a modest style with a long veil. They would even exchange rings, though they would return the borrowed pair to their owners the following day.

I had seen Bahriddin handle the ring situation, again in typical Tajik fashion, right before he had joined the bride to walk out for this ceremony. While sitting around picking at our soup, there had been a slight commotion as if the collective had just realized they would need a ring in the next five minutes. Fortunately a couple of people sitting around the table had rings on. The ring testing began in earnest with no discussion or brochures regarding the "Five C's" of buying diamonds.

It reminded me how after reading the book *Rich Christians in an Age of Hunger*, I had informed Ann with passionate, idealistic conviction that I would be buying her a simple engagement ring from a pawn shop. I probably even used the word cheap. Not one of my best courtship moves. I am happy I lived to tell the story.

Bahriddin's thick fingers proved a bit problematic, but fortunately a ringed cousin shared his finger genes. So the groom, outfitted with a ring with seconds to spare, arose prepared to join his bride. Meshavad! It will do!

Now in ceremonial position together, the bride's head was bowed, eyes on the ground in traditional Tajik fashion. Reciprocating in conventional groom fashion, Bahriddin stared blankly ahead, emotionless. I knew he was excited, but this stoicism was the unbending expectation. He was hiding his happiness well, I thought to myself. By looking at him I wouldn't have guessed he was interested in the proceedings at all.

They took up positions in front of the band. The hard-packed earthen yard was standing room only. From the looks of it, 120 percent of the village had come to the ceremony. Fortunately, no fire marshals were to be seen. A group of young girls, desperately in need of a few more extracurriculars, huddled together against the wall beside me. Their eyes were so wide I thought they might pop out. They had probably been looking forward to this wedding for months. It was probably the highlight of their year. I wondered if they had helped out by sewing some new pillows or dresses for the bride to take to her new home.

A few months ago Bahriddin, or more likely his representatives, had delivered beautiful material and a mountain of cotton along with the rest of the agreed-upon bride price. And in the consequent weeks, the bride and her community of helpers had quickly sown them into pillows, sleeping mats, and all the other essentials to properly establish her new home.

More or less fully recovered from *Rich Christians in an Age of Hunger*, Ann and I had registered at Target together using a cool laser-coding gun. This was fortunate as I'm not sure if Ann's neighbors would have wanted to come over every evening for a month to help make pillows from a mound of raw cotton. Bahriddin found our laser-registration-gun concept insurmountably odd, but intriguing. "It's all about the bar codes and resisting the urge to scan your eyes," I explained to him.

The wedding party had found their places. Bahriddin stood staring straight ahead. The bride, eyes transfixed on the ground, stood by his side, one of her hands delicately slipped through Bahriddin's left arm. At Bahriddin's right, Muslimjon stood as dispassionate as ever. A young girl, who I assumed was the maid of honor, completed the line as she stood demurely at the bride's left. Groomsman number two had been bumped, but still looked good in his suit standing nearby. The primary four stood staring out like zombies as the men looked on from the scene's edges and the prominent women peacocked around them.

I have never been able to get used to these Tajik wedding scenes. There is some unwritten law stating that a Tajik bride and groom must not show any emotion. Often you can watch them stand there like statues for hours as the dancing goes on and on and they will never crack a smile.

Men and women will dance up to the bride and groom and stick five- and ten-somoni bills in their hands or wedding hats. Still there is not a trace of human response. Personally, with the way some of the men groove on up with their cash I think I might die trying not to laugh. Perhaps the people give money out of astonishment at how statue-like the wedding pair have become. I, for one, admire the feat.

Indeed, typically the only emotion one will observe from the bride or the groom at a Tajik wedding is the usual despair and weeping through the veil onto the bridal shoes. As I recorded them standing there, Bahriddin's bride continued to look down at her feet in silence. I took the absence of tears as evidence that Bahriddin's bride was ecstatic. But to get to the conclusion of ecstatic from looking at her, you certainly had to do some cultural translation work.

A pause in the music allowed our officiating mullah and a few prominent people to take the microphone for various charges, poems, and flowery addresses. Tajiks love using exceedingly melodramatic intonation and form. It usually strikes me as about the cruising altitude of a 747 over the top and in the same vein as peacock dancing. They use this stylized accent that grates on me. Every time I hear it, I always feel like it would be like me getting up at a wedding back home and giving a speech with a British accent, not for a laugh, but to impress.

Bahriddin's Wedding

All this formality and seriousness pervading every aspect of Tajik weddings is so different than where I come from. Back home in America, I wouldn't be surprised to see people getting married wearing swimming trunks amid the general ruckus of a pool party. Sometimes I wonder if it is only a matter of time before I witness Americans getting married while sitting down in some comfy his-and-her matching recliners enjoying a light snack during the ceremony. Our cultures seem to be at opposite extremes. They're being strangled by stuffiness and we've oozed into a puddle of casualness we might never have the conviction or upper body strength to rise from.

And marriage expectations between our two cultures are even more divergent than the wedding moods. Basically, Tajik grooms and their mothers expect hard-working brides with fruitful wombs. Americans, on the other hand, seem to expect perpetual heaven on earth.

With such a chasm between our astonishingly high and their incredibly low expectations of marriage, one would expect divorce rates to be much higher in the US than they are in Tajikistan. And from my casual observations the US does seem to dominate in the arena of divorce. When you add the fact that Americans often seem to define love as one's strongest physical attraction at the present time it is actually surprising that the US doesn't have a bigger edge in this area of divorce than it already does. It's hard to see how a definition of love as shallow and dehumanizing as that could ever lead to a joyful, enduring marriage. On the other side of the world, Tajiks don't usually have love, regardless of how it is defined, as an expectation at all, which seems to work in a depressing contractual way most of the time.

I panned from the speechmakers back to the bride and groom. I zoomed down on the feet thinking I might get the action of a foot stepping. No luck. I would have to be vigilant to capture one of those. After they had signed the government papers, the bride retreated to the house, later to reemerge in traditional Tajik wedding garb. It was clear she could not see a thing in her burka—her burka that covered her entire body including her eyes. This time as Bahriddin took her arm, I realized it was out of necessity. Through the elaborately decorated burka, she could see nothing but her feet. She was dependent on Bahriddin for her next step. Somewhere under her impenetrable garb, her hair was woven with milk-dipped cotton. Earlier we had watched as women braided the dripping white cotton into her hair. I assumed this was done to symbolize purity.

All ceremonies finished, the new couple made their way toward the waiting car just outside the gate. They would take the car we had come in, leaving groomsmen one, two and, due to my demotion, myself at number three. We'd have to find another way back. Men weaved through the watching crowd carrying loads of new pillows and flowery korpacha mats. They stacked them up against the high, wood-planked sides of a rusty green truck. Hopefully the motor had not been replaced with wood as well. I could see the ornately decorated sanduk wedding trunk secured near the back.

All was music and commotion as the chauffeur bore Bahriddin and his bride away. I found a spot in another car and was soon on my way back as well. I noticed a large group beginning the long, dusty walk. That looked like more fun. Maybe next time.

When my car arrived back at Bahriddin's, our own Yamaxa-led band was in full swing. The bride had already been taken into seclusion behind a curtain in a private room within the house somewhere. Perhaps if I visited Bahriddin in a couple of months I could actually meet her. It was doubtful I would make her acquaintance on a return visit and I would certainly never ask to meet her, but perhaps if Ann and Grace came with me next time they would have the chance to meet Bahriddin's new bride. For today though, his new bride sat wearing a veiled burka behind a curtain. She would make no further appearance.

Bahriddin's Wedding

There was a lull in activity as Bahriddin's younger brother prepared to repeat the process. Accompanied by his own entourage, he would soon go for his own bride. Assuming I would not be included in that, I wandered past the steaming cauldrons and kettles and began to climb the hill towards the high barley fields rising steeply behind the house.

The music slowly faded as I ascended to a good height on the sloping field. Up here, the view would be good. As I turned to look back down at the buzzing village below, I noticed that one of Bahriddin's countless cousins was following me up. I stood waiting, enjoying the panorama of rolling hills as he approached.

A couple minutes later we were standing together looking out over the fall countryside so in need of the November rains. We took the opportunity to get to know each other better. He was short with a slender build and broad smile. His features were European, like Bahriddin's. We spoke about the new water pipe that we could see running over the hills and down the slope to the pump in Bahriddin's yard. We decided it should certainly be put in a trench and buried to protect it, and that definitely before winter.

As we talked of this and that and he attempted to practice a little bit of his halting English, I began to eagerly seek an opportunity in our conversation to share the gospel. The moment seemed right. But then, surprisingly, he began to talk about how his parents were not actually villagers. They were in Kazakhstan doing something of importance. When he added that he worked for the KGB up in Dushanbe, I stopped looking for opportunities.

There is an internal battle we face here where we stick out like evangelistic sore thumbs in a sea of Islam. It rages over the relationship between faith in God's sovereignty and my own discernment. As we are instructed in James, I pray for God's promised wisdom, ever striving to believe and not doubt. I try to examine myself closely, never wanting to label my fears as wisdom or discernment.

Boldness and common sense battle daily. I tell myself as long as I keep the gospel low key, sharing selectively and carefully, the odds increase for us to be able to stay here indefinitely and rarely lose friends or make enemies. I warn myself that I should not be responsible for getting myself, my team, and my entire NGO of over fifty foreigners dismissed from the country.

I know this same internal debate rages in all of us who have come to Tajikistan with good news. We have come to love the Tajiks. One aspect of our love is to meet their physical needs with solid humanitarian help. But the gospel is the core, the jewel, the vital reason we have come. The glorious gospel has transformed our lives. We must proclaim it to others. If it is not proclaimed, all other good works seem to fade rapidly toward an ultimate meaninglessness. Yes, we must bring water to the thirsty. But infinitely greater is their need for living water or they will die of spiritual thirst.

I believe in living water. I believe you can hold this water up to another man's mouth so that he can drink of grace just as you did before him. I would be unspeakably evil to withhold this spiritual water, especially if I am engaged in making the physical aspects of the man healthier. I am reminded that every patient a doctor sees eventually dies, that every person we might feed or clothe will one day breathe their last. It is clear that we must minister to the whole man. Christ must be made known. He alone is life.

In this internal struggle for discernment, I find myself sharing with this friend, but not that one because he works at the government. I'll invite this group of neighbors to our Christmas outreach to hear the gospel, but not that particular neighbor because he's wealthy and his brother has clout. Yes, I'll answer my student's spiritual question, but not until after class. Or perhaps I should wait one year until he turns sixteen so it won't be illegal to have such a conversation with him.

So much of ministry in Muslim lands seems to be one-on-one. This is both so that they have the confidence to really engage with the gospel and also for our longevity. On the other hand, we must be bold. Everyone on our team feels strongly that it is absolutely essential to establish our identity as evangelistic Christians in our apartment buildings, our friendship circles, and our broader communities so people will know who we are and who we live for. Then those God might be drawing will know where to come.

Beneath the small talk about my family and his, my humanitarian work, and his KGB job up in the big city, my familiar, internal battle waged. I decided to let the opportunity pass by this time. We stood for a time speaking of lesser things. After a while, we decided Bahriddin's brother would be coming back soon with his new bride. We began our descent together. As we followed the footpath back down, I was wondering if I had done the right thing. I didn't know. At least I had not been swallowed up by indifference. I would choose this angst over ever-creeping, malignant apathy any and every day. I pray by God's grace I always will.

Shortly after our return to the wedding festivities, the convoy arrived, carrying Bahriddin's brother and his new bride in the brightly decorated lead car. Before it came to a full stop near the dance floor, the ever-growing throng of villagers had already pressed in touching the car on every side. There must have been a couple of hundred people there at the car to welcome them.

Saifuddin, as stone-faced as his brother had been earlier, forced his way out into the music-filled chaos, helping his heavily veiled, completely covered new bride follow him out. Unable to see anything but her feet, she grasped tightly to his arm.

A man carrying a big knife forced a panic-stricken goat through the crowd and right up against the legs of the new couple. With the help of another man holding the goat and fending off the aggressive crowd, he bent over the bleating animal. Using his legs as a vise he grasped the goat tight and sliced its ear, letting blood pour out onto the ground before the bride and groom as they advanced. I imagine the shed blood symbolized consecration for the new marriage.

The goat's blood dripped upon the ground of what would be their new home together.

The smothering crowd parted to let a group of Bahriddin's family's closest women lead the way dancing proudly, arms uplifted in front of the new couple. The couple followed the dancers across the blood-sprinkled ground taking up a standing position in front of the new bride's sanduk. All of the new flowery sleeping mats were on display stacked on top of the ornately flamboyant sanduk. Just as Bahriddin and his bride had done a few hours before, the second couple stood together for a few minutes in front of their wedding bounty. Slowly the women relatives gave way for other friends and neighbors to dance before the new couple. The dancers stuck money in the bride and groom's hats, hands, or wherever they could find to put it. The bridesmaid helped collect. When the dancing lulled, they retired to a prepared room in the house where a veil of seclusion had been prepared for this new bride—the second of the day. I wasn't sure if the two brides would be in seclusion together or not.

It appears to be custom for the bridesmaid to stay on and sit behind the curtain with the bride for the first night, not leaving her side until the next morning. As I understood it then, it would not be until the second night that the new couples would consummate their marriages. I wonder if Tajiks have this tradition of the bridesmaid staying the first night in order to lessen the stress and make the transition to a strange new home and unknown man a little bit easier.

Sometimes Tajiks will use a cloth on the consummation night to test if the new bride is truly a virgin. Reminiscent of Deuteronomy, if she bleeds, the cloth becomes the precious evidence of her purity. If she does not bleed, she will most likely be cast off. She will be returned to her father's house the following day where, as tarnished goods, she will either eventually become someone's lesser second wife or despairingly remain living in her father's house in lifelong shame.

Bahriddin's Wedding

Of course there is no similar way to measure the purity of the man. Not that the Tajiks would, even if they could. The prevailing attitude seems to be that a woman must be untainted, but a man is just a man and reciprocal attainment cannot possibly be expected.

Though I hate the cloth practice, sometimes I feel it reflects a superior view of both men and women than we are gradually adopting in the West. The practice of the cloth, while not setting an equal standard, at least reflects some vestige of human dignity. It appears to me that purity matters in Tajikistan because humans matter. When humanity is sacred, when humanity has a creator, there can exist such things as purity and honor.

The West cannot even comprehend the cloth. Naively, we are overjoyed to be free from law, not realizing we have fled from grace as well. When a culture shakes free from God, the possibility of knowing truth, and a morality set firmly upon these, then it is forced to embrace the fruit of its worldview. The fruit of the general Western worldview seems logically to lead slowly, but surely toward nihilism. We are all free. We are all correct. We are all accidents. We are all meaningless.

Could it be that Tajikistan has a higher view of women than the West? Could that possibly be? As I observe the random drifting of Western culture, I seem to find myself wondering more and more.

Soon after the second bride had been taken into seclusion, Ann arrived with our daughter Grace. They were accompanied by some of our teammates and a few of our Tajik staff. Our group was shown special honor by being seated inside to recline on the floor around a lavish dustarxon. We enjoyed a generous meal.

With a bowl of Russian chocolates within her reach, predictably our two-year-old daughter, Grace, had a little more sugar than we would have liked. Unable to open the wrappers herself, every time she grabbed a new one she would turn to Sitora and beg, "*Aela! Aela!*" ("Open! Open!") Grace knew instinctively our friendly youth center teacher would be much more likely to honor her requests than her parents would be. Sitora eagerly obliged, placing Grace on her lap to more easily supply her excited charge with a constant flow of sweets. By the look of Grace's smeared chocolate cheeks and beaming brown smile, Ann and I decided Grace might not share our displeasure at the developments.

Ann and I knew we would not be able to stay for too long. Some of our teammates and Tajik coworkers would stay until late. My buddy Sam, sitting beside me at the dustarxon, was practicing his congratulatory wedding speech. He had peppered it with specially selected Tajik poetry.

Later on in the evening at a break in the dancing, he would take the microphone and offer Bahriddin his blessing. We shared a laugh as he imitated and embellished the ostentatious style expected during such speeches. Sam hoped to include a seed of the gospel in his speech. Perhaps he could speak to the crowd of how our Kitobi Mukadas (Holy Book) defines love in 1 Corinthians:

> Love is patient, love is kind. It does not envy, it does not boast, it is not proud. It is not rude, it is not self-seeking, it is not easily angered, it keeps no record of wrongs. Love does not delight in evil but rejoices with the truth. It always protects, always trusts, always hopes, always perseveres. Love never fails. (1 Cor 13:4–8)

It was not difficult to see that these five verses could revolutionize Tajik life if they would only allow Christ through the Holy Spirit to begin to make this kind of love a reality in their lives and marriages. I have seen Tajiks basically go into shock as they try to process this passage. They've never heard or read anything like it. I prayed for similar results tonight. I prayed for Sam. I prayed for boldness. I prayed for open hearts.

After awhile Ann and Grace were graciously invited to go in and meet the secluded brides. Ann jumped up and gathered Grace eagerly. I watched as they followed their hostess out of the room. They looked so cute together, both dressed in traditional Tajik kortas. On their way out of the room, Ann hurriedly straightened her headscarf and made sure Grace was clean of all visible chocolate. Grace's eyes opened wide, pleased at the simple adventure of going through a doorway. She looked adorable in Ann's arms, dressed in the tiny Tajik dress our neighbor had made for her out of some traditional material. I wish I had been able to see Grace's face as she saw the real princesses. I wondered how much she would understand.

The three of us eventually reunited outside to watch the dancing for a little while. The celebration was in full swing. More interested in some chicks, Grace chased the precious fuzz balls around the apple trees as we stood listening to the music.

We had arranged to head back toward Kadimobod early. We hoped to leave before Grace fully metamorphosed into a *kadu* (pumpkin), as Tajiks call the orange gourd. Tajiks do not know the story of Cinderella and we certainly didn't want a screaming Grace to explain the concept to them. So our family soon said our good-byes. With hands over our hearts, we bid farewell to whoever we could find amid the crowd. I received a few hugs from Bahriddin's relatives. I suppose we had grown closer this weekend. They seemed to feel it too.

"Nameshined? Nameshined?" ("Won't you sit?") came the echoing polite refrain from the family as we slowly made our way toward the waiting car. I said a short, stiff goodbye to Bahriddin as we left. He was in robot mode and difficult to get to with all the dancing, but I knew he was very happy I had shared all of this with him. So was I. I looked forward to sharing a better reminiscence of the proceedings when he returned to the office. He'd certainly be asking for a copy of the video I'd taken.

Grace stared—enthralled—at the dancers, the drums, and the music wafting out over the darkening village as we made our way to the car. As the evening advanced and with both brides secured in private rooms, the celebration gathered intensity. The ever-growing crowd danced to the pounding, electric, Yamaxa-dominated music. Groups squatted down to share steaming plates of osh wherever a bit of open ground could be found. Near the dance floor, the two grooms looked out over the crowd. They would stand on the out-skirts until late into the night temperately observing, respectfully acknowledging the honor the guests showed them by dancing.

As our taxi carried us away, the music fought valiantly for su-premacy, but eventually gave way completely to the gentle sounds of the night. Exhausted, Grace soon fell asleep in Ann's arms, soundly dozing through the incessant bumping. We hit the main road and began swiftly rolling through the ever-descending hills back towards Kadimobod. As I stared out the window, I knew I had left part of my heart with my friends up in these Tajik hills. I knew I would never forget my brother Bahriddin's wedding.

I did not know the future. I did not know how the Spirit would work. Perhaps the gospel would eventually cause Bahriddin to reject our friendship or perhaps my heart's desire would be fulfilled and Christ would become the eternal foundation of the deepest, truest brotherhood of all.

IX
SCHOOL DAYS

On Lessons and Their Avoidance

So much of our lives in Tajikistan revolve around lessons. We give lessons. We receive lessons. We pray to meet people open to Bible lessons. We hope for good foot speed and agility reminiscent of Barry Sanders in order to flee university students who chase us demanding twenty hours per week of personal English lessons. Ann and I have our daily *darsi Tojiki* (Tajik lesson). Ann gives Grace her *darsi xonagi* (homeschool lesson). I run here and there giving *darshoi Inglisi* (English lessons), *darshoi varzishi* (sports lessons), and *darshoi Kitobi Mukadas* (Bible lessons). And of course all the while, as a foreigner, I'm receiving heavy doses of *darshoi zindagi* (life lessons).

When I slip my shoes on by the door each morning, before I head over to the youth center offices, my familiar last sight is of Ann at the family room table pouring over a pile of language books with her Tajik tutor while Grace and Silas hone their own skills in the living room with their strictly Tajik-speaking nanny.

As I sling my backpack over my shoulder, I'm reminded of my pile of Tajik books. Despite the weight, I'm thankful. The first year we were here, we couldn't find a good Tajik-English or English-Tajik dictionary. Now with a solid grammar, a couple of newly published dictionaries, and a few other excellent resources we have scrounged up, I was happy to suffer a bit under the weight as I made the short trudge to the office.

Was it my imagination or was that group of university students I passed in front of our office building eyeing me? I swear the local university's English faculty equip their students with native-English-speaker identification flash cards or steal pieces of our clothing and train their students to recognize our scent.

Ignoring the smashed-in elevators and crumbling stair edges ever further removed from Soviet salad days, I hastily double-staired it all the way up to the third floor before daring to glance back to see if I was being followed. This time it appeared I had gotten away free and clear. I often end up having to have the twenty-minute conversation, my "cruelty deficiency syndrome" dooms me to repeat over and over for all eternity. The gist of this conversation between me and the university student always goes something like the following:

Student: "Hello, *Aka* (dear brother)!" (*With such enthusiasm that I know I either make a run for it now or face the worst.*)

Me: "Um, hello . . . " (*Trying to avoid eye contact and scanning for escape routes.*)

Student: "You are America?"

Me: "Um, well, yes, something like that, unfortunately."

Student: "You meet me! I am student! I am study language English! Each day you meet me! I am study language English! Please, Aka! You teach me three hours for each day."

Me: "Well, I'm sorry, but I already have over one hundred students. I have classes. I'm so sorry, but I don't even have time to do what I need to do already so I can't be your teacher."

Student: "Is okay. Is okay. Understand. When you home go? I come every day when come you home."

Me: "Uhhh, well, no, thank you."

Student: "You don't work some days? Then teach me! Every Sunday we learn six hours. It is enough. Six hours only."

School Days

Me: "You know, uh, that sounds great but it's just not going to work. I have a family and . . . "

Of course the conversation never ends there. Being afflicted with this softhearted disease, I seldom escape in less than twenty minutes. And they usually show up at our apartment with a dictionary later on making me wonder if perhaps I hadn't been firm enough. Ann rolls her eyes not so subtly suggesting "wimp" as she informs me we have yet another dictionary-toting visitor at the door. The eye roll usually makes me feel pretty self-conscious as I know that somewhere in the other room, Ann is listening in as I begin in on my next thirty-minute attempt to say no. Perhaps it will be better to say no over tea. I'd better get the tea myself.

Of course this natural magnetism to half our town's university students can also be quite a blessing. An informal English club can be a great way to make friends and share the gospel. And as we've found in our over 99 percent Muslim society, the gospel is, unfortunately, often a great way to offset the English magnetism.

Safe on the third floor for now, I stopped for a moment to catch my breath. The guys from the architecture department were on a smoke break out in the hall. Fortunately, most of the large windows no longer have any glass. In the spring, summer, and early fall, the wind-tunneled halls are refreshing. The pigeons and bats think so too. And let me just say that I am thankful for the precision of echolocation in a way I have never been before. The bats don't stick around in winter. On January office days when I'm huddled at a desk shaking, I feel they are clearly the higher mammal.

I spent the next hour and a half in one of our youth center's Spartan classrooms having my Tajik lesson with my language teacher, Safar. We passed the time negotiating nuances and jotting down this and that in my Tajik penmanship, which oddly enough is better than my English scribbling. I chalk up my improved pen craft to the fact that twenty some years after my first go-round, I'm more interested in learning how to write than in the joys of recess. Well, some days I am at any rate.

Safar, my fifth or sixth teacher, was lucky. By now my language proficiency was high enough that we could talk about most anything from politics to poetry. At the other end of the spectrum, I remember feeling so bad for my first Tajik language teacher. The poor man had to endure around two hours per day of "This is a brown dog. This is a blue dog. This is a yellow dog. This is a green dog." And repeat.

Often he would go into this sort of waking coma where he would respond to my eternal, banal barrages from somewhere near the limits of human consciousness. On Fridays, feeling the need to have mercy on him and help him regain his humanity, I'd mix it up. We'd play Tajik Scrabble. I made the game from cardboard, totally guessing about letter frequency and point values. Man, I got trounced in those games. But I could hardly have been surprised. After all, you can't expect to win Scrabble feeling stretched by the words "this," "is," "a," "blue," and "dog." Well, technically I suppose there is no indefinite article in Tajik. So there goes 20 percent of my vocabulary.

Now with a few years of Tajik under my belt, sometimes Safar and I would discuss topics like education. He had graduated a couple of years back from the English faculty of our town's university. Though by now Tajik was far and away the superior medium for our communication, he had fought valiantly to learn English during his university years. That was admirable since it was certainly less than an ideal educational setting.

He hadn't distinguished himself enough to be one of the few elite students who land lucrative translation positions at one of the many international non-governmental organizations (NGOs) that operate in Tajikistan. Believe it or not, these translator positions seem to be the best jobs in town. So much so that when I asked my high school students at the youth center to write a short essay in English about what they hoped to be when they grew up, by far the most common response was "an English translator for an NGO." Surprisingly, "Bollywood star" finished a distant second. So at least in our part of Tajikistan it appeared that joining the English faculty was potentially a more lucrative career move than pursuing a law or medical degree. And maybe it was even a more tempting option than a move to Mumbai.

Unfortunately for the Tajik rich kids, these crazy foreign NGOs always insist on hiring based on merit, spurning the immensely popular bribe and family-connection methods. Strangely, these NGOs actually seem to care that the applicant be able to do his or her job. This meritorious reality has thrown the Tajik system into such an upheaval that it has even caused the students in the English department to study.

Not landing one of the heavily contested NGO spots, Safar had found the next best thing. Embracing the family-connection method, his wealthy uncle had gotten him a job stocking shelves at the first chain grocery store Kadimobad has ever known. It's called Orima. I believe the chain has European ties. With Orima came our town's first bar-scanning checkout counter. The counter made big waves in Kadimobod. On several of my Orima trips I have observed that Tajiks seem to enjoy going into the store and buying one small item just for the exotic thrill of hearing the beep. If money is especially tight, they can still hang out and watch others' purchases make the magical noise. I like it too. My enjoyment is not found in the novelty of course, but in the rush of nostalgia that washes over me as the items slide over the fabulous sensor. Just imagine, if my purchases hit the internet, they might live on forever as evidence to the fact that our family really likes Russian breakfast cereals.

But before getting too excited over Kadimobod's shopping possibilities, one word of caution for the reader: never shop at Orima when Kadimobod's electricity is off. If you do, one of Safar's aunts will have to write down all the bar code numbers on your purchases so they can type them in manually when the electricity thumps back on. And yes, that process is as painful as it sounds. So basically, you are wise to avoid Orima from November through March unless you are willing to sprint to Orima every time your apartment electricity happens to come on in order to see if Orima's did as well. Like most everything in Kadimobod, this is not an efficient use of time. Therefore, the smart Orima shopper stocks up in October before the first gentle fall rains wreak havoc on the whole universe.

But the reader need not worry about remembering this advice as Kadimobod's Orima closed. The managers—realizing that apart from Ann and me there was virtually no local demand for canned tuna and potato chips—packed up their magical scanner and called it quits. Being closed saves Orima quite a bit on electricity costs, though not as much as one would expect.

But Safar hadn't stayed at Orima until the bitter end when the regionally famous scanner beeped its last and Kadimobod made a clean break from bar codes and the absurdly foreign idea of pet food. In market research, they should have noted that pet food doesn't sell well without the prerequisite concept of pets. No, Safar had hated his boss so he quit a few months before that fateful day. I hoped for Safar's sake that his boss wasn't a relative. And suddenly I could see yet another benefit of the merit hiring system.

Now free of Orima, Safar, the father of two small children, looked to me and our five to ten hours of lessons per week for his sole income. So he was in enthusiastic agreement when I told him I had time for an extra-long lesson today. I had extra time because my university student friends, lured in by the illusion of education, were off picking cotton. On threat of expulsion from Kadimobod University, my friends had been forcibly rounded up by their professors, piled into the backs of rusty trucks, and sent off to distant regions for a few weeks to pick cotton. Of course pay was not part of the obligatory equation.

School Days

Today was Thursday and Thursday was usually my sports night with the university guys. Every Thursday evening after work my two American teammates and I meet a group of university guys outside the office. Depending on the season, our big enthusiastic group would meander over to the park for some American football or hike down to the valley for ultimate Frisbee, soccer, or volleyball.

Since we seem to be cursed with the sadistic urge to constantly introduce new sports, we have found that having a critical mass of university guys who have played with us in past years goes a long way toward having a successful outing. "Successful" could be roughly defined as only ten to twenty minutes of explaining to newcomers about the imaginary line known as "scrimmage." Newcomers soon learn the seriousness of this invisible line. They must constantly know the location of this line in order to count to five *kurboka* (frog) before crossing it to slap the guy with the ball, not with one, but with two firm hands. To make their heads spin even more we introduce the concept of *blitz kardan* (to do blitz) explaining they have one blitz per set of downs. "What's a down? Why ten meters?" And suddenly their horseback sport of *buzkashi* with the decapitated goat seems beautiful in its simplicity.

But with all our college buddies suffering to get a few bushels per day amid endless cotton fields near Afghanistan, we had decided it would be best to cancel Thursday sports for a few weeks. So Safar and I had a bit more wiggle room within the Thursday schema. We had a good lesson. After Safar left, I even had time to study for a while.

From where I sat studying, I could look out my third-floor window down onto school number six. From up here, apart from the decay of the facility itself, it looked respectable enough. Unfortunately, our neighbor children go there so I am well aware of the actual state of affairs. Every fall during the first week of school Kadimobod's streets fill with the sharpest-looking students a person could ever hope to find. Droves of white-shirted, dark-slacked boys interspersed with throngs of white-bloused, navy- or black-skirted girls descend on the schools like locusts. Reflecting the local interplay of Islam and modernity, the girls wear modest pants underneath their skirts. The spotless students make their way proudly to first lessons. Or more accurately, they make their way proudly to the playground where they will stand in various lines for about three or four weeks while the school scrambles to find and refind teachers who are repeatedly wandering off. They will also use the early weeks to enter into book-buying negotiations with students and every other activity under the sun except teaching.

After about four weeks of students standing in lines and messing around, the school is just about staffed and squared away. By early October, when the school is usually ready to begin what they consider to be a serious regimen of lessons, the cotton season hits full throttle. This seems to throw things into a general upheaval with groups of students constantly walking or being bused to nearby picking fields until the middle of November. I suppose it's hard to resist free labor.

And even when it's not cotton-picking season, it is certainly not a given that teaching will go on. In Tajikistan, I have grown accustomed to seeing the neighbor kids meandering back to their apartments about two hours after they have left for school. I ask the kids about this, ask them why they are home already. Some common explanations are that only one of their four teachers was there today or that the school told them they should get some rest because tomorrow they would be needed for yard work or preparing flowerbeds in the park just in case the president or another important guest were to stop by Kadimobod. But by far the most common answer I am given is, "I don't know." Nobody ever seems to know what's going on over there at school number six. I sure don't.

Because Tajikistan's school system is overrun with many more children than the infrastructure can handle, Tajik students only study half a day to begin with. The students come in two shifts, morning and afternoon. You'd hope they'd at least make it to the end of their shift!

But with a monthly salary equivalent to the approximate cost of a big bag of flour, teachers certainly can't afford to teach. So I suppose they can hardly be blamed for not showing up if they find more lucrative work for a few days. Then there is the problem that even when the stars align and the teachers happen to be there, the two extremes of classroom management are as follows: 1) none and 2) demanding absolute silence on pain of beatings. The latter method is the Tajik ideal. In the resource-starved schools, absolute silence creates the perfect atmosphere for the rote memorization which is the Tajik educational model. But considering the chaos that characterizes most Tajik schools, there seems to be very little of the ideal going on. This makes for fewer bruises, but also less education.

The grey-haired Kadimobod men frown at the mayhem and reminisce about the good old days when the Soviets ran the education system. My friend Akai Mumin, who I estimate is approaching seventy, loves to talk about the Soviet glory days. Back then there was discipline, education, and even extracurricular activities, like sports leagues. He loves talking about those sports leagues. He's shared more than a couple stories about when his collective farm dominated some tournament or another against the neighboring collective farms.

In fact, Akai Mumin loves to recollect so much that if I have less than forty-five minutes free, I make eye contact with him at the peril of my to-do list. On one such occasion when I was sucked into the familiar vortex of the Soviet time machine with Akai Mumin, he told me a story about a local Kadimobod teacher who he seemed to hold up as his ideal.

Most importantly, this teacher of the bygone days of discipline was *zur*. "Zur" basically means powerful, dominant, and strong. Tajiks adore people who are zur. In soccer this means you must pass the ball to the biggest guy every time you touch it so he won't scream at you, not that I'm bitter. Anyway, one day a student was being disrespectful to Akai Mumin's friend, the powerful zur teacher. The teacher grabbed the discourteous pupil and dragged him over to the second-story window where he proceeded to hold him out the window by his ankles. The teacher dangled him there until he thought the boy had been sufficiently scarred.

When I heard this story my first reaction was to bask in the superiority of the American educational system. But then I remembered the American educational system. Most parts of our educational system are phenomenal, but I have also seen parts of our system that make Akai Mumin's story look like cotton candy.

Of course in America, land of increasingly bizarre, self-evident, relative truths and inalienable rights, it wouldn't be the teacher holding the student out the window. That would be reversed. In America, the student would be holding the teacher by his heels out the second-story window. And the dangling teacher might mumble a prayer to himself hoping that the student wouldn't get hurt in the altercation for fear he would lose his job or get sued. And after being pulled back in the window, the insanity would probably continue with the American teacher thoroughly checking the student's palms for bruising. If bruising were to be found on the student, then the teacher would feverishly devote himself to filling out the proper paperwork, complete with little red arrows pointing at the palms of the sketched form. Then he'd get a coworker witness to sign it as soon as possible. Can anyone say "insanity"?

At the school I worked at in the States for a couple of years, our staff would have probably been hanging out the windows regularly if not for the three bouncers our school employed; they were well trained in the classic Greek pedagogical techniques of weightlifting and "safe" restraint forms. I thought this was a bit unnecessary until I had my shirt nearly ripped off by a student. Fortunately, one of our bouncers was nearby to save my scrawny hide with an inspiring, lawsuit-resistant hold.

School Days

Tajik students, for all their rambunctious behavior, would never even think to try such a thing as ripping the shirt off their teacher. In fact, I have found attendance star charts are still incredibly motivating among my Tajik high school students. They like to put the stars by their names.

When I get past my initial shock, it's actually very cute to see our Tajik high schoolers standing around the chart whispering to each other about how many stars they have. After introducing the star chart, which by the way, offered something like a new pencil at the end of the semester as a reward, attendance at the youth center soared.

By way of contrast, I think I could be in immediate danger of at least verbal if not physical abuse if I tried introducing a star chart to a high school class back home. When word got out about the star chart, the school might even have to reinforce their perimeter by doubling the metal detectors.

The fact that there is no need of a metal detector at any school in the entire country of Tajikistan must be an indication of something important. America should get an expert on that right away. He might want to consider bringing backup to his study though. And if he wants intense data, he might consider passing out sparkle pencils to American high schoolers.

I remember trying to explain to some of my Tajik friends how we would use the metal detector wand to thoroughly search each student before allowing them into the school where I used to work in America.

Students: "Why would you do that?"
Me: "So they won't bring weapons into the school."
Students: "Why would they bring weapons into the school?"
Me: "So they can kill each other, I guess."
Students: "Why would they kill each other?"

I never really have a simple answer to that last one other than something like, "Because that's what we do in America." Ironically, the guys I had this conversation with, showing courageous resolve, still hold up America as the ideal society and consider reaching it by whatever means possible to be their highest goal.

As for me, I'm pretty convinced the chances of getting killed or maimed in the classroom are much lower in Tajikistan than America. Granted, in Tajikistan you have to watch out for holes in the floor big enough to usher you into the netherworld. But since you can pretty much ignore threats from your students, you can fully concentrate on testing the floorboards. Holes are more predictable.

Murder, after all, is still personal in Tajikistan. In America it is not unheard of for murder to be random, a raging against society in general. In Tajikistan, murder still has motives that most of us would recognize as normal for humanity down through the centuries. Cain killed his brother because jealously and hatred bubbled up within him. That is normal, evil humanity at work. That is still homicide in Tajikistan, the universal variety for the human race. I have never heard of Tajiks randomly blasting complete strangers to bits in schools and bazaars. And if that did happen, I would immediately assume there was some political motive. It seems apparent to me that it is primarily in the West that violence breaks out of senseless despair without many rational hints of personal, religious, or political motive.

I'm reminded of the time I went up to Omaha, Nebraska, to meet some Tajik students who were there studying. An American friend and I drove up and met a few of them. We spent most of our time getting to know two Tajik guys who had been studying in Omaha for around two years. Sadly, both of them had personal stories of brushes with violence in their dangerous new world.

They both work at gas stations. As an American, when I learned this I was not surprised in the least by their stories. One of the guys, Rahmatulloh, often closes the station at night. First, Rahmatulloh told me about his Tajik friend who was robbed and knocked unconscious at his gas station job. Then he told me about the time he was closing the store when a man came in and put a gun to his head. Amazingly, Rahmatulloh still closes at the same gas station. I really hope he survives America. He's not off to a good start.

Then Rahmatulloh's roommate, Jamshed, told me about the day he arrived in Omaha. Arriving by bus from New York, he was welcomed to Omaha in foreboding style. He arrived in Nebraska the day of a shooting rampage at the Westroads Mall. Everywhere Jamshed turned, he heard that some random mass shooter had just killed eight people and then himself inside this upscale Omaha mall.

I felt shame welling up inside of me as Jamshed related how he went to sleep that first night in Omaha wondering what in the world he had gotten himself into by coming to study in America. I hope the Tajiks studying in New York are finding America to be a friendlier place than the ones studying in Omaha. And suddenly the melting pot metaphor is beginning to sound scary to me. Boil the new arrivals?

It didn't make me feel any better when Rahmatulloh related how he had tried to get some information from the gas station patrons last Fourth of July. He asked them, "So this is Independence Day? Independence from whom?" He said he got mostly blank stares on that one. Again he asked, "When did this independence start?" with even poorer results. He laughed as he told me all this. I wondered if he had known the answers to these questions before he asked them and only asked them as sort of an experiment in American stupidity for his amusement.

After all these shameful revelations, I remember feeling strangely happy when we sat down to eat dinner and I realized that Rahmatulloh and Jamshed didn't have forks in their apartment. Evidently, they'd been eating by hand for over a year. I knew they had probably chosen to eat by hand to keep their connection with home, but I hung on to the idea of forks and spoons as some inventions to be proud of in that moment when I was feeling rather ashamed of my own home. Additionally, I was proud that the Tajik students up in Omaha are enamored with the malls and local Chinese buffet. America can certainly do utensils, buffets, and consumerism like nobody else!

At least I had a few things to be proud of. So I felt better after dinner as I watched Rahmatulloh blow his way through an abandoned warehouse, shooting Nazis and ravenous dogs point blank in the head. Personally, I thought the money they had spent on their PlayStation system or whatever it was would have been better spent on forks, although perhaps Rahmatulloh felt he needed the training for his gas station job.

Reflecting on my years in Tajikistan, I realize that I have become so accustomed to hearing about and voyeuristically witnessing incredible violence in America that when Tajiks talk about "ripping each other to pieces," as an often-used local expression goes, I find it a bit funny. They speak so fiercely, and then I see a small scuffle or nothing at all. Tajiks seem so innocent compared to Americans. I'm used to trench coat clad boys coming to school with multiple firearms and intricate plans made in hopes of maximizing their opportunity to kill the most people. So to see how Tajiks get so upset about little incidents sometimes strikes me as amusing.

My students' scuffles remind me of when I used to fight in my neighborhood when I was little. I know my amusement at my students' skirmishes is a sinful response, but it is interesting how skewed I have become growing up in the violence-laden cultural and entertainment landscape of the United States. Far from terrorism, every last one of my Muslim Tajik students seems so innocent compared to what I have witnessed in fierce America, where like animals it has become instinctual in too many communities to avert eye contact so as not to come across as aggressive.

Threats, Beatings, Flights, and Such

Some mornings and most afternoons are a whirl of lessons at our youth center. We have tried our best to sift through the applicants each year to find the Tajik children who are truly poor and need the additional help of our free lessons. For the most part we have screened them adequately as most of our hundred or so students are very poor. A majority of our students have one or no living parents. To read through their profiles, filled with the bits of information we have gleaned about their life situations over the years, always shocks me. I find the knowledge gives me much more patience with them. I remind myself of this when I am frustrated they didn't do the English paragraph I assigned on their greatest role model—i.e., Bollywood star—or when they take ten steps on their way to the hoop for that layup we've been practicing for five weeks now.

With the high demand for English, things can get a bit crazy each fall when we, the only native English-speaking teachers in town, open our free doors on registration day. Trying our best to stand fast against the constant pressure from wealthy parents, our questionnaires are designed to weed out the rich. We hope all of our twenty-some new spots for first-year students really go to the poor, the poor who are far less assertive on registration day. Of course everyone in the room is incredibly poor by Western standards. This extensive poverty is well illustrated by the questions that we ask as we screen the applicants attempting to find those milk-guzzling rich kids.

If it is demonstrated that they can read and write in their native tongue—which is hardly a given in spite of the fact that we don't accept students younger than *sinfi haft* (seventh grade)—we then proceed with our economic queries. The students, along with some relative of authority, take turns sitting in front of me or my American coworker, Doris, while we ask things like, "How many times per month do you eat meat? How about eggs? How often do you drink milk? Does your house have a telephone? Does it work? How many carpets do you have?" If they eat eggs more than once a week or own their own cow they might not make it in. If they arrived by car, their rejection is almost certain.

Our center's English program, which Doris so wonderfully put together, level by painstaking level, is probably only surpassed in town by the Turkish private school. Kadimobod's wealthiest children attend the Turkish school. There they learn in a rigorous setting, which as far as I know is found only in Tajikistan's handful of Turkish schools.

We have become aware of a fascinating unofficial competition that pits Kadimobod's richest students against some of its poorest. They face off in Kadimobod's scholarship competitions. Every year there are various American and European scholarship programs that come to Kadimobod to test until the one or two winners are selected and flown off to high school or college for a year-long, all-expenses-paid dream come true.

We have become well acquainted with most of these contests due to the constant requests for help, mainly from college students, in filling out applications. As much as possible I resist helping, being of the opinion that if they can't fill out the application because it's in English then that might be an indication they're not quite ready for that full-ride scholarship. And I consistently counsel that applying for Oxford Law School is a total waste of time especially since no scholarship is involved. Where do they even get these applications?

We at the youth center have become familiar with one particular contest. It rolls into town every year to hold a few rounds of testing for the local high school hopefuls. It seems to me that every Tajik student in the nation who has learned a special song that chants the words, "How arrre yoou? How arrre yoouuu?" holds their breath each year and hopes against hope that they will win one of the ten to twenty scholarships granted for the entire country. Usually our town gets two or three such scholarships each year. The kids who win them come back after their year in America as mini-celebrities.

I always thought the testing, like everything else here, must be rigged. But I reconsidered that assumption when one of our most intelligent, penniless students made a strong run at winning.

School Days

Beginning as one among hundreds, he made it through several rounds of testing and into Kadimobod's final four. As usual, the other three students were from the Turkish school. It's a good school and I didn't question their academic ability to place three in the final four.

Over the years, our final-four student, Jahongir, has become very dear to my heart. We've bonded in English class discussing everything the policeman is doing in the picture, taking turns pulling each other up from the sloshy mud pit in the middle of our January football field, trying to get him better sets to his spiking hand, and sitting together in his home, sharing a cup of tea after the loss of his father to tuberculosis.

I remember wishing him the best of luck as he and his mother took a bus up to the capital for his final interview. An all-expenses paid year of education in America was on the line, a year that would certainly pave the way for his family to drink milk and eat eggs a little bit more often.

When word came a few weeks later that three scholarships had been awarded to Kadimobod students and that he was the odd man out, I made the sad trip over to his house to sit with him and his family. He's a big ultimate Frisbee fan now, so I gave him one of the precious discs I brought with me from the States. As we drank some tea and talked about how we were going to pound that Turkish school squad in our upcoming basketball scrimmage to make us feel a little better, I thanked God for my student, my friend Jahongir. God has placed Jahongir and so many of our other precious students so deeply into my heart that I cannot imagine they will ever be removed.

In Tajikistan, speaking about religion with children under the age of sixteen is illegal. And strangely, the local university extends this, without legal authority to do so. The university commonly makes pronouncements forbidding or discouraging and sometimes vaguely threatening their students from going to study their own religion, Islam, under the tutelage of various local mullahs (religious leaders).

Yes, even Islam is taking hits from the government-backed university. Perhaps the government's fear of Islam is justified when they look around at their bordering neighbors or reflect back on their own civil war. With this pervading attitude, which strongly resists the expanding education of even their own faith, obviously it isn't well tolerated when we start sharing the gospel with anyone who isn't old enough to have graduated from university.

At first, the local government didn't seem to mind. For a few years they even approved our Bible curriculum knowing we would teach it to all of the orphans. So, empowered by the pervading mood of freedom, we shared the gospel quite openly with the hundreds of orphans and poor children who came to our summer camps each year.

"*Lagir!*" ("Camp!"), they say with a twinkle in their eyes when we run into them now as they work pumping gas or selling plastic bags at the bazaar. It was quite a place, camp. We only sent home the children who had reached the stage of active tuberculosis with lots of coughing, allowing all others to stay and experience the excessive joy of eating an egg for breakfast every single day.

But someone complained and the government made sure that was the last of camp. Seeing that the local attitude toward our team has changed, we have obeyed the law at our youth center. I waited until Jahongir and his good friend, Firuz, were seventeen before I invited them to an outreach party where they heard the gospel. So it has been strange for us that, despite following these rules we continue to be threatened with the closure of our youth center and lose students due to various rumors.

Once around Christmas, Doris had the students color a nativity scene, introducing it with a few general remarks about how it is a historical event important to roughly two billion people the world over. She went no further. We lost at least a fourth and maybe up to a third of our students after that incident as word and undoubtedly wild rumors of the evil coloring page rapidly spread to schools and mosques all over town. Our brave students, recognizing that we sincerely love them, kept coming in spite of the fact that at least one school was threatening them with beatings if they ignored the school's prohibition and continued to come to our center. Doris and I prayed and tried not to worry.

Over time our veteran students have learned to ignore the rumors that whirl up from the mosque leaders and schoolmasters who speak of how we lock up children in our basements until they convert to Christianity. We don't even have basements. And if we did have one we'd probably use it to start a mushroom project or something, which I guess could be scary in itself, at least until they tasted them. Tajiks do love their mushrooms as evidenced by the fact they race to the hills when the rains come each spring.

It was encouraging to see how angry my college friend, Alisher, was as he related to me how he had heard that particular rumor—about us holding children in our nonexistent basements—being discussed by some group of men down by the bazaar. I guess there are enough skeptical parents out there to keep our center filling back up to capacity after every fear-induced exodus subsides following some nasty rumor or threat. The saddest part to me is when I pass one of my old students on the road and try to say hello only to watch them shirk away in visible fear as if I possess some black magic with which I can control them if they make eye contact. I suppose many Tajiks, perhaps even a majority, do believe in and practice such things.

Tajiks know about binding people in the spiritual realm and pay good money for their powerful mullahs to perform the incantations to do so on their behalf. "Good" mullahs chant to bind a wandering husband back to a desperate wife. Aware of this "good" binding, one of my university friends is afraid to talk to girls because he wants to graduate. He doesn't want some girl with a crush consulting a mullah and binding him spiritually so he ends up having to marry her as if in a trance. "Bad" mullahs, it is widely held, perform greater evils than binding for love.

Knowing all this, perhaps, is why my old students shirk away. I myself believe in the power of the Holy Spirit to work in people's hearts. That's why I continue to pray for my shirking students. They might be even more afraid if they knew of the effectual power of prayer and the strength of the Holy Spirit, infinitely superior to any mullah or black magic. Perhaps they are wise to avoid me. I miss them very much. Without God's power I cannot reach them. This has always been so, but I am now more fully awakened to the reality.

Safety from Fire Safety

After lunch with Ann and the kids at our apartment, I made my way up to the fourth-floor sports room to grab some supplies before I began the mile walk down to our new sports facility in the valley on the outskirts of town. As I grabbed a couple of basketballs from the cabinet, my eyes fell upon our makeshift fire safety list. We had printed it out in Cyrillic Tajik on our youth center computer before taping it to the wall.

Seeing the fire rules always sends a chill down my spine as they remind me of the man who made sure they got there. The barrel-chested, rabid wolverine, also known as our fire safety inspector, arrives unexpectedly every year and attempts to find safety violations we will not be able to fix. The point of his visit is obviously not compliance or fire safety but the hope of lucrative bribes. So upon arrival, he gives us the yearly ultimatum that we will be shut down if we do not comply with this or that by the time he unexpectedly drops by again.

When I see him coming it's time to get my coworker Sam out of the building or, as Sam readily admits, things could escalate to blows. That would be bad, but I suspect the whole building and

perhaps the whole of Kadimobod would cheer at the justice of
Mr. Fire Safety getting smacked. So far we have avoided a fist fight,
though as I hear the screaming breaking out from every nook and
cranny as Mr. Fire Safety pays a visit to each office on his way down
the long hall toward our center, I am amazed. From the sound of
it, he should have a fight break out on every floor he roars down in
wrath amid the inner flames bursting forth from every soul in his
consuming wake.

After he leaves, the scene is always the same with the architectural department, the land department, and the internet center
employees spilling out into the hallways to chain smoke and rub
their temples together as they attempt to get their heart rates back
down to normal before they keel over. With compliance out of
the question in the rotting dinosaur carcass of a building that we
cohabit, the only question for these offices to consider seems to be
how much to bribe in order to pacify the fire wolverine.

Everyone knows the fire wolverine cares little about fire safety.
He wants bribes. So as he arrives in each office he looks for weakness in the eyes of his opponent and tries to see how much he can
get away with in fining them for things nobody ever knows anything about. Being indomitably zur, I think the Tajiks hold him in
this strange place where hate mingles with admiration. This mingling of opposite sensations seems a common response to much
of Tajik leadership. We definitely don't want to contextualize the
church in this area.

Most offices usually seem to give him bribes. Now best friends
again, he smiles and whacks them quite, quite hard on the back.
As he leaves, he passes the faulty wiring hanging in a big bunch
out in the hall, knowing if it were fixed he would have one less
item to use to his advantage the following year. I wouldn't be
surprised in the least if he was annoyed when we actually fixed the
hanging wire ball.

I think he was quite perturbed by the results the time he gave us about three weeks to get a smoke detector set up in each youth center room and we actually ended up doing so. Nobody has smoke detectors in Tajikistan. The schools do well to have desks. You basically have to resort to using Russian when speaking about the device as the Tajik language won't support the new concept without awkward linguistic acrobatics. We don't even think you can buy them. Of course we mentioned all this humbly to our fire wolverine.

Swinging in a psychotic instant to friendly mode, he said he had a few smoke detectors for sale at some outrageous price. This was certainly not an option, both for economic and emotional reasons. So as he left, our staff sat in a defeated heap wondering yet again if this was the time our youth center would breathe its last if we resisted the bribe option.

But somehow the Lord provided. We scrambled and found a visitor coming from the States who could bring us a bunch of new smoke detectors. We got them up on the walls, even splurging on good batteries that were neither frozen in the heaterless Kadimobod bazaars the previous winter nor off-brand Chinese that have been known to last an abysmal one and a half songs on my Discman. Yes, Discman. Perhaps we've been in Tajikistan too long. The disappointed shock on the fire wolverine's face when he came back and saw that we had actually found smoke detectors didn't speak well of his passion for the safety of the children that he so loves to yell at us about. He retreated to plan an attack for next year. Ahh, good times.

At least the school board inspector is better. He actually seems to care about education. Informed of our past evangelistic camp exploits, he is primarily concerned to make sure we do not slip any Christian content into our curriculum. Since he doesn't know any English, I always stand wondering how exactly he is ensuring that as he confidently flips through our books every year. I don't ask. If Mr. Inspector is happy, everybody is happy.

School Days

Our school board inspector is a passionate advocate of red pen. Using a red pen to correct student papers is a point of marvelously strange concern for him. He gets very worked up over seeing corrections in black or blue. When he signs our center's forms, thus paving the way for us to receive teaching permission for another year, we do our best to comply with his desires. We agree to mend our ways and somehow work the red-pen methodology into our youth center. Of course both parties understand the stipulation that we can only do so as long as the bazaar proves able to supply us. I suppose in a pinch, we could always make a red-pen run to the capital.

I remember one strange inspection we had at the youth center when the main inspector was ranting and raving about our pitifully inadequate facilities. He was irate that the center lacked language-listening stations, complete with the latest technology, for each student. Our coworker replied that when she had taught English at Kadimobod University, there hadn't even been chalk. At this, the inspector decided to change the subject of his complaints.

Of course in the middle of the inspector's rantings about the inadequacies of our free programs that benefit the town's poor children, his sidekick pulled us aside to ask if we could accept his own children as students at our center. There is always a bit of a mixed message at our inspections as to whether we are wonderful or evil personified. They eventually decided on evil personified, but that is a long story for a different time.

Happy to stop reminiscing about inspectors and move onto my sports lessons, I locked the closet and headed down to the street. Most of my students would meet me down at our outdoor sports center on the outskirts of town, but a band of a few boys and girls were waiting as usual. The boys, under the guise of helping, snapped up the basketballs as well as my backpack. This freed me to walk without a care, if we don't count my concern for the well-being of my stuff as a care. We all headed down to the sports land together in the early afternoon sunshine.

After two long and tedious years too painful to mention, the government had finally given us all the permissions necessary to build a nice outdoor sports facility. Much to our surprise they finally granted us a football-field-sized plot of land so we could help Kadimobod's poorest children at no expense to them. These permissions come in the form of lovely stamps that you have to get personally from roughly each and every person who has ever called Kadimobod home.

Trying not to be bitter at the local officials' hard-heartedness and unbelievably enduring lust for bribes, as soon as we received the final approval for the land we put up a simple six-foot perimeter cement-block wall, paved a basketball court, and put up some nice, imported German hoops. Then we dumped truckloads of sand for the volleyball, put in a simple awning, small changing rooms, a pit toilet, storage closets, and a guard's house. And we did it all for roughly the same price as the architectural fees for a hot dog stand in the States. Granted the hot dog stand is probably sturdier, and with superiorly designed escape routes.

We only had to pour the cement for the basketball court three times to get a finished product capable of bouncing balls that would return to your hand in a predictable manner. Perhaps the builder considered predictable dribbling to make for a less interesting game of hoops. I stuck to my ridiculously high standards, though I didn't stick with the initial builder.

Our sports facility on the outskirts of town is a wonderful place for lessons. Standing in the middle of our mini soccer field, looking back toward Kadimobod and the mountains that rise up behind her, always summons a strong response of thanksgiving from within. The sight makes me want to praise God. A few minutes outside of Kadimobod and with this view it is so much easier for me to re-member who is really in control.

I certainly don't miss the pre-sports center days of chasing teen-age boys through Kadimobod's central park trying to retrieve my

Frisbee so my class could continue their ultimate Frisbee lesson. Fortunately, the village boys don't seem so enamored with rock throwing as their city neighbors just up the hill. It is hard for me to express how wonderful a development that has been.

Even our girl students from the farthest fringes of Kadimobod make the hour walk each way so they can learn to dribble, spike, and cover second without having to worry that someone will swipe their high heels while they do it. I think the girls know their window of time is fast closing for getting exercise that is more enjoyable than hauling water across a dirt hovel or up a crumbling Soviet staircase. It is wonderful to see them enjoy it. I should probably let them giggle more during the lessons.

I hope the memories of chasing down their friends and digging the volleyball from the summer sand—not an easy task in a modest Tajik korta dress that goes to your ankles—will last. Soon enough, these experiences will end forever. Tajik women never play such games. Fun outside the confines of home is for men. They will soon don the headscarf and these days of freedom will be over. I have no doubt they will talk about these afternoon sports lessons for the rest of their lives. Yes, I should certainly let them giggle a little more.

Walking down to the land and back are always times for informal lessons. These regular walks together outside the city confines are more organic learning opportunities than sports or English conversation classes. I especially enjoy the walks back into town. After lessons, the girls always leave together in a big group. I teach them first in the early afternoon, not only so they can return home in time to do their evening chores—something that the boys unfortunately share little responsibility for—but also so they can be back home and safe before it begins to get dark.

I do not think Kadimobod is dangerous, but Tajik society protects its young women. Even so, Tajik women have a great deal more freedom when compared to women in most Muslim societies. So as long as I teach them first while the sun is still high in the sky, most of them have permission to come.

After the late-afternoon lessons, the boys—freer from work and the restrictions of darkness—help me lock up the sports center and turn things over to our 24/7 guard family. The guard's family lives in the village on the other side of the creek just down the dirt road from a flour mill and neighborhood mosque. The mill, like so many in Tajikistan, still uses the water pressure diverted from the stream to push the mill stone in circles to crush the wheat. The mosque still lacks speakers for the call to prayer.

The boys always wait for me while I prepare for the return walk into town. I check over our tiny storage and changing rooms to make sure everything is in order. I notice our absurd escape routes taped to the plastered walls. I have my doubts as to whether a three-by-three changing room adjoining a field needs an escape route. If you can't figure it out, I'm pretty sure a picture of the three-by-three room with an arrow pointing at the sketched door isn't going to help a whole lot.

Smoke detectors happily flickered their indicator lights, taking up wall space in way too many tiny rooms. I suppose you can never be too safe with the fire wolverine prowling around. I wonder if the mill should get one even though they don't use electricity. And certainly the village school with its hundreds upon hundreds of children would be a better place for these smoke detectors than our one-person-capacity changing rooms. But such is the absurdity of the fire wolverine pursuing deep pockets instead of safety. I locked up, trying my best to recall the escape route as I led our group safely out of the gate and into the open fields.

We began the familiar walk back to Kadimobod. We always walk in a tight mob discussing who has the best free-throw form, what is the best down to blitz kardan, why English spelling is insane, what latest Tajik singer has the country all abuzz, where in the world "Shtati" (Kansas) is, and expanding in all conversational directions from there.

On our walks sometimes I agree to try things like the local remedy for colds. They were considerate, going to the bazaar and buying it for me even though they don't have any money. So against my better judgment, I bent over the small brushfire and breathed in the unknown smoke billows. Pretty good for congestion, actually. I wonder what it was.

At other times, when I'm not bending over a brushfire inhaling mysterious smoke, I answer their questions about how Christians fast differently than Muslims or why I don't bow for prayers during our basketball lessons when the mosque across the stream summons the faithful's attention towards Mecca.

I recognize most of the cussing now and can finally discourage vulgarity and peer abuse. Sometimes we argue. Usually we laugh. Over the years the laughing has increasingly been together and not simply at me. This is a nice development. Maybe they are just being nice because I realize in so many ways I'm still the foreigner, the weirdo, the eternal walking joke.

I love these walks. These are the walks where relationships really begin to form as we clump along together back toward town in the cool of the summer evenings or the early darkness left by the fast-retreating winter sun. Somehow over countless walks, the odd American teacher and his Kadimobod students have become friends. We have grown to respect and love each other. I believe we will remember these walks forever. I believe they can all see that the walking joke loves each of them very much.

Cotton Pickin' Education and Worserer Fates

On most of these evening walks back toward town, our crew will have a few college guys in our midst. This is especially true on Thursdays, as we have designated that as our college sports night. At times we even open the sports center up to the whole community. But we've found that hosting over one hundred men interspersed with roaming bands of young children is not conducive to either the survival of the human race or our facility. And we certainly don't want to have to pour cement a fourth time! Fortunately most guests prefer the more durable surfaces offered by sand volleyball and soccer.

With the college guys all gone picking cotton, on this particular October Thursday evening we had a quiet walk back. As we reached town and gradually split off to head towards our different neighborhoods, I found myself missing my college buddies. I hoped they were doing alright out there in the distant cotton fields.

The fledgling Tajik democracy seems to have decided to keep the beneficial communist idea of forced free labor. Unfortunately, they have bucked the communist, reciprocal truth of rewarding the laborers by sharing the gained benefits with the community as a whole. The Tajik capitalists seem to have stumbled upon what they would consider to be a perfect combination of the two systems. Of course, as the Tajik news constantly reminds, the cotton harvest is still supposed to go toward the common national good. But no Tajik I've ever met being forced to work the fields seems to buy that.

I don't really know any bigwigs or capitalists, but I do know the student laborers. I remember the time my friend and Kadimobod University student, Aloddin, showed up at our apartment very early one freezing, fall morning shaking uncontrollably from the cold. He chatteringly explained how he had been hauled back from the cotton fields. Evidently about one hundred students had endured an all-night journey packed into the back of a few old Soviet trucks. These old trucks are most often used to haul gravel and the like, but occasionally to haltingly freight a truckload of underfed, huddling college students—Tajikistan's intellectual future—back from weeks of slave labor in the cotton fields. I told Aloddin it was a good thing he had been sardined in there with so many other students or he might have been too cold to chatter at all.

I ushered Aloddin quickly into our warm living room where I got some hot tea and eggs down him. He was a strong guy, so it concerned me to see him shaking uncontrollably. I wondered how the weaker students were faring this morning. As the shaking gradually subsided, he told me the all-too-common story I've heard so many times before. The university's faculty had rounded them up in the student commons a few weeks ago. They were then trucked out to some lonely, remote locale where they were forced to pick cotton on pains of facing a few failing grades and possible expulsion from university.

They were underfed. Usually they seemed to survive on bread and weak tea with an occasional potato or onion. American chain gangs seem to have it soft although they don't get a *deeplom* (diploma) at the end of their labors. In Tajikistan, you really earn your deeplom, although not in the traditional manner of rigorous studying.

Aloddin had come for his stipend. I didn't doubt he wanted it so he could buy some much-needed food. He was one of our sponsored kids. In one of our projects we had recently expanded from sponsorship of elementary and high school aged kids to include around a dozen college students. Slowly but surely, our sponsored kids are graduating out of the Soviet-begun, internat educational system. They usually graduate this high school equivalent without any prospects other than flying to Russia to do grunt work for some decent pay. Some of them are orphans. All are from very poor families.

Older Tajiks have told me that during the Soviet Union, the internat system offered the best education around. All wanted to attend these boarding school type institutions. Interestingly, it appears that during the communist era many of the Tajiks who received the best education were orphans. This is certainly an educational situation that has been a rarity in history. But to also cast a questioning shadow on the motives of the internat system, this was probably done because orphans and the castaway children of the very poor provided the cleanest slate on which to educate and indoctrinate. But those days of an excellent internat education are past. Now the internats do well to keep the children fed and clothed, activities we are often quite involved in helping with when state funding falls short.

Aloddin came from our favorite internat partner school. The internat is from a small town down near the Afghanistan border. This internat's leadership actually welcomes our presence and help, even in the area of education. Unfortunately, at other internats it is extremely difficult to get our help to actually reach the children. It is common for their staffs to constantly demand more money while belittling our visits and all of our other efforts as pointless and sometimes unwelcome.

Sometimes we'll be working away happily, coming alongside an internat with this and that when we'll receive an ultimatum from the internat leadership that if we don't give them X amount of cash or X amount of new computers in the next few months that they will be severing ties. So ties have been severed. This is unbelievably sad for anyone who has ever visited the bleakness of a Tajikistan internat where the simple actions of giving every child a few eggs and an orange once a week or providing a brand-new pillow for each cot are received by the children with great joy. It baffles us since we try to serve humbly, seeking to be their servants for the good of the children. We did build a computer lab down at Aloddin's internat. Without a threatening ultimatum, it was actually a pretty good experience for all involved.

Another one of our sponsored college guys from Aloddin's internat had come back from the cotton fields a couple weeks early. He had somehow escaped the watchful eyes of the warden-professors. Incidentally, I wonder if tenure in Tajikistan includes exclusion from supervising cotton-picking excursions. Imagine how much research professors could get done without the hassle of having students for half of every fall semester. I must admit it's an intriguing reverse-sabbatical program. Aloddin's buddy hitched rides all the way back to Kadimobod. When I talk to them, these escapees, they never seem worried that they will actually fail or get expelled. Perhaps they have made arrangements on the side. That's quite likely as "arrangements on the side" seem to be what Tajik universities do best.

Being around Kadimobod University students for a few years now, I have begun to learn the intricacies of the labyrinthine grading system. Final exams usually go on and on for weeks, especially after spring semester. If the semester ends in late May, I am not surprised to hear of students still taking their final exams into July. I guess the beginning of fall semester is the cutoff.

And fall semester is even more absurd with a couple of weeks to get organized in September in order to hopefully have a few weeks of classes before cotton picking starts. By the time they return from the cold fields and have a few recovery days to help in their fight for survival, they usually seem to only have enough time to attend a few weeks of classes before the murmuring and rumoring of finals is upon them.

There are a few possible reasons for this painfully long and random phenomenon known as finals which forces all my buddies to hang around Kadimobod for most of the summer rather than head home. The first possible explanation for unending final exams is the most positive. It explains the delays by pointing out that they are probably a result of the standard Tajik testing method. In Tajikistan, exams are oral. Each student will go before his professor one at a time. Maybe that takes a long time. I don't think so, but let's say it might so that we can have at least one positive explanation for the endless process.

When the Tajik student comes into the professor's office for his final, upon the desk there will usually be three slips of paper facedown. The student picks one randomly off the desk and flips it over. On it there will be a single question concerning some aspect of the semester's course work.

Most of the student's grade depends on his answer to this single question. Some professors will allow five to ten minutes for the student to sit and think about his answer. Other professors want an immediate answer. It is to the advantage of the professor to have three extremely difficult questions awaiting the student as professors usually seem able to survive in teaching only by the gifts they are able to secure from their students.

And that is a second possible reason the finals process takes so long. If the student does not know the answer to the question then the negotiation over the price of a passing grade and the additional price for an excellent mark has begun. This process may take quite a while as most students are poor and have to run all over town gathering and scrounging up little loans so they can get cash to their professor. Other students go down to the bazaar for some noncash goods that might shake that good grade loose. If sufficient bribes cannot be found, then the student must return to the professor for further consultations and the process goes on and on and on.

Most professors seem to be subtle in this process, suggesting appropriate gifts to get them in the proper mood to consider the student's grade. Many students know this and bring a sack of flour or a couple kilos of meat with them to their final. Then it can simply be seen as a gift and all that nasty bickering over price can be avoided. If the gift is accepted, this really speeds the negotiation process along.

Other professors are surprisingly direct. I even heard of one professor who told his class straight out that it would cost this many somoni for *bahoi 5* (an A grade), this many for *bahoi 4* (a B grade), and so forth. That professor must have tenure.

His brazen straightforwardness no doubt saves him a lot of time in back-office negotiations, not to mention making his trips back home every evening more enjoyable. It's not easy to carry a couple fifty-kilo sacks of flour across campus. Perhaps the student receives extra credit if they offer home delivery? I would think every professor would insist on home delivery after having to drag a couple of crates of vegetables across the commons. The commons certainly must be entertaining during finals. I don't think that livestock usually enters into the grade-negotiating equation, but if it did Kadimobod University might have a primal scream to rival Northwestern's finals week tradition. If I understand Northwestern's tradition correctly, during finals there is a moment when all the students know to corporately stick their heads out of their windows and let out their frustrations by screaming. I assume the Northwestern intellectuals would scream louder and with a more directed purpose than livestock, but they certainly couldn't beat nervous goats visiting a university for the first time for sheer bleating endurance.

Another possible explanation for the endless finals phenomenon is that it takes time to locate and round up students. Students who have failed to attend a single class during the semester due to laziness, confidence in their family connections, or being out of the country—say in Russia working—certainly have a harder road ahead of them toward securing passing grades. But they need not despair. Indeed, even in such an educationally vacuous situation, as long as the right price is arranged, a student may be able to retain that summa cum laude glow and still be back at that warehouse job in Dushanbe or Moscow before the start of next semester.

With the Tajik professors being very open minded in their definitions of distance, education, and distance education, it is likely that more often than not something can be arranged. However, and this is of utmost importance, it is a nonnegotiable necessity to wear a tie and have a nice leather binder when you go to negotiate your grades. Otherwise the university elite might have reason to doubt the sincerity of your desire for a university education and you might just find that no arrangement can be made.

I have actually heard of students hurrying home from Russia just in time to take all their exams. And let's not kid ourselves, there is no online education going on over that distance either. I worry that these students and soon to be grads might not be getting a full college experience, education being the most notable portion lacking. But at least students still seem to have to take finals in order to pass finals. It is nice that the university still has its standards.

I met an agricultural student from the village who told me straight out he doesn't bother going to class. He works hard on farming out in his village and saves enough to have a healthy profit even after visiting his professors to arrange his grades at the end of every semester. The conversation I had with him one summer out in his village was quite funny as long as you don't depend on Tajikistan for your future. As I remember it, it went something like this:

Me: "Oh, so you're a student at Kadimobod University?"

Student: "Yes, a third-year student."

Me: "So when will you head back for classes? Do you live in the dorm?"

Student: "No. I live here all year."

Me: "But how do you go to classes? You can't drive back and forth every day."

Student: "I don't go to classes."

Me: "You don't go to classes?"

Student: "I only go for finals at the end of each semester to get my grades. I already know everything they teach. I'm studying agriculture. I'm a farmer already. I don't need to go."

Of course locating the students at the end of each semester isn't easy. Calling them back from their various villages and work in the countries of the far north requires a lot of time. This is another possible reason why final exams drag on for five or six weeks.

But what really makes me angry is when one of my friends will tell me how they actually studied hard, diligently went to all classes, and nailed the final question on the oral exam only to be told by their professor that they would have to pay a bribe anyway in order to get their grade. As a reward for knowing the material, they seem to be given a discount. My intelligent, studious friend, Iskandar, rants about this injustice. When he slows down a little bit, I can even make out what he's saying.

Though I don't have much information, I fear that grad school isn't much better. When another one of my intelligent friends, Zohir, was applying to grad school, I was happy to help him out with his foreign language requirement. So we sat a few times to hash over some simple English. Even though he had never studied English before, in just a couple of months he had surpassed most of the Kadimobod English majors I know.

I wished him luck before he departed to take entrance exams at his graduate school of choice in the capital. Naturally, I thought my work was finished. So I was surprised when he called me on his cell phone the following day. In hushed and anxious tones, he told me he was in some prestigious hallway because he had been given ten minutes to sit alone and prepare his response to the English question he had selected for the foreign language portion of his exams. He asked for my help. I was pretty surprised, though not as surprised as I would have been if I had never lived in Tajikistan.

His shock at my refusal to give him a few minutes of extremely specific English instruction sounded so astoundingly sincere that I actually felt a little guilty as I promptly hung up on him. He got into grad school even though his "phone a friend" lifeline proved a wash. I couldn't help but wonder if he had a few other lifelines lined up for the other portions of his entrance exams.

At least some professors seem to resist the whole system. My friends speak of professors who actually teach and make them study. For me it's all a haze but it seems there are some good professors out there investing in the next generation. I hope a healthy percentage of them are the ones training the doctors.

The infinite intricacies of the whole process seem to be sort of hush, hush. I can never really get my mind around the whole situation. Other institutions seem to follow the same pattern of never-ending stalling and misinformation to get you all lathered up in a sweat of desperation before the negotiations begin. So you need a thousand government stamps before building on your new plot of land? Is it really your plot of land? Either way, good luck with that. Want me to stamp it? How badly?

The rule makers don't seem to know the rules and that's to their advantage. If you know somebody or, better yet, are somebody, all the necessity of stamps seems to miraculously become unnecessary. This allows the movers and shakers to continue to shake away. They're zur. But at least university enrollment saves many from the more perilous fate of military service. It seems like avoiding the service is the primary motivation for countless young men in attending college. This is easily understandable once you've heard a couple of gaunt returning soldiers tell their tales.

Military service, I believe for a term of two years, is mandatory for every Tajik young man unless they are the family's primary breadwinner or are enrolled in higher education. The rules, or at least their enforcement, seem quite vague, but better to enroll in university or at least some sort of college program just in case. This way you have a good defense when the local recruiting office gets put on a tough recruiting deadline. So what if you have to pick cotton! A month or so every year of forced labor certainly beats two solid years. At least this seems to be the consensus of everyone I know.

We believe that being enrolled in university protects you from getting dragged away by the military. I choose to use the word "drag," not for dramatic effect, but because that is an accurate description of how enlistment often seems to transpire.

Kadimobod's decaying military recruiting office is in a building on the street directly behind our apartment building. What they lack in cool posters of buff guys driving tanks they make up for with a few fleet-footed personnel. This swift platoon is charged with chasing down unfortunate Tajik guys who happen to be walking down the wrong road looking about the right age.

School Days

It's scary to watch the panic-stricken youth running for freedom knowing the next two years of his life probably depends on the outcome of this race. Will he be watching Russian-dubbed *Spiderman* at home tonight with his buddies or will he be bumping along on a bus headed for some less-than-inspiring civil engineering project, hoping somebody will let his mom know? It all hangs in the balance as feet pound pavement.

I've watched before as the youth sprints on looking over his shoulder to see how many yards he has on the two guys thudding along in their big black recruiting boots. Most times, the recruiters grab them before they're aware of danger. This prevents the dramatic exertion of the footrace.

As with diplomas, for the rich and sometimes even for the middle class, military service is negotiable. The parents parked in their nice new cars outside the shabby, two-story recruiting center will no doubt retrieve their captured sons before they're shipped off to the Pamir Mountains for twenty-four months of ditch digging and the like. But inevitably the parents who arrive on foot wearing shabby clothes leave without their boys.

Unfortunately, college enrollment and being underage are not necessarily foolproof ways of avoiding getting nabbed on our street if the recruiters have a pressing quota of patriotic recruits to meet. I remember hearing about how they nabbed an unusually mature thirteen-year-old boy. It took his mother presenting his legal documents proving his age before they opened the holding cell to release him back to his mommy. Being a man-mountain is not without dangers.

Unfortunately, one of our sponsored college students got nabbed. Leaving our apartment one Saturday where he had just had lunch with us, evidently he wasn't paying attention when he walked down our fateful road. He found himself being dragged off to a holding cell for processing. Even though it happened just a couple of hundred yards from our apartment, I didn't know.

His father called to inform me about what had occurred and to see if I could help. I grabbed a wise neighbor to counsel me. We walked around the backside of our apartment building to try to intervene. We decided to build our defense on the grounds that he was presently enrolled in college and should therefore be exempt. My neighbor told me to stay put on the street while he went inside. Foreigners make everything more complicated, and send bribe prices through the roof. I waited outside and tried to avoid getting "recruited" myself.

Being enrolled in college, Alisher should have been free to go in no time, but oddly, they would have none of it. It appeared his education would have to wait. After a few days, I resigned myself to the fact that Alisher would probably not be coming over for lunch again for a couple of years. A good host does not want to have their guests end up getting dragged away to slave labor. Looking back I'd have to say it was one of my least successful luncheons ever. When I'm not feeling angry, I feel quite guilty as it was only because he was over visiting us at our apartment that he came into range of Kadimobod's Venus human-traps in the first place. I hope he'll forgive me for not bribing him out. If he's angry at me, it looks like he'll have two years to count to ten.

I heard later that his father had negotiated to get him assigned to a locale of lower altitude and better conditions. I was very glad to hear it. I miss Alisher. I hope he continues coming to church when he returns. I wish I had known to savor our last lunch a little bit more.

Old Tajiks savor their recollections of past Soviet times. They remember those good ol' Soviet days when there was discipline and order in education, when cotton picking wasn't such an empty endeavor, when people were actually trained to do their jobs, and when military service could be anticipated more than an hour in advance. I hear the old men as they sit around and speak of those days. To the Tajiks, those were the days.

School Days

After locking up the sports equipment in the main office, I headed towards home. As I approached our apartment building, I could make out an old man walking toward the wavering light emanating from the furthest crumbling stairwell. I realized it was Boboi (Grandpa) Umed going over with his electrical tools, no doubt to attend to something urgent. Boboi Umed lives in the apartment above us. He's an electrician, Soviet trained. That means he knows what he's doing. So every time something in our stairwell or stairwells further afield explodes, he figures it out and has us up and running again in no time. He walks around with his tools competently fixing everything. But he's getting so old. It worries me. Sadly, he's made it clear he doesn't want to speak about spiritual light, but we all certainly rely on him for visible illumination. What will we do when he's gone? What will Tajikistan do when his generation is gone? But that's in the future. Right now we should simply say, meshavad, as the local philosophy goes. Not being Tajik, that mantra doesn't do much for me. Tajikistan will miss the knowledge and skill of this fading generation.

I must admit it is annoying that the neighbors won't believe me when I tell them that the Russian czar and his family were not and are not living happily in Europe. Oh well. At least some of my neighbors believe the United States participated in the Second World War. But who cares about Soviet propaganda, neighbors spying, or religious persecution if you can have boxed milk, heat, and mail service! And so we look together at the shambles that is Tajik education and collectively abuse that Gorbachev buffoon who ruined everything. But at least at the moment we are relatively happy because a thousand Boboi Umeds are hobbling around Tajikistan saving our hides, even allowing Americans to savor the fading Soviet education.

X

UNITY IN CHRIST

I remember clearly our final Easter in Tajikistan. The events that would lead to our team's expulsion were already in motion. Both the willing and unwilling witnesses' testimonies and accusations were being gathered by the authorities, as we joined the Tajik believers to worship our risen Lord.

> *Iso Ehiyo shud!* (Jesus has risen!)
> *Albatta, Ehiyo shud!* (Indeed, He has risen!)

The words still ring in my heart as I remember my Tajik brothers and sisters. That Easter morning they joyfully proclaimed His victory along with us. And now that our team has been pushed out of Tajikistan, they continue to speak boldly in a difficult place.

Ann and I sat along the wall as our Easter service began. It would be a more intimate Easter in Kadimobod this year than in years past. Our small church had decided that rather than doing a large outreach event at a local Kadimobod hall or in our teammate's largest room, as we had done for Christmases and Easters past, this spring we would change the celebration's focus from evangelism to fellowship. We skipped the sweeping invitations to all neighbors and friends in favor of concentrating our attention on one another. We, the community of believers and the innermost serious seekers gathered with us around the dustarxon tablecloth, looked at one another and prepared to worship.

Leading the local church in Kadimobod, Chuponi Suhrob ("Shepherd" Suhrob) opened his Tajik Bible to Kitobi Ibrion (the book of Hebrews). Sitting cross-legged on his living room floor, he shared passionately with us how the curtain has been torn, how we can go confidently into the most holy place because we have been washed clean by the blood of our eternal High Priest, Jesus Christ.

Looking around as Chuponi Suhrob shared the Word, I slowly realized that if ever the young Kadimobod church was ready to stand on its own, it was now. My thoughts were increasingly drawn to such things as the pressure on our team increased. Already we knew that part of our team would not be able to return to Kadimobod.

Pastor Suhrob sat across the dustarxon tablecloth proclaiming the glorious gospel message more clearly than anyone on our team could ever have hoped to do. I'd had enough moments where I'd confidently said to a group of Tajiks something like, "For the wages of sin is chicken" to appreciate God's providential preparation of Suhrob.

The gospel overflowed from Suhrob's heart, a Tajik heart of faith. As the seekers listened, I praised God that this testimony of His love for the Tajiks was coming straight from one of them. It was beautiful to behold. I looked around at his audience. I prayed for God to raise up more Suhrobs. There were far too few in this country. But I thanked God they were beginning to emerge.

I also thanked God that He had chosen to use our team to begin building the church in this area. Why? Because as I looked around with joy at a Tajik church that was beginning to blossom, I realized that there could be no mistaking who the glory, honor, and praise belong to. This was God's beautiful work, not ours.

I've often thought that our team is like Gideon's meager three hundred in this place. It appears we have been providentially selected for the purpose of more prominently displaying God's glorious victory by setting it against the backdrop of our cultural and linguistic inadequacies. We break pots, wave our tiny torches, and blow our trumpets into the night while God routes the army. I have learned over the years that though we make strides toward incarnating into Tajik life, we will always be foreign. We will always be Western. We will always be strangely individualistic, task oriented, and filled with a myriad of other inadequacies. But in our tremendous weakness, His glorious strength has stood out all the more.

Several of the Tajik believers from Kadimobod were so afraid, discouraged, or uncommitted that they had not even come to worship with us on this Easter morning. And then there were other believers who could not be with us because they were away working in Russia or Dushanbe. But the Tajik believers who had come made my heart excited. The Lord was doing something mighty. My heart pounded joyfully as I sat there observing from my spot against the wall. This morning Ann and I were witnesses to the courageous response of these faithful in spite of recent persecution and darkening days.

We knew these Tajik believers came despite the fact that a local paper had already begun to write concerning our Christian activities. They would continue coming even after the printing of an article naming each one on our team as well as the prominent local believers. This article attacked with lies and slanders before ending with a vague reference to others who had been killed for doing such evil Christian activities in the past. The reporter wrote that he hoped a similar fate would not befall all of us.

As the believers and seekers sat there listening to the word on this Resurrection Day, Pastor Suhrob had not yet stood before the local government for his six-hour grilling. This persecution would come in just a few weeks. He let his light shine so bright. In spite of intimidation and orders to the contrary, Pastor Suhrob humbly but firmly informed them that he would continue to lead the local church.

As I looked around the room that Easter morning, I was so impressed by the boldness of the Tajik believers. Persecution was brewing. Things were swirling. Sometimes when things swirl, the foreigners get the boot, but, of course, the locals stay. They knew this. They were holding on to the Rock. If anything, they were our examples in faithfulness.

It angers me that the Tajik believers' families and neighbors derisively label them *dinfurushho* (religion sellers). The newspaper articles would make similar claims stating that we Americans paid them to convert, that we gave them all new cars to become believers. No one seemed to notice that hardly any of the Tajik believers had a car and none of the foreigners did. No, most were poor.

The term *dinfurush* speaks of selling one's faith for material gain. In reality, the opposite is usually true. When a Muslim accepts Christ as his Lord and Savior and begins to live for Jesus, usually great material and relational hardships await. Tajiks know this. That is why an important early conversation with seekers is always about counting the cost. The truth is that in Tajikistan it is easy to be a Muslim. It takes great courage and endurance to be a Christian.

Yet Tajik churches must be sensitive to the accusations. We, as foreigners, have learned that though the local believers are incredibly poor, any monetary help must be given with great discernment. The testimony of the church is at stake. Sometimes Ann and I put an offering in the cardboard collection box that sits on the floor in the corner. Once we put ten somoni in the box. We found out that amount is probably too much to donate as all the children in the church somehow guessed where the ten somoni came from. They were all talking about our offering even though it was less than four dollars. If we want to be generous, we will have to find better ways.

Though Pastor Suhrob was speaking from Hebrews, the whole scene felt like a chapter out of the book of Acts. When I read Acts, it no longer feels like history. It feels like the present. It feels like Kadimobod. Here we were, first church in a brand-new area, the first of the firstfruits. Sitting to my right, older brother Firuz listened intently, his grandchild on his lap and wife by his side. As I looked at Firuz, I remembered back to before Ann and I had ever even set foot in Tajikistan. In America we had put a tape in our VCR and stared at the shaky footage, amazed as Firuz and his wife Ruksora took turns standing knee-deep in a rusty house church bathtub to profess faith in Christ. As far as we know, that day they became the first Kadimobod Tajik believers to be baptized. As we watched the tape, I remember thinking the book of Acts was alive and kicking. I remember thinking we had to join them.

Now, years later, I sat looking at older brother Firuz. We had come to know each other well. We had spent years sowing the seed of the gospel together all over Kadimobod. We had sown alongside our brothers and sisters, both American and Tajik. All of us had spent years together praying for good soil, praying for faith, praying for the Spirit to move in countless hearts. Echoing the prayer of the Israelites recorded in Isaiah, we prayed for God to "rend the heavens and come down, that the mountains would tremble before you!" (Isa 64:1).

I sat trying to control the excitement that I felt as Pastor Suhrob shared the gospel yet again with these interspersed seekers who are so close to our church's communal heart. I have learned that you don't have to look far into Tajik culture to find a redemptive analogy. Pastor Suhrob could jump right into the meaning of sacrifice this Easter morning because most of the seekers who were sitting here listening to him had participated in or had at least seen an animal sacrifice in the last few months, most notably on Idi Korbon (the holiday of sacrifice). Tajiks already believe a lamb is a wonderful sacrifice because it is to them, in some sense, a pure animal. They already have opinions about such things. They all know from personal experience what it looks like, what it sounds like, what it smells like, what it feels like when an animal's blood is spilt in sacrifice.

In so many ways, the Tajiks should be ready for the gospel. Many Old Testament practices continue all around us. Tajiks need to understand the providence behind their practices. They need to see what God was preparing beforehand when He put these ways in place all those centuries ago before, in the fullness of time, He sent His Son to die for our sins.

When some Tajiks, who I don't even know very well, start a conversation by asking me point-blank about the state and details of my circumcision, I know they are not asking in concern for my health but to see where I stand spiritually. Now that I'm pretty much over my past embarrassing responses to these questions, I can seize the opportunities. When I explain to them how in the Tavrot (books of Moses)—the Tavrot that they already deeply respect but rarely know anything about—the law states that the person bringing the sacrifice must put his hand on the animal's head, we can immediately begin in on why that might be. Why must the man's hand touch the animal's head as it dies?

And that is definitely a different place than I would ever dream of beginning when sharing my faith in America. Sometimes I consider what might transpire if I tried to share the gospel with an American as I did with a Tajik. Suppose I was to start talking with an American coworker or new ultimate Frisbee buddy about why it is that I believe we no longer need to offer animal sacrifices or how, though I am circumcised, it is not for religious reasons because what God truly wants is circumcision of the heart. Flashing lights might be in my future if I stuck around for ultimate Frisbee after that. Or at least I would have an inordinate amount of empty grass around me to operate in during the game. I suppose being wide open could be beneficial if my team ever decided to risk tossing it to the freak.

I begin to appreciate the common ground, the common presuppositions I share with Tajiks. It's refreshing to start in the common stream of Abraham rather than trying to explain who Abraham is or that I am not an idiot for believing that there is such a thing as truth. My goodness, that's an incredibly frustrating place to have to start! It's quite wonderful that Tajiks would find me absurd if I started in on how I believe there are such things as good and evil. Their look at such a ridiculously obvious assertion would clearly communicate, "Well, duh." Coming from the West, that is such an astoundingly exhilarating, "Well, duh."

Though Islam throws up a massive amount of its own unique roadblocks against the gospel, I still appreciate the cultural preparations all around me. Prepared seekers were among us. Being Tajik, being Muslim had in some ways helped prepare them for this morning's good news. They had shown great boldness in coming.

I looked over at two Tajik seekers close to my heart. I started thinking about one of them, my friend Komil, as I observed him listening to Pastor Suhrob's message. Through the years, the talks over the gospel had seemed endless. Sometimes Komil would tell me that yes, he thought he did believe these things—believe in Jesus. Then he would say how he must wait until he finished university to ever say so in a public way.

Sometimes I was encouraged when he would tell me about how he had argued with his uncle about some issue where he defended a Christian position. But he always stopped short of telling that uncle or even me that he truly believed. Komil always stopped short of repenting and making the final step. I found it odd that Komil was willing to defend the faith and even suffer a little bit for that defense and yet not willing, even privately, to join that fellowship of faith himself.

I remember recently how I challenged him with Jesus' parable of the pearl of great price. Would he sell all he had to buy it? Would he truly give his life to Jesus? As I looked around the crowded living room I realized so many of the other seekers were like Komil. They loved our fellowship. They loved to learn from the Bible. They loved to hear of Jesus. They loved worship and to hear of the lavish love of God. They had all contemplated the cost for a long time. But fear or other factors always stopped them from truly becoming part of our body. Many flitted about the edges of our church. Many others who used to flit about the edges have flown further away. But still we pray. The Tajik believers continue to pray for so many by name.

I, like so many on our team, have been praying for years and years now that God would orchestrate my relationships. I have been praying that He would put people in my path who are ready for the good news. I pray He would use me in His plans for many Tajiks. I believe in His providence. I look back on so many seeds sown. It gives me great hope to think that God has heard our repeated prayers. He is in control of where each seed falls. He is in control of the types of soil it falls on. He is in control of soil preparation. I pray for His grace and mercy in the lives of all of the Tajiks who have become so precious to us.

I struggle with patience, waiting to see what the Lord might do. If the Lord so chooses, Kadimobod will be awash in the power of His grace and the glory of His salvation. I do not know what the Lord will do or whether I will live to see it, but I am slowly learning to rest in Him. I know at one time none, absolutely none, of my ancestors believed in Jesus either.

I have learned that joy is impossible if you have a weak view of God's providence. God is almighty, the Almighty. As that sinks into my marrow, the joy begins to bubble up. In Tajikistan I find myself so often oscillating between peace and guilt. I read Mark 4 and try to learn to submit to the joy found in the rhythms of God's natural and spiritual world. If I sow the seed, even if it be as small as a mustard seed, then the harvest will come for the power is not in the sower, but in the seed and in God's created, Spirit-filled order. As Paul says in 1 Corinthians, "neither he who plants nor he who waters is anything, but only God, who makes things grow" (1 Cor 3:7). But what will the growth be? Will the harvest be tenfold or twentyfold? Sometimes it feels that it will be 1/1000th of a fold. Remembering a different metaphor, I wonder too about the prerequisite of that great harvest—the dying of the seed. What will that mean for me, for my family, my fellow workers, the local believers? I struggle as God begins to teach me how I can be a sower in contented repose awaiting the harvest He controls and at the same time be the wheat kernel falling to die. Repose and anticipation of death or suffering often seem to me a most unlikely pair.

Before Pastor Suhrob had begun to speak from the Word this morning, we had sung together from our church's simple photocopied songbooks. There was no Arabic, Latin, or English to deter them from entering into the joyful proclamations that Jesus has risen from the dead for the Tajiks. I especially enjoyed the songs we sang that were not translated from English but were taken from the creative works of a few faithful Iranian believers. These Iranian melodies, probably unbeknownst to them, have made their way from Iran and their Farsi-accented offerings to their linguistic brothers in Central Asia who employ them with their distinctive Tajiki dialect.

I have thanked Iranian believers for this blessing that they have inferred on their Tajik brothers and sisters. I hope that God-enabled Tajiks will rise up and put worship to music that will someday flow blessings toward the Iranian believers in return.

And I hope these musicians rise up soon because over the years in Tajikistan we have sung enough a cappella to kill a cat. We have grown impatient for instruments and for the gifted that will never destroy rousing praise by accidentally starting an octave too low leading to nether tones which can only be whispered in strained grunts or more fully by the blessed among us who have the vocal empowerment granted by a bad head cold.

And yet, I have grown to deeply love the simplicity of this Tajik house church where we don't have to argue about the color of the carpet because there isn't any, where no one rushes out the door afterwards unless they hail from the West, where all of our church's finances are held in a shoe box, and where encouragement and fellowship are made essential and potent by persecution.

Apart from our simple song folders, the only book we really have is the Bible. I have learned its sufficiency anew. The community has so few distractions to lead us away from going directly to the source and studying what it teaches. I deeply appreciate the vast amounts of resources in the West and I often wish for many to be available in Tajik, but I also treasure the newfound gem of simplicity and the undistracted focus on God's Word that is born from it.

Unity has yet to be compromised by deep fractures. Since there are only a couple dozen believers in all of Kadimobod, the believer who tends to think along lines slightly different than you will hardly break away unless he wants to start a separate house church with one or two people. In our situation, nonessentials are treated as such. The small band locks arms to pray and fast that God would penetrate this place. And they are encouraged knowing similar groups of believers are growing in cities all over Tajikistan.

Yet the beginnings of divisions are surfacing in areas where the Tajik church is more established. It is strange that anything would keep the few Tajik believers from holding on to one another in a place where they exist as a few diamonds scattered in the vast sands of Islam, but we should not be surprised. The Corinthian believers taught us that even a tiny minority is quite capable of fracturing into many pieces.

Even so, there is such hope. Here in Kadimobod, the Tajik believers have increasingly, and on their own initiative, met in their homes to spend the night in corporate prayer. They fast. They pray. Passion and commitment grow. Even though the truly committed core is hardly more than eight or ten Tajiks, with the feel of their church so similar to the house churches they read about in the book of Acts, it is hard for them to miss how much God can do with a faithful handful once they entrust themselves to abiding in His hands.

After Pastor Suhrob finished sharing, the Tajik women carefully gathered up the songbooks and the Bibles. They were replaced by a beautiful dustarxon upon which the meal was soon laid out. Akai Firuz leaned against the wall as he enjoyed a peola of steaming tea with fresh bread. Believers and seekers mingled over simple *shurboh* soup.

Not all of those who had wanted to attend had been able to make it this morning. Notably gone were young believers Sobir and Muhabbat. Their wedding just last month was most likely the first joining in Christian marriage of Kadimobod Tajiks. It is strange how an event of that magnitude will pass in the relentless whirl of life failing to arouse our sense of wonder and thankfulness as it should. Of course this shows our need for further sanctification for the Bible clearly teaches that we are to be an amazed and thankful people.

Of course such historic events which are now beginning to take place throughout Tajikistan have opened the door to discussions about which cultural traditions Tajik Christians should continue to observe in their weddings and which practices should be abandoned. Wisely, our team leader has already begun to help Tajik believers from all over the country engage in such discussions.

Throughout the country the young Tajik churches are beginning to wonder what a Tajik Christian family should look like. This new category—Tajik Christian family—demands careful thought. The Tajik way of life, century upon century of intricately intertwined tradition, history, literature, and religion, lies before them in need of a wise sifting. It is a daunting task. What should they do? What should they refrain from doing? What is important? How will they become distinctively Tajik Christian families in faith and practice? But those heavy analyses were for other meetings. For now we continued our unofficial exploration of what it means to be Tajik Christians as we interacted during our meal.

After the meal, it was time for fun. The children—their Bible lessons and lunch finished—burst out of their room and into the hallway. They ran here and there throughout the apartment. I watched our little Grace running and dancing in the heart of it.

I looked at Ann. We smiled to hear Grace shouting out her perfectly pronounced Tajik slang and imitating the moves of Shabnam, her favorite Tajik pop star. Perhaps she'd had a little too much Tajik MTV. Hopefully she wouldn't turn this gathering into another opportunity for a Tajik dance recital as she had done at our last party here. Silas trailed behind Grace and the big Tajik kids wherever they went, trying his best to be just like them.

The ladies cleared the dustarxon floor cloth while games started up. We played several group games that our teammate Lydia had prepared. "Mafia" was especially illuminating as we got to see which ones of us are the most adept liars. Unfortunately, I didn't do too badly. Most of all, we laughed. I remember the joy.

I remember Pastor Suhrob's two oldest sons enthusiastically joining in the games. I watched them intently. Many around the table had poured themselves into their lives, beginning to teach them how to grow in the young faith they had professed. They came one evening a week to our apartment for discipleship. We ate a lot of cookies together on those visits. We were going through the book of Luke. Every week they memorized what we thought was the most important verse to know in the passage. They were growing. It was exciting to see because I know if the Lord truly captures their hearts, well, I can only imagine. I often try to. I asked Pastor Suhrob if it wasn't time to baptize them. He said he wanted to wait until they were older. Later, when it became clear we had to leave Kadimobod, I told Pastor Suhrob that he must let me know when they would be baptized. I desperately want to see that incredibly special day. I pray the Lord provides a way for it to happen.

After the games had wound down and the last bits of cool tea were sipped from the peola teacups, people slowly began to rise from the table and make their way toward the door. We put our shoes on, said warm goodbyes, and walked out into the stairwell. Soon enough we were all back in our own homes.

Unity in Christ

Our last Kadimobod Easter faded. The memories live on. But more than that, the church lives on and will continue to do so because its members are eternal. By the grace of God, Tajik churches continue to grow, continue to spring up around the country. We know that even though we have been painfully separated far sooner than we ever thought, all of our lives are under God's control. One day we will become fellow and eternal heirs in the kingdom, re-united with our Tajik brothers and sisters. For now, we miss them very much. We hold on to the memory of our last Easter together. The importance of prayer grows in our understanding. We pray for them, our family. We aspire to constantly look on the situation of our separation with eyes of hope, for He is risen. He is risen indeed!

EPILOGUE

Bui jui Mulion oyad hame,
Yodi yori mehrubon oyad hame.
Obi Jaihun bo hama pahnovari,
Hingi moro to mion oyad hame.
Mir moh astu Buxhoro osmon,
Moh sui osmon oyad hame.
Aih Buxhoro, shod boshu derzi,
Shoh nazdat, mehmon oyad hame.

Aroma of Mulion stream comes,
Remembrance arrives of your affectionate lover.
Waters of the Jaihun in all their breadth,
Reach to our horses' chests.
King the moon and Bukhoro the sun,
The moon comes in the sun's direction.
Oh Bukhoro, be glad and live long,
The king draws near you, a guest will come.[1]

I remember sitting with my friend and language teacher, Zohir, as he explained the meaning and history of this poem to me line by line. Zohir taught me that the great Tajik poet, Rudaki, had accompanied his king, the king of Bukhoro, to a far region of his domain, a part of modern Afghanistan, where they stayed and held court for a long time.

Longing for home, Rudaki composed and shared this poem with his king hoping it would awaken a yearning that would prove strong enough to carry them home. Deeply moved upon hearing the poem, the king commanded that they would in fact cross the expansive Jaihun River—today's Amu Daryo—and ride north toward the familiar aroma of the streams near Bukhoro.

I reflect on this poem now as I sit here writing at a coffee shop back in America. Unlike the ancient king of Bukhoro, it was not a poem that called us home. Exhausted and wisely counseled to return home, we left two months before our final two teammates were forcibly deported from Tajikistan. But that is another story. For a graciously given window of time, the aroma of our team's faith overflowed into our Tajik neighbors' lives.

But many in Kadimobod grew weary of the good news. We hold on to the truth that ultimately it is the Lord who is in control, allowing or perhaps directing all of our team home far sooner than we ever would have imagined.

After the initial months of relief from all the strain of those last heavy days in Tajikistan, I now begin to realize that I feel great loss and separation. I realize the Lord caused a great love for the Tajiks to grow in my heart. I believe, I pray, the love will be lifelong. I hope that my life in prayer faithfully reflects this God-given love.

I believe in the centrality of prayer in ministry. God, primarily through our amazing teammates in Tajikistan, taught Ann and me to pray fervently. Recently our team leader wrote that when the first of our teammates began to move to Kadimobod in the late 1990s, the situation was such that "from the first century till the twentieth century, this valley had minimal, if not nonexistent gospel witness." As far as we were able to discover there was only one family of Tajik believers in all of Kadimobod. They had come to faith when another group began making evangelistic visits in the mid-1990s.

When Ann and I arrived a few years later to join our team, we entered into an atmosphere where prayer was central. Surrounded by a sea of Islam and graciously humbled by the hurdles of language and culture, we had far fewer illusions than we tend to entertain in America that we could do anything without His power. But I still had much to learn.

C. S. Lewis writes, "The load, or weight, or burden of my neighbor's glory should be laid on my back, a load so heavy that only humility can carry it, and the back of the proud will be broken."[2] In Tajikistan, I understood more clearly than ever that God must be allowed to truly be God in my understanding. That was the beautiful, appropriate, penitent humility that led me from a constant, oppressive feeling of overwhelming burden for the Tajiks to an understanding that the fruit of the Spirit, notably peace and joy, must be the daily reality of my life regardless of my surroundings.

Though we would probably never wish for it, I believe our team understands the precious gift of our refinement. This difficult refinement that took place in us as we lived in Tajikistan was often achieved through suffering. This suffering, perhaps counterintuitively, has brought us far deeper into the experience of the joy of the Lord that is our strength.

Over the years, we were graced to be a part of the beginnings of a fledgling church where we saw several handfuls of Tajiks come to faith. A core of Tajik believers has become the center of the church, the church that continues to glorify and proclaim His name after our departure. We pray to trust more fully in His providence.

I have a pair of small pages I use as a bookmark for my Bible. Most days I pray through the first page upon which is scribbled the names of my Tajik brothers and sisters in Christ. And most days I continue on to pray through the second list, a list of my neighbors and students, my friends and the "seekers" we deeply love. It is a joy to be quickened to passion in prayer, a joy I deeply appreciate having gone through many spells of prayerless indifference in my Christian journey.

God is awakening me, awakening Ann, awakening our team, the believers, the Tajiks, awakening us to long for our true country. Increasingly as I hear His Word, I long to mount the horse, wade the rivers, and ride hard for home. Ann and I were latecomers to Tajikistan. We usually rode behind our teammates and the few mature Tajik believers as they blazed the trail in Tajikistan. And now in prayer and encouragement we urge on the Tajik church in Kadimobod and the Tajik church universal as they take the lead they rightly should take.

Tajikistan has instilled in me the sense that I must not ride toward my own personal Bukhoro in America, my homeland, nor toward the Tajikistan I have grown to love. Such riding is vanity and futility. Though Ann and I still long for and pursue another opportunity for ministry, it is clearer to us now that in all of our pursuits, by His Spirit, we must ride hard toward Him alone who will one day race toward earth, mounted on His volant white horse. Regardless of the Bukhoro we choose to ride towards, the King draws ever nearer to them all. Depending on our relationship with the King, that is either a dreadful or magnificent thought.

Amen. Come, Lord Jesus. The grace of the Lord Jesus be with all. Amen (Rev 22:20–21 NASB).

NOTES

A Day in Pursuit of Air Conditioning

1. Richard Adams, *Watership Down* (New York: Scribner, 2005), 45.
2. Tom Bissell, *Chasing the Sea* (New York: First Vintage Departures, 2004), 97.
3. Francis A. Schaeffer, *How Should We Then Live?* (Wheaton: Crossway Books, 2005), 249.
4. Alexander Solzhenitsyn, "A World Split Apart" (commencement address, Harvard University, June 8, 1978).
5. Dylan Thomas, "Do Not Go Gentle into That Good Night," in *An Introduction to Poetry*, ed. Louis Simpson (New York: St. Martin's Press, 1967), 315.
6. Aldous Huxley, *Brave New World* (New York: Harper Collins, 2006), 229.
7. G. K. Chesterton, *Collected Works* (San Francisco: Ignatius Press, 1986), 363–64.

The Giant Saint

1. Sadriddin, Maxsumi, and Hoji Muhammad ibni Muhammadali. *Mazor of the Great Sulton Uvais Karin at Hovaling* (Kulob: n.p., n.d.), 22.
2. G. K. Chesterton, *Collected Works* (San Francisco: Ignatius Press, 1986), 257.

3. Sadriddin, Maxsumi, and Hoji Muhammad ibni Muhammadali. *Mazor of the Great Sulton Uvais Karin at Hovaling* (Kulob: n.p., n.d.), 16.

Normal Life
1. Edward Bellamy, *Looking Backward: 2000–1887* (New York: Penguin Books, 1986), 120.

100% Unnatural
1. William Rose Benet and Conrad Aiken, *An Anthology of Famous English and American Poetry* (New York: The Modern Library, 1944), 562–63.

A Winter's Night
1. C. S. Lewis, *The Weight of Glory* (New York: Harper Collins, 2001), 46.
2. Laura Ingalls Wilder, *Little House on the Prairie* (New York: Harper & Row, 1971), 250.
3. Neil Postman, "Five Things We Need to Know about Technological Change," (speech, Denver, Colorado, March 27, 1998).
4. Conversation with Ann James, 2008.
5. Gene Edward Veith, "Praise the Lord, Pass the Ammo," *WORLD Magazine*, October 25, 2003.
6. Traditional Tajik Navruz song.

Bahriddin's Wedding
1. Traditional Tajik folk poem, author unknown. My Tajik language teacher introduced me to the poems in this story. He explained that these are poems from the common people. He learned them from his grandmother. As traditional folk poetry, neither he nor his grandmother ever knew of a more specific source or author than the oral tradition all around them. Translation is mine.

Notes

2. Traditional Tajik folk poem, author unknown.
3. Traditional Tajik folk poem, author unknown. (This poem portrays a woman looking in the mirror trying to give herself a pep talk to face up to her neighbors and get an education anyway.)
4. Traditional Tajik folk poem, author unknown.
5. Traditional Tajik folk poem, author unknown.

Epilogue

1. Abuabdulloh Jafar Ibni Muhammad Rudaki, (poem, circa AD 900). Translation is mine.
2. C. S. Lewis, The Weight of Glory (New York: Harper Collins, 2001), 45.

BIBLIOGRAPHY

Adams, Richard. *Watership Down*. New York: Scribner, 2005.

Bellamy, Edward. *Looking Backward: 2000–1887*. New York: Penguin Books, 1986.

Benet, William Rose and Conrad Aiken. *An Anthology of English and American Poetry*. New York: The Modern Library, 1944.

Bissell, Tom. *Chasing the Sea*. New York: First Vintage Departures, 2004.

Chesterton, G. K. *Collective Works*. San Francisco: Ignatius Press, 1986.

Huxley, Aldous. *Brave New World*. New York: Harper Collins, 2006.

Lewis, C. S. *The Weight of Glory*. New York: Harper Collins, 2001.

Postman, Neil. "Five Things We Need to Know about Technological Change." Speech given in Denver, Colorado, March 27, 1998. http://www.mat.upm.es/~jcm/neil-postman--five-things.html (accessed August 23, 2011).

Sadriddin, Maxsumi, and Hoji Muhammad ibni Muhammadali. *Mazor of the Great Sulton Uvais Karin at Hovaling*. Kulob: n.p., n.d.

Schaeffer, Francis A. *How Should We Then Live?* Wheaton: Crossway Books, 2005.

Simpson, Louis. *An Introduction to Poetry.* New York: St. Martin's Press, 1967.

Solzhenitsyn, Alexander. "A World Split Apart." Commencement address, Harvard University, June 8, 1978. http://www. americanrhetoric.com/speeches/PDFFiles/Alexander%20 Solzhenitsyn%20-%20World%20Split%20Apart.pdf

Veith, Gene Edward. "Praise the Lord, Pass the Ammo." *WORLD Magazine,* October 25, 2003. http://www.worldmag. com/articles/article.cfm?eid=17A2645C-910C-7B37-E86F43A318D44CA3

Wilder, Laura Ingalls. *Little House on the Prairie.* New York: Harper & Row, 1971.

CPSIA information can be obtained
at www.ICGtesting.com
Printed in the USA
FSHW021157041021
85183FS